Radical Cities

Radical Cities

Across Latin America in Search
of a New Architecture

Justin McGuirk

VERSO
London • New York

For Dina

First published by Verso 2014
© Justin McGuirk 2014

1 3 5 7 9 10 8 6 4 2

Verso
UK: 6 Meard Street, London W1F 0EG
US: 20 Jay Street, Suite 1010, Brooklyn, NY 11201
www.versobooks.com

Verso is the imprint of New Left Books

ISBN-13: 978-1-78168-280-7
eISBN-13: 978-1-78168-655-3 (UK)
eISBN-13: 978-1-78168-281-4 (US)

British Library Cataloguing in Publication Data
A catalogue record for this book is available from the British Library

Library of Congress Cataloging-in-Publication Data

McGuirk, Justin.
  Radical cities : across Latin America in search of a new architecture / Justin McGuirk.
    pages cm
  ISBN 978-1-78168-280-7 (hardback)
  1. Architecture and society – Latin America – History – 21st century. 2. Cities and
towns – Latin America – Growth. 3. City dwellers – Political aspects – Latin America. I.
Title.
  NA2543.S6M39 2014
  720.1'03098–dc23
                        2013051123

Typeset in Fournier by MJ & N Gavan, Truro, Cornwall
Printed in the US by Maple Press

Latin America is Africa, Asia and Europe at the same time.

Félix Guattari in *Molecular Revolution in Brazil*

'What do you want to be?' the anarchist asked young people in the middle of their studies. 'Lawyers, to invoke the law of the rich, which is unjust by definition? Doctors, to tend the rich, and prescribe good food, fresh air, and rest to the consumptives of the slums? Architects, to house the landlords in comfort? Look around you, and then examine your conscience. Do you not understand that your duty is quite different: to ally yourselves with the exploited and to work for the destruction of an intolerable system?'

Victor Serge paraphrasing a pamphlet by Peter Kropotkin, in *Memoirs of a Revolutionary*

Contents

Introduction   1

1. From Buenos Aires to San Salvador de Jujuy:
   Dictators and Revolutionaries   37
2. From Lima to Santiago: A Platform for Change   67
3. Rio de Janeiro: The Favela Is the City   99
4. Caracas: The City Is Frozen Politics   139
5. Torre David: A Pirate Utopia   175
6. Bogotá: The City as a School   207
7. Medellín: Social Urbanism   231
8. Tijuana: On the Political Equator   259

Acknowledgements   285
Index   287

Introduction

Saturday, June 30, 1962.
9:35 a.m. President Kennedy arrives at the housing project.
Tours project - brief ceremony.

This I found in the John F. Kennedy Library's digital archive, in the schedule of the president's official visit to Mexico City in 1962. I'd been told that on this trip he'd been taken to see Nonoalco-Tlatelolco, a vast housing estate, the biggest of its kind in Latin America. And that made sense. In the 1960s, what else would you show the US president to flaunt your modernising nation if not industrialised ranks of housing stretching as far as the eye could see? Mechanisation, social mobility and economic power all wrapped up in one potent image.

My source was wrong, however. A few pages further into Kennedy's itinerary briefing it emerges that it was the Unidad Independencia housing project that he visited, not Tlatelolco, which was still under construction. You can almost feel his hosts' frustration. Two years later, the city would have an infinitely more impressive site to show off. The photographs of Tlatelolco taken when it was completed in 1964 are some of the most powerful images of social housing I've ever seen. Row upon row of megablocks stand proudly over the low-rise sprawl of Mexico City. With their gridded, ultra-repetitive facades, they resemble banks of mainframe computers, or server farms before the fact.

Here was the modernist utopia built on a scale that Le Corbusier had dreamt of but was never able to realise. This city within the city comprised 130 buildings, providing 15,000 apartments. At its height, Tlatelolco housed nearly 100,000 people. It was the kind of solution that the problem of Mexico City seemed to demand, a problem of population explosion fuelled by industrialisation and the accompanying mass migrations from the countryside. What was a population of a little over a million in 1940 was on its way to becoming 15 million by 1980.

Tlatelolco's architect was Mario Pani. Like other prominent Latin American architects of his generation, he was trained in Europe, indeed in Paris, where he attended the École des Beaux-Arts in the 1920s before imbibing the spirit of Corbusian modernism. An earlier housing project, the Presidente Miguel Alemán estate, built in 1948, even uses the zigzagging blocks of the Ville Radieuse, Corbu's blueprint for an ideal city. But while on one level Pani was being derivative, on another he was bringing those unfulfilled ideas to fruition. For Tlatelolco took the modernist idea of social housing to its logical, many would say absurd, conclusion. If, in the mid twentieth century, the city of the future would comprise rows of megablocks sitting in parklands and gardens, then the future looked like Tlatelolco.

Indeed, Pani's plan had been to build 'five or six Tlatelolcos' on that site, with an extension of three million square metres. In his eyes, much of Mexico City deserved the wrecking ball so that a new vision could flourish. Invoking Le Corbusier to the end, Pani never accepted that the Swiss genius might be, to borrow Henri Lefebvre's description, 'a good architect but a catastrophic urbanist'. In 1964, Pani was still progress.

In Luis Buñuel's film about a group of delinquents in Mexico City, *Los Olvidados* (The Forgotten), there is a scene in which a youth who has settled into a life of crime murders a rival and steals the money out of his pockets. It's a primal scene, like watching Cain kill Abel, except that in the background is the steel frame of a modern building. Is it housing? It's impossible to say. But, rising out of a wasteland, this space-frame is surely a symbol of approaching progress. In Buñuel's unremittingly bleak portrait of life in Mexico City in 1950, crime is depicted as the inevitable result of poverty. The fleeting shot of that construction site is arguably the only moment of hope: it suggests change, modernism riding to the rescue.

It is not Tlatelolco that is being erected in the film, but it might as well be. The estate was built on the site of an overcrowded slum district, and Pani's design, commissioned by the government, was intended to rehouse its inhabitants while bringing in middle-class residents to create social diversity. In short, it was an old-fashioned slum clearance. Pani matched the extreme density of the slum he was replacing, which was 1,000 inhabitants per hectare, but with sanitised, vertical machines surrounded by acres of public space. We can quibble with the vision, on both urbanistic and aesthetic grounds, but where it went wrong was in its outcome. Intended for the poor, Tlatelolco ended up being occupied largely by bureaucrats and workers at the state rail and health companies. As usual, the slum-dwellers were shunted elsewhere. This was the key failing of a scheme that came to be notorious for altogether different reasons.

At the heart of the estate is a historic site. The ruins of a pyramid mark the spot where the Aztecs were finally defeated by the Spanish, and right next to it stands the sixteenth-century church of Santiago Tlatelolco that heralded the new era. Pani incorporated these pivotal monuments into a centrepiece called the Plaza de las Tres Culturas, a broad square rimmed by his brutalist apartment blocks. The three cultures meeting here were the pre-Columbian, the colonial and the modern, providing a symbolic ensemble that tied a modernising Mexico to its past. But Pani's architectural allegory was to be overshadowed by tragedy.

In October 1968, only days before the Mexico City Olympics, students chose the Plaza de las Tres Culturas to stage a pro-democracy demonstration, challenging authoritarian president Gustavo Díaz Ordaz and the single-party political system that produced him. Jittery about any signs of unrest as the Games approached, Díaz Ordaz called in the army, and hundreds of students were killed by soldiers firing into the square from the surrounding apartment blocks. The poet Octavio Paz described it as a repeat of an Aztec rite, 'several hundred boys and girls sacrificed, on the ruins of a pyramid'. This was the first blow to Tlatelolco as an emblem of modern Mexico. The second came in 1985 when an earthquake brought one of its buildings crashing to the ground. The collapse was most likely caused by the construction companies cutting corners, a common problem at social housing estates across Latin America. A dozen other buildings had to be pulled down due to structural damage, and the whole complex had to undergo a major structural overhaul. This was ultimately the more devastating blow to Pani's vision.

Today, Tlatelolco is almost unrecognisable. In the butcher's shop overlooking the square, among the *corrida* posters and the bull heads – the butcher is an ex-bullfighter – you'll find blown-up photographs of the place soon after it was built. The checkerboard facades are now gone, covered by thick concrete skins. These new casings were superimposed after the earthquake to reinforce the buildings, adding another archaeological layer to an already historically loaded site. Some buildings, if you compare them to the butcher's photographs, have quite clearly changed shape, as if several floors were shaved from the top to make them more stable. Around the corner there is a memorial on the site of the fallen tower block.

After poring over his photographs, I feel I ought to buy something. I ask for a Coke but the butcher won't let me leave with the bottle, so he decants it into a clear plastic bag and sticks a straw into it. Sipping on my bag, I stand in the middle of the Plaza de las Tres Culturas taking in the collision of ideas. On one side the black, volcanic rock of the pyramid and the church, and on the other gridded concrete – degrees of mysticism and rationalism, but three faiths nonetheless. There's a plaque commemorating Hernan Cortes's taking of Tlatelolco in 1521, described as 'the painful birth of the mixed-blood country that is Mexico today'. If this square symbolises the birth of a nation, it also marks the birth and sudden demise of utopian modernist planning in Mexico.

I start walking to the other end of the estate, nearly two kilometres away. The scale of Tlatelolco remains intimidating. After the earthquake the neighbourhood went into decline, becoming a no-go zone in the 1990s. It doesn't *feel* like a no-go zone today, however. The gardens are lush and well tended – in this respect the tropical climates of Latin America were forgiving to the brutalist housing adopted from Europe, nature softening an unforgiving architectural style. It seems safe to walk around. Admittedly, that is pathetically unscientific, but the feeling is measured against estates in other cities across the continent where no local would accompany me or where they wouldn't dare step out of the car if they did. Nevertheless, my impressions are academic, because residents are concerned about crime. Drug dealing and gang violence are a problem, and apparently half of all residents have either been victims of or witnesses to a crime. Furthermore, there are still concerns about the structural soundness of some of the buildings.

This is a familiar story. Housing estates in Europe and America have faced the same problems and seen public opinion turn against them the same way. Though rarely a fault of the architecture itself – and more often a case of poor maintenance, mismanagement and blighting by poverty – the architects were blamed. Their sins were catalogued and generalised: treating people like ants, making cities ugly, replacing variety with standardisation, repetition, repetition, repetition. Citing 'failure', governments used these sins as an excuse to stop building social housing, relying on the private sector to fill the gap and allowing their neoliberal policies to make cities more unequal places. In London as I write, housing estates that are some of the most visible symbols of a welfare state in operation from the 1930s onwards are being pulled down to make way for 'luxury developments' built by private developers. Much like in Latin America, the poor will be pushed to the periphery, or in some cases out of the city altogether.

So why is Latin America special? And what can we learn from it? As we shall see, the countries of South and Central America were home to some of the greatest experiments in urban living of the twentieth century. Latin America, let us not forget, experienced mass urbanisation long before China and Africa, which today produce almost panic-inducing statistics of urban population growth. In the 1950s and 60s the equivalent statistics were coming out of Brazil,

Mexico, Venezuela and Argentina. It has become a cliché to say that more than half the world lives in cities, but many countries in Latin America have had 80 per cent urbanisation for decades. It was in an attempt to deal with the scale of urban migration that Latin American architects picked up the gauntlet thrown down by the European modernists. If standardised, industrialised housing was the future, then it would be adapted to the scale of the New World.

Let's leave aside Le Corbusier for a moment. His famous Unité d'Habitation in Marseille – the closest he came to realising his own vision of mass housing – provided a mere 337 apartments. Instead, think of some of the largest archetypal housing estates in Europe and America. The ill-fated Pruitt-Igoe project in St Louis, Missouri, comes to mind. Designed by Minoru Yamasaki in 1952, it provided 2,870 apartments. Even Le Mirail, an entire modernist new town near Toulouse in France, designed by Candilis Josic Woods in 1961, only provided 5,600 homes. Compare these to Carlos Raúl Villanueva's extraordinary 23 de Enero housing complex in Caracas, which in 1957 comprised more than 9,000 apartments. Or indeed compare them to Tlatelolco, with its 15,000 units. In response to Tlatelolco, the British magazine *Architectural Review* wrote: 'Even after years of inoculation against the shapes of Niemeyer, Northern Europeans can still be taken aback by Latin American bravura.'

For all its bravura, Latin America is where modernist utopia went to die. Today, 23 de Enero is paradigmatic of the problems that beset this ambitious and single-minded vision of mass housing. Crime-ridden and overcrowded, it is a virtual law unto itself, a place where the police seldom go if they can help it. Around and in between the *superbloques*, a carpet of slum has grown, an organism that now seems to bind the blocks together in some symbiotic relationship. These are the kinds of hybrid forms that are developing in Latin American cities, where the rationalist vision of the mid twentieth century is giving way to the ineluctable logic of the informal city.

By the early 1970s, modernist housing estates were already widely discredited in Europe and America. The architecture historian Charles Jencks famously pinpointed the demolition of Pruitt-Igoe in 1972 as the end of modernism. This was not quite the case in Latin America, where ambitious social housing projects continued to be built until the end of the decade, often by military dictatorships who used them to reward their support bases. In fact, I would argue that it was another, earlier event that signalled the end of social housing as an ideal, and with it the end of the architect's reign as the most powerful force in city-making.

In 1968, the president of Peru, Fernando Belaúnde, initiated a project with the support of the United Nations that set out to solve the growing problem of Lima's *barriadas*, or shanty towns. PREVI – Proyecto Experimental de Vivienda – was a different kind of proposal, opting not for the heavy artillery of the megablock but a more intelligent scheme of individual houses that residents could expand as their families grew. This, of course, is one thing that an apartment in a tower block cannot do. The idea had come out of the research of an English architect, John Turner, who had studied the *barriadas* and was making a convincing case not to see them as slums that needed clearing, but as creative and efficient solutions to the needs of the poor. Why move them to new blocks on the edge of the city, far away from their jobs and with rents that they couldn't afford? Controversially, Turner proposed that it was actually an advantage for the poor to build their own homes. The instigators of the PREVI scheme met him halfway, with a hybrid solution. The government would provide a framework of good architecture that was specifically designed to be expanded by the residents – it was modernism combined with the slums.

What was remarkable about PREVI was the stature of the figures who were involved, a dream team of the architectural avant-garde from around the world. It included the Englishman James Stirling, the Dutchman Aldo van Eyck, the Japanese Metabolists, Charles Correa from India and Christopher Alexander from the USA, among many others. For reasons that we shall discover later, the project was only partially developed and it was subsequently scrapped. Largely forgotten until recently, PREVI remains one of the great almost-moments of twentieth-century architecture. It was, in effect, an attempt to save architecture – to resuscitate it as a force for social change. But it was the last time that the best architects of a generation were brought to bear on the question of social housing.

From that moment on, arguably, a different agenda took hold in the cities of Latin America. It had become only too clear that it simply wasn't possible to build housing blocks fast enough to cope with the scale of the problem, or cheaply enough to avoid bankrupting nations. Turner had argued that, effectively, the poor were literally better off looking after their own interests and building their own informal settlements. 'No government – however wealthy, as the Venezuelan "superblock" project shows – can possibly finance more than a small proportion of the total demand for housing,' he'd written in 1963. According to such realpolitik, slums were not the problem, they were the solution. Perhaps unsurprisingly, the same conclusion was eventually reached by governments themselves, which were increasingly unable or unwilling to throw the same resources at housing as they had done in the past. Not that politicians in Latin America were reading Turner, or even knew who he was. The collective shift in mood away from paternalistic responsibility was happening at a much higher level. Pursuing the neoliberal policies advocated by the International Monetary Fund, many governments left the problem of housing to the free market. It was the same mistake that Margaret Thatcher made in Britain, only incalculably more serious, because the housing deficit in Latin American cities was measured not in thousands but millions.

The laissez-faire approach to cities gained traction in the 1960s. Turner's position can be seen in the context of Jane Jacobs defending the boisterous streets of Greenwich Village, members of Team 10 studying Dogon villages in Mali, and the Situationists lampooning Le Corbusier and his tower-block 'morgues'. This attitude was exemplified by the 1964 exhibition 'Architecture Without Architects', curated by Bernard Rudofsky at the Museum of Modern Art in New York. Celebrating the timeless beauty of ver-nacular buildings, it offered proof if proof were needed that we had been getting along perfectly well without architects for thousands of years. And what were the favelas and *bar-riadas* if not products of the same intuitive craftsmanship?

In the 1970s, the favelas of Rio de Janeiro and São Paulo, the barrios of Caracas, the *villas miseria* of Buenos Aires and the *barriadas* of Lima started to take on a different order of magnitude. Dropping the notion of housing as a right, governments across Latin America opted instead to try and manage the growth of informal settlements. One approach was to provide what was known as 'sites and ser-vices', where plots were mapped out on the ground and some basic infrastructure provided, but people would build their own houses. Leaving housing to free-market econom-ics, they increasingly opted for non-architectural solutions to raising people out of poverty, such as social welfare programmes. The days when architects such as Pani and Villanueva could erect modernist cities within the city, all with the full support of the paternalistic state, were over. Their seats were taken by economists and policy-makers.

The story of modernist social housing in Latin America is often presented as one of heroic failure – of bold archi-tects in the service of well-meaning welfare states. In truth, the politics often left much to be desired. The most avid builders of social housing were the military dictatorships that held Venezuela, Argentina, Chile and Brazil in their grip for long stretches between the 1950s and the 1980s. When housing estates weren't merely tools for driving the economy, they were used to relocate squatters from prime sites to the periphery, creating polarised cities. And yet one can say that social housing was undertaken with conviction. What happened afterwards, however, oscillated between abdication of responsibility and crisis management. It would be impossible to generalise here about urban policies across the continent, because the approaches were as unique as the politics and the local conditions. A more detailed and nuanced picture will emerge in the various episodes of this book.

For now, let's allow ourselves to make some sweeping generalisations about architecture culture in the intervening years. With the demise of social housing as a government priority, not just in Latin America but in America and Europe, architects, I would argue, lost their social purpose. The housing blocks that had accompanied industrialisation gave way to the office towers that heralded the service economy. Modernism gave way to postmodernism, and the transparent glass of rationalism became the impenetrable mirrors of a new corporate culture. The avant-garde — namely those too young or too academic to have surfed the PoMo office and hotel boom — withdrew into experimenting with architecture as an autonomous art form, informed by deconstructivist philosophy and complex geometry. Continue zooming through time and you'll see the development of computer-aided drawing software and a resurgent global economy on converging tracks until – voilà! – the 'starchitect' is born.

What happened in the first decade of the 2000s is easy to parody, and will continue to be, until a more forgiving future inevitably resuscitates the starchitects as heroes. The era of the 'icon', whether we mean blobs and other parametric forms or indeed icy minimalism, was the result of pure architectural form-making finally finding a globalised market. Both the corporate elite and a booming culture industry were hungry for it. And architects were brazen about the new world of opportunities available to them when it came to making the buildings of their dreams come true. Even its intellectuals, notably Rem Koolhaas, invoked a culture of ¥€$, in which the architect and the client mutually fulfilled each others' wildest fantasies – a philosophy that under his young acolyte Bjarke Ingels became the slogan 'Yes is More'. If in the 1970s the Marxist architecture critic Manfredo Tafuri was already bemoaning the fact that capitalism had effectively stripped architecture of its ideological purpose, then he hadn't seen anything yet. What he already viewed as the 'drama' of architecture reached its apogee slightly later: 'that is, to see architecture obliged to return to *pure architecture*, to form without utopia; in the best cases, to sublime uselessness.'

That phrase 'form without utopia' is the key to early twenty-first-century architecture. In the 1960s, the architectural avant-garde was dedicated to producing social housing – and Europeans such as Alison and Peter Smithson were hugely influential to a generation of Latin

American architects building social housing on a scale that the Smithsons never did. The question is, what drove this dedication? Was it the fact that they were idealists, or that social housing was where the work was (and the ¥€$ of the 1960s was in reply to government housing authorities)? I believe the answer is both. To see their output as simply gainful employment is to strip it of the ideological content that it plainly demonstrates. By contrast, the pinnacle of architectural ambition in the first decade of the next century was the museum.

Call it 'the Bilbao effect' or what you will, the museum as a tool of urban regeneration, not to mention urban branding, becomes the focus of architectural discourse. Now, the idea of architecture at the service of the culture industry is a perfectly noble one. To see Spain churning out one museum after another in those years – perhaps simply because the architecture was better and more restrained than the images streaming back from China and Dubai – evinced a faith in the idea of architecture as a civilising force in the city. With hindsight, the fact that Spain was bankrupting itself in the process only goes to prove that the system supporting all those museums was weak. Indeed, the very process of branding-based cultural regeneration was complicit in the neoliberal attitude to the city, where the ultimate motive is always rising land values and profit. If architecture is just speculation, then could there be a more fitting legacy of that period than Spain's 3.5 million empty homes? This is the capitalist drama that Tafuri had warned us about, the drama of architecture for its own sake: no ideology, no utopia.

It's so easy now, isn't it, to blame architects for servicing an economy of the spectacle? In our mid-recession world, the starchitects are soft targets and 'spectacle' has become an easy epithet. But this book will take you to places that are also, in their own way, spectacular – even social housing. Affonso Reidy's Pedregulho housing in Rio, built in the 1950s, has a curvaceous facade that was designed to make a spectacle of itself. This was a tropical utopianism at work. Equally, the sight of Tlatelolco stretching into the distance, a man-made event approaching the fearsome scale of the sublime, is also a spectacle. Both of these have the power to convey visually a political will at the service of the people, to communicate modernisation and the right to housing. The fact that they came to represent other things altogether – failure, a one-dimensional approach to city-making, crime – is history's lesson. Perhaps our judgement of spectacle depends not so much on *how* architects design as *what* they design. It is the social dimension of mass housing that allows us to forgive the failures, indeed to feel nostalgic.

But this is not a revisionist history of Latin American social housing. This is a much more optimistic book than that. What I've argued thus far is that the architecture of spectacle, brought to its knees by the financial crash in 2008, was the culmination of a process that begins with the abandonment of social housing as a utopian project. After Latin America's own Pruitt-Igoe moment – with the scrapping of PREVI, the tainting of Tlatelolco by student massacres and earthquakes, the slumification of 23 de Enero and countless estates across the continent – there is effectively a three-decade hiatus when the architect is no longer involved in the question of how to incorporate vast populations of the poor into the city. This is not to say that architecture with a social purpose disappears, because at the community level there were all sorts of initiatives in operation. But in the last decade a new generation of architects has emerged in Latin America, and they have returned a sense of hope to the idea that the architect can make a meaningful difference in the cities of the developing world. This book is about that generation.

A Generation of Optimists

As the editor of an architecture magazine in the mid Noughties, I could have published a building almost every month from Chile. There was a steady stream of museums, university buildings and lapidary houses perched on dramatic clifftops. It became almost a challenge not to include yet another second home from this sliver of a country where copper wealth and architectural talent were combining to produce a glut of archi-porn. But one project announced itself as not just another glorious double-page spread in a magazine. It was a housing scheme in the very north of Chile designed by Alejandro Aravena and his practice, Elemental. This was social housing, built for a poor community with the barest of budgets. What was ingenious about it was that it seemed to rewrite the equation of social housing, providing each family with merely half a house and letting them build the other half according to their means and within a defined structural framework. It was clever, adaptive and it allowed – just as PREVI had – people to participate in the end result. Moreover, what was unusual about this, as a social housing project, was that it had been initiated by Aravena himself, along with his then partner Andrés Iacobelli. They lobbied the government to let them try their model until finally they were dispatched to that needy community in the north. Then, they had to solve the small matter of how to fund their scheme. Here, the impetus, from conception to final product, had come from the architect.

I soon realised that Aravena was not the only architect tackling social projects in Latin America, nor in being the driving force behind them. In Venezuela, Urban-Think Tank (U-TT), a practice founded by the Venezuelan Alfredo Brillembourg and the Austrian Hubert Klumpner, were building what they called 'vertical gyms' in the slums of Caracas. These structures, which provided much more intensive use than the little football pitches they replaced, had a galvanising effect on their communities. Urban-Think Tank, when I first encountered them, were also building a cable-car system to the hillside slums, connecting the informal city to the city centre and radically improving the mobility of the slum dwellers. Again, a pair of architects initiated this piece of urban infrastructure, which remains one of the Chávez government's most visible legacies. As we shall see, the story of how they pulled that off is one of high-level political wrangling and street-wise survival skills.

In Brazil, the Argentinian émigré Jorge Mario Jáuregui has spent the better part of two decades working to improve the quality of housing and public space in the slums of Rio de Janeiro. As one of the active proponents of the Favela-Bairro scheme, Jáuregui was doing slum-upgrading long before it was a fashionable pursuit among architects. His methodology was to use public spaces and transport to build connections between the informal and the formal city. The basic principle of Favela-Bairro, that you can soothe social divisions with urban form, was to be hugely influential.

In Colombia, we encounter a different story. Rather than the activist architects mobilising support, we witness what was effectively the radicalisation of a political class that adopted spatial solutions – architecture – to solve social degradation. The political achievements of Colombia in the 1990s and 2000s were set in motion by an extraordinary figure. Mathematician, philosopher and twice the mayor of Bogotá, Antanas Mockus was an eccentric political genius who used unorthodox methods to bring a notoriously troubled capital back under control. Inheriting a city plagued by crime, violence and traffic, he set about trying to instil a new civic culture. He reduced road accidents by hiring hundreds of mime artists to direct traffic, and by distributing football-style red cards among the people so they could shame their fellow citizens when they drove selfishly or dangerously. He reduced violence by introducing a policy of exchanging guns for toys and by offering symbolic vaccinations against violence, as though it were a disease. Dressing up as a red-caped 'Super Citizen', his methods owed more to performance and art than to conventional politics. But on the bedrock of civic stability that he established, his successors went on to do great things for Bogotá, in terms of actual transport and infrastructure.

Against that backdrop, there were equally extraordinary (if less bizarre) things happening in the country's second city. In the 1990s, Medellín was the murder capital of the world. A sequence of mayors, Sergio Fajardo in particular, and other civic leaders decided that they had had enough of the violence that warring drug cartels had wrought on their city, and that new public spaces, civic buildings and infrastructure would help turn the city around. And it did. But in a sense what was more radical than the new buildings and plazas themselves, impressive though they are, was the organisation of the different civic stakeholders into a united front. There is a lot of talk these days about 'bottom-up' solutions that give ordinary citizens a voice, but the transformation of Medellín was the result of 'top-down' activism.

On the US–Mexico border, where Latin America hits North America, a different kind of architect is at work. Teddy Cruz is not building housing, at least not quite yet, but his observations about this politically sensitive border zone – where the poor of Tijuana build houses out of discarded garage doors from San Diego – have made him the most influential thinker of the generation that I am describing. Rather than building, he has theorised the role of the activist architect, outlining a new form of practice based on self-initiation and an engagement with the messy business of policy – all of this of course is to compensate for the failures of public institutions. He is currently attempting to initiate a community-led development in the San Diego suburb of San Ysidro, but a Teddy Cruz action is just as likely to be a 'performance' that involves leading politicians across the border through a drainpipe so they can understand the local conditions that their policies determine.

Elsewhere, in the north of Argentina, we encounter a hardcore architectural activism that has nothing to do with architects. In Jujuy, a radical social movement called Túpac Amaru, led by a formidable Kolla Indian woman called Milagro Sala, has been building entire communities for the poor. Again, what is remarkable is not just her role as a catalyst but the organisational structures she implemented to create these communities. Túpac Amaru created its own brick and metal-working factories and employed the residents themselves as its construction force. This autonomous activism was in response to the repeated false promises and corruption of the politicians. And perhaps what is most astonishing about her is how she managed to reverse the equation of social housing, so that instead of providing the minimum that you can get away with she provided the maximum. That meant vast swimming pools and Jurassic theme parks – what better way to make the poor feel rich, she says, than a swimming pool? The houses are branded with the face of Che Guevara in a total vision that amounts to a radical socialist Disney urbanism, but a powerful work of activism nonetheless.

There are other episodes in this book in which the poor take matters into their own hands, becoming urban activists without the help of architects. In Caracas, we shall visit a forty-five-storey skyscraper that has been squatted by 3,000 people. Built as a banking headquarters, Torre David was left uncompleted in the mid 1990s when its developer died. After standing abandoned for a decade, a group of families from the slums invaded it and turned an emblem of exclusive real estate into a symbol of redistribution. The new inhabitants organised themselves, brought in electricity and water pumps and turned a derelict skyscraper into a vertical village. It's a powerful story but, again, it is no utopia. Walking up and down thirty storeys every day to get to your front door – Torre David has no elevator – is the price you pay for swapping precarious living on the city's edge for penthouse living in the city centre. Torre David is an anomaly, an accident of extreme circumstances, but it is precisely the kind of formal-informal hybrid that cities of the developing world need to explore if they are to start imagining a future that is different from the present.

Learning from Latin America

There was a time when, in the eyes of those exporting the policies of the Washington Consensus, Latin America was a byword for precariousness, corruption and illegal practices. Today, we are just as likely to think of Wall Street in the same terms. By contrast, Latin America's economies are relatively stable, demonstrating the kind of growth that the US and Europe would die for, and its governments represent a bastion of progressive politics that has not yet had to dismantle its welfare systems in the name of austerity. But it is on the question of the city that Latin America may have most to offer. The fact that Latin American nations endured the levels of urbanisation that they did in the mid twentieth century, in conditions of scarcity, has made them a prime testing ground for radical ideas in urban development and management. For if growth was the paradigm of the twentieth century, so scarcity looks likely to be the pre-eminent condition of the twenty-first century.

In 1955, New York's Museum of Modern Art held an exhibition entitled 'Latin American Architecture Since 1945', encapsulating an era when Latin America was viewed by many as producing the most exciting architecture culture in the world. Following on from an earlier celebration of southern exuberance, 'Brazil Builds' of 1943, the show presented the region as embracing modernity with a zeal that MoMA's visitors were supposed to envy. Here were the poets of reinforced concrete. In the spirit of the times, the curators foregrounded individual genius and, above all, style.

Six decades later, Latin America has far more useful lessons to impart, about strategy rather than style. No other region of the world has demonstrated the kind of collective effort and imagination that Latin America has in addressing the chronic symptoms of rapid, unplanned urbanisation. Whether we're talking about tackling housing, crime, transport, segregation or the lack of political participation,

this continent has set precedents that could have a transformative effect in other parts of the developing and,
indeed, the developed world.

Take the city of Porto Alegre in Brazil, which in 1989
initiated a policy of participatory budgeting that gave citizens an active role in determining how public money was
spent. Within seven years, spending on health and education had risen from 13 per cent to 40 per cent. This was
a potentially revolutionary reversal of top-down politics.
Its effectiveness has diminished in recent years (following
a swing to the right in the 2004 local elections), but Porto
Alegre is now a touchstone of bottom-up urban management, and the policy has been implemented by more than
140 municipalities across the country, and 3,000 across the
world. Also in Brazil, we might cite Curitiba, where in the
1970s and 80s Mayor Jaime Lerner (an architect) brought
in a series of often unorthodox policies that transformed its
public transportation and made the city, in current parlance,
more sustainable. Most famous of these is the so-called
Bus Rapid Transit system, which revolutionised mobility in the city, but his reforms also included offering slum
dwellers free bus passes and groceries in return for collect-
ing their own trash. The Curitiba experience was highly
influential on Mayor Enrique Peñalosa's implementation
of the TransMilenio bus service in Bogotá, just as Antanas
Mockus's programme of civic education in Bogotá helped
pave the way for the rehabilitation of the public realm that
was so transformative in Medellín. This exchange of ideas
between Brazil and Colombia, along with the unexpected

use of cable car systems in the slums of Caracas, Medellín and now Rio, and the experimental housing methods introduced in Chile and Argentina, are all evidence of a continent-wide programme of reform. They also amount to a new urban repertoire.

If there is one area where the Latin American experience contains a global lesson, however, it is in its attitude to the informal city. What do we mean by 'informal'? The short answer is slums. The slums are not defined as informal because they have no form, but because they exist outside the legal and economic protocols that shape the formal city. But slums are far from chaotic. They may lack essential services yet they operate under their own self-regulating systems, housing millions of people in tight-knit communities and proving a crucial device for accessing the opportunities that cities offer. Acknowledging the informal as a vital part of the city's ecosystem has been the great U-turn of urban policy over the last two decades.

We've seen how the paternalistic attempts to impose order on the city in the middle of the last century failed. This was not just because of a lack of resources and political will, or a one-dimensional approach to urban design. They failed because the slums were too dynamic a force in the city to be subsumed and were consistently underestimated by both planners and architects, who understood them only scantly. The geographer Neil Smith put it succinctly when he said that one of the reasons why the informal city was misunderstood was because it was seen as 'pre-formal', as 'a transitional form of urbanism, en route to formalisation.'

That is the classic old-school planner's mind at work. Today's architects and planners have a far less rigid idea of what a city should be like, and have no pretentions to controlling the form that it takes. As Urban-Think Tank puts it: 'The totally planned city is ... a myth. Therein lies the historic error of urban planners and designers and of architects: they fail to see, let alone analyse or capitalise upon, the informal aspects of urban life, because they lack a professional vocabulary for describing them.'

Acting on this historic failure has seen the abandonment of one medical metaphor for another. If the modernists were surgeons, whose job was to 'cut out the cancer of the slums', then the prevailing trope of our age is 'urban acupuncture'. Needles rather than scalpels are the tools of today's planners, stimulating the city's nervous system with tiny interventions that can have a catalytic effect on the organism as a whole. 'Urban acupuncture' is what Jaime Lerner was practising in Curitiba, or what U-TT practise when they insert a vertical gym in a barrio.

Accepting the informal city as an unavoidable feature of the urban condition, and not as a city-in-waiting, is the key lesson that this generation of Latin American architects can offer the world. The challenge they are now addressing is not just how to rehabilitate the slums, by inserting necessary services and improving quality of life, but how to integrate them into the city as a whole, creating the connections and flows, the points of communication and inclusion that will dissolve the lines of exclusion and collision. Urbanism in the informal city has to be smarter than in the past; it needs to be flexible, so that it can handle unplanned change. Inevitably, this involves the participation of the communities who live there.

In 'The Right to the City', Henri Lefebvre argued that only social classes with 'revolutionary initiative' could solve the problems of divided cities. We've seen how the rise of neoliberal policies favouring private interests has segregated the city. In that sense, the forces of neoliberalism were revolutionary, but so too were the forces of self-determination that allowed millions of barrio dwellers to create their own communities, on a vast scale. Reversing the tide of segregation and rebuilding cohesion is one of the great tasks of the century. Architects and planners will play a role, but they must channel the transformative potential of the slum dwellers. As Lefebvre foresaw, the working class is 'the only one able to put an end to a segregation directed essentially against it.'*

Latin American leaders have been highly effective at empowering the informal city as a political force, but less so at integrating it. In other words they've often treated the slums as a power base, rather than as the home of millions of citizens with the right to the city. One thinks of former Brazilian president Luiz Inácio Lula da Silva, whose Workers' Party (PT) was fastidious in registering slum dwellers on the electoral roll, and whose Bolsa Familia scheme of family loans lifted millions out of poverty by encouraging them to become good consumers – both of

---

* 'The Right to the City', in Henri Lefebvre, *Writings on Cities*, Oxford, Blackwell, 1996.

which granted the PT unprecedented popularity. Or one could mention Venezuela's Hugo Chávez, who relied on residents in the Caracas barrio of Petare, arguably the world's largest slum, and other impoverished strongholds to keep his Bolivarian revolution alive, even while he did little to house them or to demarginalise them.

In those cases, architects and planners have encouraged the politicians to go further – to provide slum dwellers with property rights, to build them public spaces or to connect them to the city centre with a cable car. Lefebvre was right to say that 'the architect is no more a miracle-worker than the sociologist. Neither can create social relations.' They *can*, however, create the channels for those social relations to occur naturally. They can create lines of communication, transport links and reasons for middle-class citizens to overcome their fears and go to the slums. Overcoming prejudice and stigmatisation is essential to making cities more cohesive. Until these methods become more mainstream, we can refer to the architects who practise them as 'activists'.

The Activist

There is a famous scene in Ayn Rand's *The Fountainhead* where Howard Roark, the archetypal modernist übermensch, is waiting for the phone to ring. His rent is overdue and he is desperate for his banking client to call with a commission. Howard Roark is not an activist. An activist does not wait for the phone to ring. If there is a precondition to activism, it is being proactive. Your client does not even know you exist, cannot afford your services and has come to expect no help from you anyway, because your client is the urban poor. So in the first instance, being an activist architect means pinpointing a difficult context and, with the support of the local community, creating an opportunity to intervene; it means self-initiating.

So what is an activist architect? The word 'activist' enjoys a currency that it hasn't had since probably the 1970s. It may be something to do with the fact that we have witnessed the emergence of a protest generation, whether that refers to the revolutionaries of the Arab Spring or to British students occupying their universities in protest against government funding cuts. But in truth you no longer qualify for this epithet merely through political protest. Every blogger with more than a half-baked political opinion, every TV chef campaigning for better school meals and every creative 're-activating' a disused warehouse (even if the ultimate beneficiary will be a developer) is an 'activist'. In an *Evening Standard* list of the most influential people in the London property market even Prince Charles was described as one, which means that the word has shed its radical connotations and now applies even to reactionary pillars of the establishment leading rearguard actions against modernity.

However, I believe the term retains some value. I also believe that it helps us define a radical new approach to making architecture – radical not in terms of a political position but as a form of practice. We've seen, as illustrated by the ideas of John Turner, how in abandoning social housing as a pre-eminent urban policy the politicians effectively threw out the architectural baby with the bath water. When Lefebvre wrote in *The Production of Space*, in 1974, that 'Today, more than ever, the class struggle is inscribed in space,' it was no coincidence that it was in precisely the period when the political establishment was giving up on space as a tool for addressing class divisions. Where social housing at least offered some form of equitability in the city, there is no greater dividing line between classes than the border between a favela and a middle-class neighbourhood. In proposing design solutions for slums, whether it's housing, transport or public squares, the generation in this book is reprising spatial solutions – design – to social problems. It is rescuing space as a tool of politics.

By definition, this means that its members are political animals. However, they are neither 'radical' nor 'political' in the manner that their predecessors were in the 1940s, 50s and 60s, when prominent architects such as Brazil's João Vilanova Artígas and even Oscar Niemeyer were card-carrying communists. They are not communists, nor do they espouse 1960s-style resistance or agit-prop (discounting the Túpac Amaru movement, which engages in both). Whatever their personal politics, they are unlikely to wear it on their sleeves, because when it comes to the city they are nothing if not bi-partisan. They know enough history to recognise that Latin America in particular has suffered from the oscillation between political extremes, flitting from socialist dreamers such as Chile's Salvador Allende to ruthless dictators such as General Pinochet and the military juntas of Argentina, Peru and Brazil – each successive regime cancelling the projects of the former. Today more than ever, being an effective player in the city means being politically nimble, even if – as we shall see in Chávez's Venezuela – not joining the party can cost you dearly. As Urban-Think Tank are fond of saying: 'Urbanism is frozen politics.'

Like characters from Greek tragedy, the modernists' over-confidence made them the victims of hubris. They had ideology, they had answers, they had political backing from the heights of Mount Olympus, they had history and technology on their side. The modernists had not only a methodology but a *style*. The activists are not so sure of themselves. Nothing is predictable. They will try the most outlandish, previously unthinkable things. Build someone half a house? Build a cable car network worthy of the Swiss Alps in Caracas? Build swimming pools and theme parks for the poor? Use public spaces to rehabilitate the murder capital of the world? Lead politicians across the US–Mexico border through a drain? Ridiculous! But effective.

In positing the activists as the humbler, shrewder successors of the modernists, are we saying that idealism yielded to pragmatism? Not quite. At first, that was how it seemed to me. On one level, Aravena building people half-houses appeared to be the very definition of pragmatism. Asking hard-working people to finish the construction of their own homes? Where is the idealism in that? Similarly, the activist architect has to try and find solutions with budgets so small that they would leave your average architect feeling helpless, not knowing where to begin. Maximising scarce resources is the activist's stock in trade. At the same time, she or he cannot afford to be precious about form. The only thing they can guarantee is that the outcome will probably not look how they intended it to. Reality – slum-community aesthetics, contractor deviations, political interference – so often intervenes. What matters is the effect, not the aesthetic.

So, yes, pragmatism. Yet there is no shortage of idealism: it is simply not dogmatic. I prefer to think of them not as pragmatic idealists (compromisers) but as idealistic prag-matists. Pragmatism, as a means to idealistic ends, requires more imagination. It means that, where necessary, methods must adapt themselves to the prevailing conditions, that flexibility and lateral thinking are prerequisites, that there is no orthodox answer.

Modernism had a proud tradition of revolt, of categorical rejection of the past. The activists are not so contrary. They may even be a little nostalgic for the utopian efforts of the modernists, but they would never advocate such authori-tarian visions as a suitable way forward. City-making in the twenty-first century is not a tabula rasa activity; the solution is always contingent on what is already there. The first rule of the activist architect is that the informal city – the slum – is a fact, and accepting it as a functioning, pro-ductive piece of the actual city, and not something to be replaced, is the only way forward. The activists are cau-tious. They observe the conditions, they accumulate data, and then they experiment. The modernists began with bull-dozers; activists begin with a prototype.

What can we say about the activists' methodology? The essential tool of the activist is agency. Here, the architect is a creator of actions, not just forms. The form may or may not be important, but the one thing that the architect *must* do is create an opportunity to act. That means choosing a context (in Latin America it will most likely be in the informal city), identifying a problem and creating the conditions necessary to intervene – not for their own glory but for the benefit of the residents. This is not a book about objects, but about actions. It is not about passive forms but active forms: systems, networks, connections, infrastructure – all of these are more important arguably than the dumb object-housing of the modernists. If we idealise 'urban acupuncture' it is because, having witnessed the onslaught of the modernists, a piecemeal approach appeals to our sensitivities. And yet there has to be something that makes all these micro-projects greater than the sum of their parts. As Jorge Fiori, an eminent teacher at London's Architectural Association, once put it: 'Acupuncture only makes sense if there is a body', and the city is the body. In other words, micro-projects only have a significant impact beyond their immediate site if they are part of a network of actions across the city.

Unlike their forebears, these architects are not the agents of a welfare state, and they can no longer count on whole-sale political support. The world is a more complicated place: they have to negotiate cities governed increasingly by private interests. In the early twenty-first century it is possible to be political and yet to believe in the market as a tool. They have to play off the private against the public to get the most out of both. They have to insinuate themselves into politicians' plans. They have to be radical while pretending not to be (there is no greater turn-off to a politician than the idea that you want to try something radical, something risky). They would never call themselves 'activist architects'.

Above all, they have to be extroverts. This may turn out to be one of the fundamental shifts in the character of the architect in the twenty-first century. They have to create networks. Just as they need political allies, they must ingratiate themselves with local communities. That might mean engaging community leaders or joining in a game of street basketball. But to work in the community's interests you need the citizens on your side, because the days of telling people what's good for them are over.

I should stress that South and Central America are certainly not the only places where activist architects operate. There are extraordinary people self-initiating social architecture in Africa and India, even in Europe and America. But there is a particular history of radical urban experiments in Latin America that lends itself to a rich and satisfying narrative. Concentrating on a single region – vast and diverse though it is – also lends this journey a certain coherence. And though this is a specific angle on a specific part of the world, I believe the lessons are universal, the influence will be global, and the implications for design as a whole apply across disciplines. Having made those remarks earlier about the profligate architecture of the first decade of the century, it seems clear now that the culture is changing. A new generation of architects is emerging with ambitions to make a difference. And I hope they immerse themselves in this story.

1

From Buenos Aires to San Salvador de Jujuy: Dictators and Revolutionaries

On 11 December 2010, the homepage of Argentina's *La Nación* newspaper was dominated by a terrible, sublime image. It depicted a group of figures standing around a supine body. In the twilight, most are black shadows, but two men are picked out in centre stage as if by a spotlight: one, shirtless and flabby, is leaning over a fallen comrade whose head is bathed in blood. The image has the stark drama of Caravaggio's *Beheading of Saint John the Baptist* – the price of a moment's violence revealed in the gloom. However, the *mise en scène* here is a park near a housing estate called Villa Soldati, in a southern suburb of Buenos Aires. This is the aftermath of a pitched battle between residents and homeless immigrants squatting in the park. Several people were killed or wounded that day, thanks to a cocktail of social tensions and Nimbyism. And the roots of it all lay in the failure of the government's housing policy – a failure that stretches back decades.

Buenos Aires is a city of political theatre. Party politics is played out in the street by means of weekly demonstrations and rallies by one group or another – a workers' union here, the Peronist Youth Movement there. Demonstrations take on a carnival atmosphere, with songs and the banging of drums that in other countries would accompany the weekend march to the football stadium. *Porteños*, as the citizens of this port city are called, live their politics with the same passion as their sport, especially since the economic crisis of 2001, which radicalised a generation and put the nation on guard against the ineptitude of its leaders. The greatest political drama since the national bankruptcy took place six weeks before the running battle at Villa Soldati. Néstor Kirchner, the former president, husband of the incumbent president and a talismanic figure, died of a heart attack. The nation mourned loudly and publicly, thronging the avenues feeding into Plaza de Mayo for the chance to file past his casket in the Casa Rosada. The graffiti, more often than not political in Buenos Aires, took on a mystical quality: it became common to see '*Néstor vive*' (Nestor lives) scrawled on city walls.

Kirchner, to his credit, believed in social housing. After more than a decade of neoliberal policies that finally brought the country to ruin, here was a man with a social agenda. In 2004, Kirchner's government launched the Programa Federal, the first social housing programme in fifteen years, which set out to build 120,000 houses nationwide over two years, to the tune of $7 billion. And yet this and subsequent programmes, at least in Buenos Aires, failed to slow the growth of informal housing. The *villas miseria*, or slums, continued to expand. The most notorious of them is Villa 31, noteworthy not so much for its size – it is home to roughly 120,000 people – as for its location in well-heeled Retiro, in central Buenos Aires, where it is an all too visible symbol of the failure of successive governments to provide adequate housing for the poor.

The violence at Villa Soldati was another high-profile symptom of that failure. It was sparked by tensions between the residents of Villa Soldati and squatters in the neighbouring Indoamericano Park, which was aptly named, since it was largely Bolivian and Paraguayan Indians who had set up camp there in the hope of eventually turning tents into houses. Essentially it was a battle between the housed – who didn't want 'their' park turning into another slum – and the homeless. These newcomers had not had the benefit of the kind of mass housing programmes that were such a major feature of Argentina's political agenda in the 1970s, when Villa Soldati was built.

Viewed from the nearby flyover, Soldati is a rather extraordinary-looking place. It has a dystopian, retro-futuristic air, a blocky termite mound rising up towards angular water towers that poke up like periscopes. Designed for just over 3,000 people, it was merely one of numerous megaprojects built immediately before and during the military dictatorship that took control of the country in 1976. The most infamous of them is Fuerte Apache – or Fort Apache, a nickname apparently taken from the Bronx police station in the 1981 movie of the same name – built to house 4,600 people and now a dangerous slum. Like a rotting modernist casbah, it's a no-go area rife with gangs and drug crime. From this cauldron emerged a minor miracle, the footballer Carlos Tévez, known as 'El Apache', who escaped his fate to earn millions at Manchester City and Juventus.

If Fuerte Apache is potentially life-threatening to the outsider, then Soldati is merely threatening. But not all of this generation of social housing deteriorated quite so drastically. The biggest of the estates in this part of the city, Villa Lugano, is still in perfectly serviceable condition. Designed in 1975 for 6,500 people, it was a paragon of European housing ideas from the previous decade. Influenced in particular by British brutalists such as Alison and Peter Smithson, Lugano's megablocks have parades of shops raised one storey off the ground – a faithful rendition of that much-loved modernist trope, 'streets in the air'. Lugano is a perfect example of why streets in the air were often a bad idea: the actual streetscape is killed off, leaving boulevards lined with parking garages and blind walls.

One has to remind oneself that Soldati and Lugano were the products of what, in hindsight, now seems like a golden era. For all the political chaos that reigned in Argentina during the 1970s – when, before the military takeover, governments were falling to coups almost annually – it was still a time when the establishment broadly believed in the right to housing for all. It was certainly the last decade when architects enjoyed the support of the political elite. Indeed, it was the last decade that architects could legitimately claim to be fulfilling a social mission at all. Lugano may have been a cut-price copy of European ideas from the 1960s, but it still represented the best architectural thinking available at the time. Its architects, a practice called Marull, Pereyra & Ruiz, had a generous social vision in mind. In the library of the Sociedad Central de Arquitectos in Buenos Aires, I looked up the original plans in a faded architectural journal and discovered some artists' impressions of the estate. They evoke a leafy modern citadel peopled with genteel types promenading or reading the paper – a place not unlike London's Barbican. It's a rather sweet vision, with no bearing on reality.

Conjunto Piedrabuena

Villa Soldati, Fuerte Apache and Villa Lugano are all on the southern fringe of Buenos Aires, dotted along the airport highway. But it was a fourth, in the same vicinity, that I decided to inspect more closely. Conjunto Piedrabuena had piqued my curiosity the first time I drove past it. It wasn't just that it was a monumental relic of a bygone era; it was also not a piece of carbon-copy European modernism. This was oddly exotic. Its huge slabs were arranged in giant arcs, each connected by an octagonal tower like the eye at the centre of a panopticon. Despite the prison metaphor, there was something instantly compelling about the place and the way in which it commanded the landscape. With its scalloped bays, this was not the product of a simple modernist grid, this was more complex, more original. Its heft was softened somehow by the cracked walls and rusting shutters – yet more modern infrastructure become romantic ruin.

Conjunto Piedrabuena, named after the naval explorer Comandante Luis Piedrabuena, was designed in the late 1970s by the acclaimed practice of Manteola, Sánchez Gómez, Santos & Solsona. The architect in charge, however, was a young Uruguayan partner named Rafael Viñoly, who has gone on to be Latin America's most commercially successful architect. A purveyor of corporate glass and steel, Viñoly is building one of the biggest and ugliest office towers in London. Originally dubbed the Walkie-Talkie, it was renamed the Fryscraper when it emerged that its curved facade had a habit of harnessing sunlight to melt cars. It came as something of a shock that this most corporate of architects had a pedigree in radical social housing. On the other hand, Viñoly's career is also a perfect illustration of the shift in the architecture profession's priorities over the last thirty years.

In a bakery at the base of one of Piedrabuena's housing blocks, I meet Luciano. He is twenty-eight and short but with a stevedore's build and ginger hair pulled back in a ponytail – he looks more Irish than Argentine. Framed against a fridge full of elaborately iced cakes, he tells me that he has lived here his whole life, along with three generations of his family. This will be true of most of the residents. Family ties are strong in South America, and perhaps more so in a place like Piedrabuena than in central Buenos Aires, precisely because it is isolated, out on the edge of the city. It is more like a small town in some ways, and thus follows more provincial ways. Most of Luciano's generation will have lived here their whole lives, and there are few new arrivals from outside these family units. There have been plenty of new arrivals within them, however. These 2,100 apartments now house nearly 20,000 people.

The first wave of residents mainly belonged to the military or the police. That may not have been the intention when Piedrabuena was designed, but by the time it was inhabitable, in 1980, the military dictatorship had the country firmly in its grip – and housing was one way of buying loyalty. In fact the complex was never completed. This becomes apparent when we ride the lift up one of those striking octagonal towers. Of the fourteen floors in this block, the lift only stops at the fifth, eighth and eleventh. To save costs, there were no exits built into the lift shaft on the other floors, so most residents have to walk up or down a couple of flights from one of the exits. These were only the goods elevators – Luciano thinks the residents' lifts weren't even installed.

The complex is arranged into horseshoe-shaped coves overlooking what, now in summer, are rather parched green areas. The idea behind this arrangement was to organise the estate into neighbourhoods, as if to gather residents into the vast open arms of an embrace. Set within each curved rank of tower blocks are smaller ones, only four storeys high. The gap between these concentric curves creates shaded streets – a novel design that appears to work rather well. Elsewhere there are ramps at the foot of the blocks that were evidently designed to create amphitheatre-style seating for public events. That may be wishful thinking – the plazas have become impromptu car parks – but there are a couple of guys sparking up an oil-drum *asado*, or barbecue. At the centre of the complex, four raised walkways intersect above the main road. Luciano says that this is where kids in the estate head to when they're being chased by the police, because it provides escape routes in four directions.

As we walk around I am conscious of people noticing us, keeping one eye on me, speculating on who I might be with my notebook in hand. But accompanied by Luciano, I have privileges. Everyone knows him here – everyone knows everyone. This microcosm is Luciano's universe, the back-drop to his entire life. And he is proud of it. He has a tattoo of Piedrabuena across his lower back. This place is not just his second skin, it *is* his skin.

Luciano describes himself as an artist, and when he's not doing odd jobs to get by he makes short documentary movies about the estate and posts them on YouTube. When I ask him how Piedrabuena has changed in his lifetime he responds with a catalogue of degradation. Most recently a staircase collapsed. Before that there was a gas explosion that left most of the complex without heating or water. You can see where it happened because one of the blocks is being supported by a timber buttress. The surfaces of the buildings are now criss-crossed with a circuit board of new gas pipes, and yet there are still 700 people left unserved.

To get anything done here, residents have to kick up a fuss: they demonstrate and barricade the roads. 'But they're workers,' says Luciano. 'They don't have time or energy to do this for every basic need.' And this is the story of how the great social housing projects went wrong – not on the architectural side, whatever one may think of such complexes, but on the political front. These megaprojects were treated as one-off expenses rather than long-term investments. Of course three decades with no maintenance would lead to degradation.

One can't help but wonder what the future of this place is – or, rather, how long before that future comes to pass. There is a Pruitt-Igoe moment coming, the only question is when. Up underneath one of the water towers that crown the elevator cores, I notice whole chunks of concrete coming away. The walls generally are fissured. Piedrabuena is a prime site for lovers of modernist ruins. Inevitably, they shoot hip-hop videos here. Part of the appeal must be the murals. Luciano takes me on a tour of them, mostly passable renditions of art-historical masterpieces. *Guernica* and Hokusai's wave are here, as are Dalí's melting clocks. They are the works of a local artist known as Pepi, who has since moved out of Piedrabuena. In front of an ersatz version of Goya's *Execution of the Defenders of Madrid*, Luciano says: 'Normally if you want to see this painting you have to pay to get into a museum, but we can just sit here and enjoy it with a beer.'

'Follow the money'

One Friday morning, thirty years after working on Piedrabuena, Rafael Viñoly is sitting in his London office trying to recall what it was like. He has just flown in from New York, and will be flying back there this very evening – a fact that, on its own, reveals one way in which the architecture profession has changed since he began his career. I want Viñoly to summon up the atmosphere of the late 1970s. I've set up Piedrabuena as a heroic failure, a relic of a time when political idealism and architectural ideology were aligned. But perhaps I am taking too rosy a view of a time when social housing still featured so prominently on the political agenda, and when politicians still trusted architects. From the point of view of today, with a clear view of the free market's failure to provide an answer, it looks like idealism. Am I being naïve?

'It was idealistic in the sense that we weren't thinking about branding,' says Viñoly. 'We weren't conscious of the buildings as a support for political advertising. The thing about Latin America, and Argentina in particular at that time, was that this subject was used as a political tool.' Straight away, a picture emerges of social housing as a vote-buying exercise. 'Follow the money,' says Viñoly, like Deep Throat, the garage-lurking Watergate source in *All the President's Men*.

If you follow the money in Piedrabuena's case, the trail ends at a repressive dictatorship waging a 'Dirty War' against any form of political opposition. It's a thought that rather takes the shine off the idea of social housing as an idealist product of the welfare state. Piedrabuena was a perfect example of housing being used to create a politically homogenous community – in this case of military and police families – loyal to the government.

One of the interesting features of the megablock approach to housing is precisely that sense of social engineering. The architects could have built the blocks smaller, creating less dense environments, but Viñoly recalls that they wanted to achieve a sense of the collective. In a country where the two primary sources of social cohesion were religion and the unions, the designers of Piedrabuena and other such estates were proposing another form of collective consciousness: the building block. Or, in Piedrabuena's case, 'the cove', that horseshoe arrangement of blocks that constituted a neighbourhood. Viñoly says he still finds a dignity in this approach, and argues that the way he and his colleagues tried to create communities is 'still valid'.

However, the housing programmes were more than exercises in buying political loyalty. From the early Perón era in the late 1940s onwards, the social housing industry became a major factor in driving the economy, creating employment and contributing a significant percentage of GDP. As such, they had a financial logic as well as socio-political motives, and of course in Argentina that logic was open to considerable abuse. The construction industry was hugely corrupt. Construction companies would inflate the budgets for the utilities, roads and earth-moving and pay off the politicians who got them the jobs. And then there were the conditions in which these projects were procured, with the architects working too fast and aiming the designs straight at the bottom line. 'There was this incredible confusion of dictatorial, demagogic governments,' says Viñoly, recalling his mid-thirties. 'And you were working in an environment where if you stopped two minutes to think ethically, you probably couldn't stand it.'

It gets worse. From 1977, the junta was on a mission to eradicate the *villas miseria*, which then accounted for 10 per cent of the population of Buenos Aires. The generals' motives were largely political, since the slums were hotbeds of Peronist and socialist dissent, though they were also freeing up valuable land for development. After systematically dismantling the system of civil liberties, the regime set about evicting 200,000 people, accounting for 94 per cent of the city's slums, often without even providing any alternative housing. This ruthless policy merely transplanted the *villas miseria* to the periphery or to other regions.

So the generation of housing estates to which Piedrabuena belongs was not even accessible to those most in need. Instead, they served the lower middle class. And this was often the case with social housing projects across Latin America. The loans and mortgages needed to afford a new state-provided apartment were beyond the means of the poorest. And when people were forcibly rehoused, it was always on the periphery, hours away from their jobs, in homes they struggled to pay for.

The fact that Viñoly can say that he still finds Piedrabuena 'valid' means that there is a thin residue of idealism left from his days designing social housing. But he's thinking of the architecture, not the disastrous urban policy of building citadels on the periphery that were completely disconnected from the city. He is not thinking of a system that generated housing with no mechanisms for effectively managing or maintaining it, so that inevitably estates became formal slums, overcrowded and run-down. With the slums out of sight, the land freed in city centres was opened up to investment and speculation. Meanwhile, the investment in the new peripheries devalued with each passing year.

The paternalistic system of state-built housing was not always as politically ruthless or as corrupt as it was in Argentina during the dictatorship but, as we shall see, it was quickly abandoned when new ideologies came into play in the late 1970s and 80s. But if the top-down approach to urbanism was destructive and ethically compromised, are there any examples of bottom-up community building that are not slums? Are there any cases of self-organisation with urban aspirations, social amenities and government recognition?

In the far north of Argentina, I encountered a strange yet radical example.

Túpac Amaru

In Villa Lugano I noticed an insignia painted on a wall. More than graffiti, it was a logo several feet across depicting a man's head in what resembled an American pilgrim's hat, the crown of the hat forming the apex of the letter A.

Underneath were the words 'Túpac Amaru'. I had no idea what the symbol represented, or what those two words meant (presumably nothing to do with the rapper Tupac Shakur, I thought). I only caught it fleetingly from the car window, but it stuck in my mind.

A few days later I discover what it was. In a conversation with the architectural historian Pancho Liernur, he mentions a social movement in the northwest of Argentina. This organisation is building more houses than the volume housing industry in the region – whole communities built around giant swimming pools. A cooperative founded on people power, and consisting of tens of thousands of equal members, it sounds like a socialist revolution made manifest. It builds its own schools and hospitals and has its own factories and security force. In fact, it sounds almost autonomous, like a state within a state. The movement is called Túpac Amaru.

History has made space for two Túpac Amarus. The first was the Incan king beheaded by the Conquistadors in 1572. The second was his descendant, who, two centuries later, led an indigenous rebellion against the Spanish in Peru. He was also beheaded, but only after his captors had failed to get four horses to pull him apart. Túpac Amaru II is the man in the hat. That he is a hero to the indigenous people of Peru, Bolivia and the northwest of Argentina is no great surprise. But that this rebel-martyr's face should be branded on thousands of houses built for some of Argentina's poorest people suggests a political discourse that is founded on revolution. Indeed, as I'm about to discover, it is not just

Túpac Amaru's image stamped on these houses, but Che Guevara's, too. What kind of housing wears its revolutionary credentials on its sleeve? And how does this ideology manifest itself as architecture? As Liernur and I talk, I'm already planning my journey to San Salvador de Jujuy, the heart of Túpac Amaru country.

I leave Salta, the cultural capital of northwest Argentina, in a shared taxi driven by a man who is bursting out of a red T-shirt. Flying past fields of tobacco and sugar cane, our driver steers with one hand while stuffing coca leaves in his cheek with the other. We are close to the Bolivian border, which is the main source of cocaine traffic into the country, and we pass regular police checkpoints.

What am I after in San Salvador, the driver wants to know. I tell him that I'm going to interview a lady called Milagro Sala. Really? Do you have an appointment? He asks that because Milagro Sala is something of a legend in these parts. As the founder of Túpac Amaru, she is revered by much of the population of the Jujuy region, and is without doubt the most powerful woman in the northwest of the country. She is also, however, the subject of wild gossip and the victim of a smear campaign that would end most political leaders' careers. The driver himself doesn't know what to believe, and neither do I. Certainly her life story is extraordinary.

As a baby, Sala was abandoned in a box outside a hospital. She ran away from her adoptive home at fourteen to become a street hawker, but fell into petty crime and eventually wound up in prison. There, she emerged as a natural leader, organising a hunger strike over the quality of the food and helping to teach inmates to read. Her subsequent political image is part revolutionary leader and part Mother Teresa (Milagro, by the way, means 'miracle'). And yet I've also heard that she's been a prostitute and drug addict, and that her children are also addicts. The right-wing media portrays her as presiding over a mob, and even the taxi driver seems to believe that her followers only receive housing if they pledge to take part in mass demonstrations at her bidding, making Túpac Amaru sound like a cult. Not all of these character assassinations are hearsay. Only three months ago, Sala was prosecuted for allowing her followers to attack a university campus where local senator Gerardo Morales was speaking. She was convicted and fined 70,000 pesos. As to how much of her reputation is based on fact and how much on malicious rumour, I am about to try and find out.

In San Salvador, the streets are lined with jacaranda trees in blossom. I notice 'Túpac Amaru' spray-painted on several walls. With the same spray can someone has crossed out the word *puto* (fag) and replaced it with *igualdad para todos* (equality for all). Pulling up outside the headquarters of Túpac Amaru, the driver says, 'Be careful of these people. They're dangerous.'

Across from a cinema turned Evangelical church, Túpac HQ is a modern building with a bust of Che at the entrance. The foyer contains an exhibition about the Inca way of life enacted with clay figurines. One graphic diorama depicts the four horsemen trying to rip Túpac apart, another the murder of his wife in front of him. A few steps further and the images of Che proliferate, on murals, in frames, next to Eva Perón. Then there are the pictures of Milagro. Here she is in jeans next to a dolled-up President Cristina Fernández de Kirchner. Here with President Evo Morales of Bolivia.

We are greeted by Raúl Noro, Milagro's husband. In his late sixties, Raúl is not only much older than her, he is also white. Milagro, and most of her followers, are indigenous Kolla Indians. Several hundred of them are gathered in the meeting hall, where Sala is fielding questions from the stage. This is a routine meeting of the representatives of the local community chapters. These are known as *copas de leche* (cups of milk) and they are the building blocks of the organisation. Each *copa de leche* acts as a local charity, attending to the community's needs, whether it be food, shoes, housing or unemployment benefit. But they are also the means of mobilising and organising Túpac Amaru's 70,000 members. The movement is known for direct action, and when they hold one of their demonstrations they can shut down central San Salvador, which no doubt accounts for some of the animosity towards them. In this particular room, the atmosphere is more matronly. The audience is mainly women. All are wearing a white apron stamped with the Túpac logo.

With Milagro engaged, Raúl and his son Federico, who is in charge of press relations, show us around. The headquarters are impressive. The first thing that strikes me is the sports court that is effectively the building's atrium. You can look down on it from any of the four floors above, with the sound of football-playing children rising through the offices. The fact that a sports court forms the heart of the bulding is not just an original gesture architecturally, it says something about the unconventional way Milagro thinks. And it's not the only good idea: there is an Office of Good Ideas, where people can come and make suggestions to the Túpac management. There is also one called the Department of Human Rights, which finds employment for recent migrants. In the media room, which cynics might call the propaganda room, a man is busy copying DVDs of the various documentaries about Milagro to hand out to visitors.

They also have a radio station, and soon they'll have their own TV channel. The library, meanwhile, covers the essential classics of political thought, and literature from Cervantes to Kerouac. They hold tutorials here for struggling students, or indeed any students excluded from public education – Milagro insists that everyone in the movement should finish secondary school. Out back is a large public swimming pool. Raúl's pride and joy, however, is the room with the MRI scanner, into which he ushers us with some ceremony. This is not your average political headquarters or community centre. This is difficult to categorise.

Milagro appears, hugs us, then disappears. When she's not standing, she runs. Then she's back, holding a woman's hands in her own and promising to do something for her as the woman's eyes well up with gratitude. Finally leading us into her spacious office, she orders Cokes all round. She is tiny and of indeterminate age. She has a gamine's look about her but a mannish face and the voice of a teenage boy. 'Tell me,' she says.

I want to find out how Túpac Amaru has managed to house tens of thousands of people without hiring any construction companies or architects. I want to know how the funding works. I want to see the communities that she is building. But somehow none of this can be done before I find out more about Milagro Sala, since the housing is the product of a philosophy that is apparently indistinguishable from her persona.

'I left home when I was very young, when I discovered that my mother wasn't my mother and my father wasn't my father,' she says. 'We were raised with strict discipline, and taught that white was white and black was black. My mother didn't like lies. She always said that as a family we didn't need to hide things. So when I found out that my parents weren't my parents and that they had lied to me, it affected me deeply. So I put some clothes in a backpack and left – I was fourteen.

'I started walking around the hospitals asking if someone had my birth certificate. And while I was searching for my real mother I was selling things on the street. The police would chase me away. Once a friend lent me a shoeshine box and I went out to work with it, but the police ordered me to stop because I was a woman and I wasn't supposed to be doing that. I got really angry because I was trying to work in an honest way and they wouldn't let me. I also used to sell homemade ice cream out of a Styrofoam box. Once my mother saw me and got out of her car and smashed my box. She said she hadn't brought me up to be an ice cream vendor.

'Of course, when you're on the streets you know all sorts of people. I met people who were stealing things. We used to go and steal and then run away to our barrio. The police would come into the neighbourhood looking for me but the people there wouldn't let them take me away, they protected me. But one day there was a special police operation in the neighbourhood because some guy beat up a prostitute. There was lots of prostitution in that barrio – I wasn't a prostitute, okay? – so the police came in and took everyone away. I was jailed for eight months.'

Prison was the making of Milagro the social leader. Disgusted by the quality of the food, which was cooked by kids from the neighbouring young offenders' institution, she organised a hunger strike, pressing the women's right to cook for themselves. They asked for the local judge to come and negotiate with them, and, when he refused, Milagro organised the taking of the prison. It was her first stab at direct action, and the judge soon capitulated to the inmates' demands.

Back out in the world, Milagro took her next steps with the Peronist Youth movement. In a bid to get a local representative in parliament, she orchestrated the storming of the party congress, and again got her way. However, with a parliamentary seat that was hers for the taking, she balked at the opportunity because she felt undereducated, and handed the job to a comrade with a degree. 'But he betrayed us and the cause. And that's when I understood that you can't give away your responsibility, you have to take it in your own hands.'

In the late 1990s, through the Peronist Youth and the local unions, Milagro helped organise demonstration after demonstration against the government. President Carlos Menem, much derided by the left for his cosiness with the International Monetary Fund, was busy selling off the state's assets, from natural resources to pension funds, and fostering the unsustainable conditions that led to the economic collapse of 2001. Taking to the streets against corruption and the rising levels of unemployment that plagued the northwest even before the crash, this local protest movement managed to unseat five governors of Jujuy. 'When we removed the first of these governors we thought things would change,' recalls Milagro. 'But they continued with the second and the third. And that was the moment when we realised that we had to organise ourselves, and not to expect anything from the government anymore. And that's how Túpac Amaru was born.'

A Revolutionary Movement

A social movement rather than a political party, Túpac Amaru set out to address the needs of the poorest. Its founding principles are self-organisation and the right to employment. These were deployed to great effect from Túpac's earliest foray into building houses. With the election of Néstor Kirchner in 2003 and the gradual easing of the financial crisis, money started to become available for

social causes, some of which came through housing subsidies. Despite having no experience in this field, Milagro
managed to access some funding, and devised the system
that now finances all of the organisation's social causes.
Needy families were marshalled into working parties to
build their own homes. This recourse to collective action
was followed by another brilliant move that doubled Túpac
Amaru's efficiency: it built its own factories for producing bricks and steel, obviating the need to buy building
materials.

Today, Túpac Amaru's entire operating budget is based
on subsidies it receives from the government for building
social housing. It is contracted to build 1,000 houses per
year, receiving 93,000 pesos ($23,000) per house. And it
builds those houses four times faster than private construction companies that receive 136,000 pesos per house. One
reason for this is that Túpac employs five workers per unit,
using the housebuilding programme as a means of generating employment. This must be one of the few schemes in
the world where you can be paid to build your own house –
and then be given it for free.

The headquarters in which we now sit, with its MRI
scanner and public pool, along with the extent of Túpac
Amaru's social activities, from feeding the poor to education, attest to its extremely shrewd use of government
money. But given that it is building its own communities
and providing them with their own hospitals and schools,
and policing them with their own security guards, is Túpac
not creating a state within a state? And while Túpac is

handling the region's responsibilities better than the governor, is the government not concerned that it is nurturing a revolutionary organisation?

'We are and we aren't a revolutionary organisation,' says Milagro. 'We are not revolutionary in the sense that we don't carry weapons and we don't believe in violence. But we *are* revolutionaries in that we understand that we can change how people think. Through dignified work and a change of consciousness and by guaranteeing health, education and work, people can become better. We don't want to be in competition with the government. Because it is the state that has the obligation of guaranteeing health, education and work to the citizens. So the organisation works with the state but we focus on the people with most needs, people who don't have easy access to a school or a hospital or a house. Túpac Amaru is wherever there is a need.'

Perhaps, rather than an extraordinary anomaly, this diminutive Kolla woman is best understood in the context of a new breed of socialist-style South American leader wielding genuine grassroots power. Thinking back to the photograph of her with Bolivia's Evo Morales, whom she calls 'comrade Evo', one recognises another indigenous leader of humble origin who rode a wave of popular discontent. Morales and Hugo Chávez, together with Brazil's Lula and Néstor Kirchner himself, brought a socialist dynamic back into the mainstream of the continent's politics. On a much smaller scale, Milagro is more politically radical than any of them. The key difference, however, is that she purports not to be interested in power.

Milagro is also, it should be said, a far cry from the politicians who have governed in Jujuy, whom she accuses of using their offices to line their pockets. This, she believes, is the source of some of the attempts to smear her. 'Before, the poor were a business. They could own a house but they had to pay a lot for it. Even the *Plan Trabajar* [unemployment benefit] was a business. It was used by politicians to buy votes. If an unemployed person was supposed to receive 150 pesos, he had to leave fifty for the person giving him the money – there was a whole business around that. Now we don't allow it to be a business. And also the politicians used to receive a very big budget to build houses, but they wouldn't do it. So the movement started receiving a budget for it and actually built houses.

'What politicians can't stand is that in the past they would go to a neighbourhood wearing elegant suits asking people for votes, and they would pay them with a glass of Coke and a *choripan* [a sausage sandwich] and people would just look at the floor and say "yes". Now people are no longer impressed with that, and they can answer back. That's why they defend Túpac Amaru in the neighbourhoods.'

This explains why the political class is against her, but not why a taxi driver warned me that the movement was 'dangerous'. 'We have a problem with the bourgeoisie,' explains Raúl, 'because we work with people on the street.' Before I have time to probe that idea, Raúl reminds Milagro about her next engagement.

Welcome to the Country Club

At the entrance to Alto Comedero, a few kilometres out of San Salvador, is a sign that reads 'Bienvenida al Cantri'. That 'cantri' is a phonetic misspelling of 'country', but the joke is no worse for that. 'Welcome to the Country Club.' Driving in, you'll encounter a vast swimming pool and a Jurassic-themed playground. These extravagant amenities nestle among row upon row of single-storey houses. From a distance the terraces resemble a piece of working-class Manchester or Liverpool, like a Latin *Coronation Street*. Here, though, what appear to be chimneys are water tanks branded with the face of Che Guevara.

There are 2,700 houses in Alto Comedero, home to 7,000 people. The buildings themselves are unremarkable. This is a standard-issue *media agua*, or half-pitch, design handed out by the ministry of housing. Each single-storey unit consists of 50 square metres with two bedrooms, a garden in front and a small courtyard out back. There were no architects involved here – the local architects' association demanded too hefty a fee.

My guide, Diablo, remembers the movement's very first housing scheme, the one that paved the way for all of this, when Milagro won a grant to build 148 houses, despite having no construction experience. And he remembers the middle-class scuttlebutt about it. 'Those shitty blacks will end up spending that money on anything except houses,' he recalls people saying. 'But Milagro said, "We have to work day and night to finish these houses, and if we work hard there will come a time when we all have our own homes." '

What makes Alto Comedero truly unique is not the architecture so much as the luxurious amenities and the surreal place-making. Everywhere you look, Túpac Amaru's revolutionary cosmology has been turned into a didactic branding concept. The water tank on the roof of each house is stamped with a face. It might be Túpac Amaru himself, or Eva ('Evita') Perón, that talismanic Argentine heroine, or Che. This is the holy trinity of the organisation's iconography – a blend of T-shirt radicalism, Argentine populism and ethnic pride.

The houses stretch along untarmacked roads in ranks of pastel pinks, beiges and yellows. They are a picture of orderliness, a neat patch of urbanity set against the foothills of the Andes. Alto Comedero is a far cry from the *villas miseria* around it, where people have built their own homes as best they could. Ordinarily, the only way people can acquire a house of the quality of those in Alto Comedero is on a state programme. But you need to prove that you earn 2,500 pesos a month to get yourself on a waiting list that may be eight years long, and then, when the time to start building your house finally comes, you need to cough up a 12,000-peso down payment. The genuinely poor can't even reach the first rung of that ladder.

But it's not just the houses that separate the inhabitants of Alto Comedero from the other suburbs around San Salvador. The real difference was hinted at by the 'country club' sign at the entrance, and is revealed a hundred yards down the road. At first I am pleasantly surprised to pass a basketball court and football and rugby pitches. But then comes the Jurassic theme park. In this vast playground roamed by fibreglass dinosaurs, children shriek as they spill down slides attached to woolly mammoth trunks and triceratops tails. The production values aren't quite Steven Spielberg (everything's made in the local workshops), but still. Teenagers, meanwhile, cluster under palm frond pavilions fitted out with barbecue grills. This is childhood heaven.

Then another suprise. When Professor Liernur told me that Milagro was building swimming pools, I'd imagined modest rectangles, not this sprawling aquatic park with giant walrus and penguin figures and a bridge across the middle. Watching a child take a running dive-bomb at it was enough to validate the entire concept.

It was the tale of the swimming pools that first alerted me to the idealism at the heart of the movement. When I asked Sala why they were so important to her, she replied, 'It's because of the discrimination we suffered when we were children. Kids with dark skin weren't allowed into swimming pools, whereas the ones with pale skin' – and here she pinched her husband's white cheek – 'were.'

This swimming pool is a symbolic middle finger held up at the politicians and the private housebuilders. Social housing is ordinarily a matter of achieving the minimum, of providing only what is essential so that state expenditure can be minimised and private profits maximised. But how do you define 'essential'? Swimming pools are a relatively cheap way of making poor people feel rich. The brilliance of the Túpac Amaru model is that what the movement saves by creating its own factories and cutting out all the middlemen – the developers, construction companies and architects – it can reinvest into the community as social gestures. You can't put a price on the impact that this swimming pool has on a community's outlook. It will affect residents' sense of self-worth and the targets they set for themselves.

What we have here is a peculiar sort of urbanism, a combination of exurbia, Disney theme park and radical socialism. And it only gets stranger. Beyond the pool is a giant stepped pyramid. This is an exact replica of the ancient temple at Tiwanaku in Bolivia. Admittedly it's made of breezeblocks, like something on a Hollywood film lot, but that doesn't stop Mapuche Indians from Patagonia coming all the way up here to celebrate Inti Raymi, the Inca festival of the sun. This is the strangest aspect of Alto Comedero. Raúl pointed out to me that one of the differences between Túpac Amaru and a Marxist movement was its spiritual dimension. Milagro herself is not religious, but she understands that keeping alive Kolla traditions is one way of bonding a community together.

In a sense, Túpac Amaru is striving to revive two now largely defunct ideas: Inca culture and worker culture, the one ancient and the other modern. In contrast with Europe, where labour movements have been in decline since the 1980s, they are still a force to be reckoned with in Argentina, and the unions wield huge political influence. But it would be hard to say they represent workers' culture in the purist, holistic sense that Túpac Amaru does. When Túpac builds a community, everyone participates, and women don overalls and hard hats alongside the men. On one of the compound walls is painted the slogan, 'We fight for work with dignity.'

On my way out, I visit Alto Comedero's two resident factories. The textile factory, with its ranks of unmanned sewing machines (today is a holiday), produces workwear and school uniforms, one of the movement's diverse sources of income. The metalworking factory, among other things, manufactures window frames for the houses and furniture for Túpac's schools and hospitals. The building is stamped with Che's face, as high as a house. The factories are not just a clever way of cutting the costs of housebuilding, they are the community's main source of employment. One of Milagro's prouder achievements is having created 5,000 jobs in the region, along with another 5,000 indirectly. Set aside the economic imperatives at work here, and there is an innocence to all of this. Alto Comedero represents an aspirational, Christmas-list urbanism: a swimming pool, a theme park, a temple – nothing is off the menu. Somehow Milagro has found a way to create a lifestyle for the poor whose outward trappings resemble those of the rich.

Alto Comedero has the exclusive feel of a gated community, but without the gate.

It's incredible to witness what can be achieved with government funding when it's given directly to a well-organised community. This is a far cry from the extortion that was simply routine in the construction of housing estates such as Piedrabuena. Indeed, the comparisons are not flattering. This community has a sense of ownership and empowerment that the residents of Piedrabuena – who have to fight to get their gas reconnected – can only dream of. In this instance, bottom-up organisation has delivered free homes, employment and social amenities that even most middle-class communities cannot boast. Viñoly's concept of creating social cohesion through the megablock sounds technocratic when you think of the multiple ways that Alto Comedero creates unity – through employment, leisure, spiritual belief and, perhaps above all, a sense of collective achievement.

Yet what is most striking about Alto Comedero is that it operates seemingly independently of the market. These people own their houses, but they did not buy them. Nor was there a developer generating profit out of this enterprise. Instead, government funds are made to work hard, with the benefits distributed to the community – and any profits converted into playgrounds and other social amenities. Effectively, what we have here is a socialist system in microcosm, with workers contributing to a productive system and sharing the rewards equally. Alto Comedero is an increasingly rare zone of exception where social mobility is not dependent on rising property values and speculation. Túpac Amaru's achievement lies in carving out a few squares of independent territory on the neoliberal gameboard. The question is, could it work on the scale of a city without having to rip up the very principles of modern society?

2

From Lima to Santiago:
A Platform for Change

Lima is a city that casts no shadows. It was local architect Manuel de Rivero who pointed this out to me. And it's true that the light is hazy, as if the sky were a giant diffuser. 'Like in a museum,' says de Rivero. Lima is also extraordinary in other ways. It has easily the best cuisine in Latin America, for instance, and it almost never rains. But what is most striking about it, for a city of nearly 9 million people, is that it is 70 per cent informal. Away from the colonial centre and the fancy restaurants of Miraflores, the city stretches out in a seemingly endless swath of dust-coloured self-built housing.

It's not an uplifting sight, but de Rivero has a nice take on it. 'People think it looks like a disaster,' he says. 'Of course it's a disaster, it's just starting out!' This notion that the majority of the city is simply nascent, the first phase in a gradual transformation, is one that has been posited in Lima before.

In the 1960s, the British architect John Turner made Lima's *barriadas*, or informal settlements, a cause célèbre. Writing in a special issue of *Architectural Design* magazine dedicated to the topic in 1963, which he edited, Turner wrote that the owner of a *barriada* house 'sees it as the architect sees his building in the delicate stages of its birth – not as a present mess and, for the uninitiated, an apparent chaos, but rather as the promise of things to come.'

Across Latin America, governments were failing to cope with the pace of urbanisation, and building housing estates that were tokenistic compared to the scale of the proliferating slums. Studying how the poor were managing to house themselves, Turner took a deeply controversial position. He argued that governments were wasting their time, and that the poor were much better off building their own homes than letting the state look after them. Even though they might be 'shocking to the outsider', wrote Turner, 'the *barriadas* are, undoubtedly, the most effective solution yet offered to the problem of urbanisation in Peru.'

Like a latter-day Ruskin, Turner was vehemently opposed to industrialised, standardised housing, which he felt resulted in 'aesthetically hideous, socially alienating and technically incompetent architecture'. On the one hand, that was not such a rare opinion (it was certainly held by the majority of his countrymen, and probably still is), but his solution ran counter to the received wisdom. Turner proved over and over again that living in a self-built shack near the city centre was best for rural migrants, because they could save money and be close to work and opportunities. Being dislocated to a housing estate one or two hours away on the city fringe, however, made it harder to earn a living at exactly the moment when they had to start paying for housing – a double whammy.

Turner's reasoning was not just micro-economic but also macro-economic. It was clear that governments could neither meet the demand nor the expense of housing estates for all. Nor could they suppress the enormous pressure for land and housing. Logically, then, the only solution was to support the building of informal communities. But across Latin America in the 1960s, the opposite policy – slum clearances – prevailed. Turner described it as a 'black joke' that governments were demolishing people's homes in order to solve their housing problem.

In his subsequent books, Turner would argue that the 'supreme issue of our time' was a choice between autonomy and heteronomy – between self-determination and letting the government determine one's affairs. With regard to those living in *barriadas*, he made the point by claiming, famously, that 'Housing is a verb.' In other words, much more important than how a dwelling looks is how it serves the owners' needs: does it put them where they want to be, does it keep their costs to a minimum? It was a choice between what he called 'the supportive shack' and 'the oppressive house'.

It was also apparent to Turner that the combined wealth of the poor – if all their assets were capitalised – was far greater than any government's, and that all the poor needed was assistance in deploying their resources in the ways that suited them best, not in the manner that suited the government. This is a premise that the Peruvian economist Hernando de Soto has reasserted more recently, in calling for slum dwellers to be given land titles. In *The Mystery of Capital* de Soto writes: 'Without formal property, no matter how many assets they accumulate or how hard they work, most people will not be able to prosper in a capitalist society.' But this is not what Turner was arguing. As an anarchist, he was no advocate of standard right-wing economics. And de Soto's theory, which has been highly influential, is ultimately destructive, resulting in the inevitable gentrification that forces the poor out of the expensive inner city. Instead of the market value of housing, Turner was asserting its 'use value'.

Most significantly of all, Turner took the view, long before it was fashionable, that the slums were sites of resourcefulness and creativity. As we shall see, this was a position that would later backfire when the World Bank used it to support a neoliberal agenda that effectively relieved governments of the duty to address the housing problem at all. However, before that turn of events, Lima's *barriadas* still seemed full of promise. They became such a touchstone that the critic Charles Jencks included the *barriadas* on his map of twentieth-century architectural movements, next to Archigram and the Metabolists. And aside from their international renown, they influenced a remarkable project in Lima itself.

PREVI

In a northern suburb of Lima is a housing estate that might have changed the face of cities in the developing world. Its residents go about their lives feeling lucky that they live where they do, but oblivious to the fact that they occupy the last great experiment in social housing. If you drove past it today, you might not even notice it. And yet the Proyecto Experimental de Vivienda – PREVI for short – has a radical pedigree. Some of the best architects of the day slaved over it. Now it is largely forgotten.

In 1966, President Fernando Belaúnde, a former archi- tect, agreed to hold an international competition to solve the city's housing problem. The list of participants reads like a roll-call of the 1960s architectural avant-garde: James Stirling, Aldo van Eyck, the Metabolists, Charles Correa, Christopher Alexander and Candilis Josic Woods. These are only the most famous. There were thirteen international teams and thirteen Peruvian – it was a housing Olympiad of sorts.

The conditions were exceptional: an architect presi- dent, an all-star cast, and funding from the UN. This was it, this was architecture's last chance to prove that it had an answer to the sprawling slums of Latin America. Never again would so many prominent architects weigh in on the issue of social housing.

PREVI was conceived by a British architect called Peter Land. He had the idea of creating an experimental housing project which, in contrast to the tower blocks that defined

1960s social housing, would be on a more human scale. Inspired by Peru's traditional courtyard houses, he imagined them tightly packed in high-density neighbourhoods. The advantage of houses over tower blocks was that residents could expand them over time as their families grew. This was one of the lessons of the *barriadas*, the capacity for incremental growth. And so PREVI was conceived as a formal neighbourhood that could grow upwards informally. Turner was not involved, but his notion that citizens should have agency over their living conditions was central to the concept.

Land was fortunate, you might say, that he happened to know both President Belaúnde and the president of the Housing Bank, Luis Ortiz de Zevallos. They were both architects and former colleagues of his from the University of Engineering in Lima. They backed his idea enthusiastically, and pulled all the strings they could to get the UN to fund it. In 1968, everything was ready to go. However, that October, Belaúnde was overthrown by a military coup. The junta now in power nearly scrapped PREVI. More populist than Belaúnde, the generals favoured agricultural revolution and the expropriation of land to give to the poor. To the junta, PREVI looked like just another housing project – but because the UN was backing it, the experiment was allowed to proceed.

In 1969, the international architects were flown in to Lima to study the *barriadas* and prepare their competition entries. The idea was that one of these house designs would be chosen to roll out on a massive scale. But in 1970 the judges struggled to pick a winner. They'd narrowed the field to three finalists – the Metabolists from Japan, Atelier 5 from Switzerland and the German Herbert Ohl. In the end, they decided to build a pilot project to test the performance of *all* of the entries (except, ironically, Ohl's, which proved too complicated). The pilot scheme would consist of nearly 500 houses, so that the designs could be put through their paces, and in the second phase the best would be produced by the thousand. Except the second phase never happened.

For that reason, many considered PREVI a failure. Imagine investing in twenty-four different designs and construction methods – some of which involved expensive prefabricated concrete systems – in the hope that the economies of scale would make up for it when the scheme was standardised. PREVI became an anomaly: a housing laboratory containing so many design ideas, so diverse and adaptable, that it can probably never be repeated.

In the end, the government resorted to far more rudimentary measures to address the housing deficit. Attempting to systematise the *barriadas*, in suburbs such as Villa El Salvador the plots were simply marked out with chalk lines in the dirt so that people could just get on with it – an approach that made the sophistication of PREVI seem almost decadent. Meanwhile, PREVI was poorly documented and, given how isolated Peru was at this time, not widely published. It was promptly forgotten.

Walking into PREVI today, it is rather difficult to get a sense of the scale of the place. When it was completed in the mid 1970s, it was a sharply defined community of neat, white modernist houses surrounded by desert. But Lima expanded beyond this milestone long ago, and now it's a challenge to discern what is PREVI and what is not. It doesn't help that, four decades later, the houses themselves are almost unrecognisable.

The street leading into the complex runs along a series of open fields and playgrounds. Facing these is a four-storey school. This, it turns out, began life as a single-storey house designed by James Stirling. You can tell by its PoMo porthole windows, like the ones he would later use in the Southgate Estate in Runcorn, outside Liverpool. Stirling's basic urban unit was a square block made up of four courtyard houses. The idea was that the owners would expand upwards, leaving the courtyard open for light and air. In fact, there's an entertaining drawing (made by his young apprentice Leon Krier) depicting the house growing into what looks like an Italianate villa with an atrium. Of the sixteen houses here, needless to say, none looks quite like that. They have evolved in their own ways – and not undecorously, with balconies and gables – to often three times the original size.

If Stirling's windows are a giveaway, elsewhere in PREVI it's not so easy. The entire day is spent trying to pinpoint which house is whose. 'Is this a van Eyck or an Alexander?' Decades of expansion have swallowed many of the clues. The original houses are encrusted with geological layers: extra floors, pitched roofs, external staircases, faux-marble facades, terracotta roof tiles and lurid paint jobs.

It's like a form of archaeology, mentally scraping away these accretions.

That was the genius of PREVI: it was designed as a platform for change. The houses were not the end but the beginning. As frameworks for expansion, they evinced one of the key principles of the *barriadas*, which is that a house is a process and not a static object. Of course there was a tradition of the working class modifying their modernist offerings, as Le Corbusier discovered to his chagrin in Pessac, but it was never intended. Here, even though some of the architects tried to stipulate *how* the houses could grow, growth was the whole idea. It was potentially revolutionary.

There are 467 houses in PREVI, covering about twelve hectares. Each of the twenty-four typologies is arranged in a neat terrace or a tessellated cluster of up to twenty units. And each quadrant is divided from the next by a street or alley. One alley will lead you along Alexander's houses and around van Eyck's, another will start behind Correa's and turn through the Danish architect Knud Svenssons's. It's a collage urbanism, like an expo where instead of a pavilion each nation was asked to exhibit a residential street.

A couple of blocks on from the Stirlings, I find myself in a little square overlooked by half a dozen houses. From the seams on the prefabricated concrete walls, they are easily recognisable as by Svenssons. The owner of the white house with the blue trim opens the gate and leads me across a patio into her home.

In 1977, when Juana Mazoni saw her new ceilings, she

knew this was a special house. She ushers me into her living room, which is tennis-ball green, and an Aladdin's cave of plump sofas, lace doilies and gilded mirrors. In contrast to this heavy nesting is a concrete waffle ceiling – a piece of brutalism touchingly hung with a chandelier. Continuing the tour, Mrs Mazoni proudly shows off original doors and details. The house has three patios – three! – each looking onto a walled courtyard, making it bright and yet private. She feels privileged to live here, she says. Somewhere she even has a faded photo of her and her husband with Svenssons. He promised to come back and help them build another room above the living room (to replicate their beloved waffle ceiling). They're still waiting.

The Mazonis are a rare breed in PREVI. They are preservationists, not expansionists. Because their son moved out when he went into the army, they never needed to convert those patios into spare bedrooms for the grandchildren. Consequently, theirs is one of the few houses in the neighbourhood that remains almost exactly as it was first built.

This particular model was designed to be industrially produced and to provide enough courtyards so that owners could extend without losing light and air. But each typology reflects the particular preoccupations of its architect. Christopher Alexander, who went on to make his name with the hugely successful book *A Pattern Language*, spent two weeks living in a *barriada* before designing his house. He was a meticulous researcher of behaviour, and he observed that Peruvians apparently prefer open spaces that they can divide up with curtains to create temporary rooms. The house I visit, owned by a man who keeps fighting cocks on the roof, has indeed kept the ground floor as an open-plan space, and has extended the dining room into the rear garden.

Aldo van Eyck, meanwhile, noticing that women were the heart of the home, placed the kitchen in the centre of the floor plan. He also took a more proscriptive approach to how the owners should expand. Creating triangular courtyards, he assumed that the prospect of triangular rooms would discourage people from building on top of them. He was wrong, of course. Neither outdoor space nor orthogonal walls are sacred to a family of eight with another generation on the way.

Every family in PREVI has a story about their house. They may not know the architect's name, but they know which international team designed it. It's common to refer to the different typologies by nation: so-and-so lives in one of the Dutch houses, or in a French house. It's a form of orientation. But more than that, the families within each section have a sense of solidarity. During the football World Cup (in which Peru rarely features) they will support the country whose house they live in. Sometimes they even organise their own tournaments, on the pitch by the gate.

It's almost possible to read the success of each typology based on how extensively it has been transformed. The Metabolist houses – designed by the trio of Kisho Kurokawa, Fumihiko Maki and Kiyonori Kikutake – appear not to have been that successful. Though long, they are uncomfortably narrow, and their ground floors are generally rented out as shops and restaurants rather than homes. Made of cheap breezeblocks, it's hard to imagine that they could have had the same budget as James Stirling's generous courtyard houses, with their prefabricated concrete walls.

In the opposite corner of the estate, however, is a series of houses that have undergone extraordinary transformations. Designed by the French team of Candilis Josic Woods, the prototypes are like kernels that have exploded into popcorn. One of these great piles has a suburban grandeur that is almost surreal in this context. With its tinted windows and hacienda styling, it wouldn't be out of place in Bel Air. Reportedly it belongs to a general.

And therein lies one of PREVI's great successes. Residents didn't move out as their financial situations improved. They stayed, and turned a housing estate into what feels like a middle-class community. This is one of the principles that Peter Land had laid down at the outset, the notion that 'the ownership of a small lot and a compact house with privacy builds equity with time and is the basic building block of "democratic urbanism".'

As a piece of urban design, PREVI was always more compromised. This was a compact testing ground for prototypes, the equivalent of a tasting menu. The different typologies were never intended to be knitted together in this patchwork fashion. But that too has its advantages. PREVI avoided the monoculture produced by the logic of standardisation, becoming what has to be the most diverse social housing scheme in the world. Its unpredictability creates the illusion of an organic piece of city. The pedestrian streets lend it a calm and sociable air. The alleys open into little squares with gardens designed by van Eyck, some of which are neglected while others have a disarming charm. One woman describes the place to me as 'a lovers' labyrinth'. 'There are so many places where lovers can hide,' she says. The old man walking with her adds, with a glint in his eye, 'Me too!'

Four decades after PREVI was built, there is still a pressing need across the developing world for creative housing solutions that meet the needs of the expanding urban poor. It should be possible to create affordable neighbourhoods on a human scale that are adaptable and walkable. And yet it is telling that the closest we have come to a generation-defining housing competition in recent times is Ordos 100, a vanity project by a Chinese billionaire in an uninhabited patch of Mongolian desert.

However, in Latin America the lessons of PREVI are being reprised. If PREVI marked the shift from a dogmatic modernist approach to housing the poor to one that celebrates the evolutionary, organic nature of informal settlements, that ethos has now been embraced by a new generation of socially motivated architects. We shall meet several of them later in this book. But one in particular, a Chilean, has brought the PREVI principle back to life.

Half a House

It's still early morning as my airport taxi tears along the *Panamericana* to Iquique. In this desert, at this hour, there is little to distinguish the dusty earth from the sky, as though my window is coated in nylon stocking. The city, when we get there, is still asleep except for a couple of surfers lying on their boards out in the sea. Iquique, a mining, gambling and surfing hotspot in Chile's far north, has a faded air for a town that's on the up. Off-season, it feels like Morecambe transposed to the Pacific. Che Guevara and Alberto Granado stopped here hoping to catch a boat to Peru on their motorcycle adventure, but didn't stick around. Today, the city is living fat off duty-free shopping and China's insatiable appetite for copper, but apart from the odd condominium tower you can't really tell.

I came here to see ninety-three homes that can claim to make up one of the most radical developments in social housing design for more than a generation. The Quinta Monroy houses have become a touchstone in the discourse around housing in the developing world. They are the product of a ruthlessly simple idea: if you only have half the money you need to build a family a house, then you build them half a house. That mathematical logic drew worldwide interest, attracting both adulation and criticism.

The architect who designed the scheme is Alejandro Aravena, the principal of the Santiago-based practice Elemental. I first met him in 2008, and he was earnest and eloquent, a natural communicator. I have seen him lecture on several occasions to rapt audiences who wasted no time in rising to their feet in ovation. With his good looks and Manga-style hairdo, the forty-five-year-old has had plenty of media attention, and his work has been published everywhere.

Aravena, a product of Santiago's Universidad Católica and Harvard, set up Elemental in 2000 with his then partner, the transport engineer Andrés Iacobelli. From the outset the practice was unorthodox, since it was a partnership with Aravena's alma mater and COPEC, the Chilean oil company. He and Iacobelli knew they wanted to do something about social housing in Chile, and they knew that with the size of government housing subsidies at that time, the options were limited. Nevertheless, they had a radical idea.

They lobbied and pestered the government to let them test it until, finally, in 2003, they were dispatched to Iquique, where ninety-three families were squatting illegally on half a hectare of land near the centre of town. The task was to settle the families there legally, in real houses. And so Elemental's contribution to the canon of social housing came from an almost impossible conundrum. With just $7,500 per family in government subsidies both to buy the land and build the houses, there was enough money to do one but not the other. 'We tested every single known typology available on the market,' Aravena told me on our first meeting. 'None of them solved the question. That's why social housing is always two hours away on the peripheries. That's the drama of Latin America.'

His answer was to build each family half of a good house, the half that they wouldn't be able to do on their own: namely, the concrete structure, the roof, and the kitchen and bathroom. The total living area would only be 30 square metres – ten square metres smaller than the national average for social housing. However, the houses were arranged with voids between them, so that when they had a little extra cash the families could extend, adding extra rooms until they had a sixty-square-metre house.

Within a couple of years of moving in, all of the families had done just that. The gaps either side of Elemental's concrete cores were bridged with new facades of plywood, timber, plasterboard or whatever was to hand. Each had different windows and colour schemes. It was standardised concrete modernism alternating, like the fronts and backs of playing cards, with favela-style spontaneity. It was PREVI Mark 2, only this time dirt cheap. All kinds of great claims were made for this system, by myself included. Long before I'd set foot in Chile, I was calling it a masterpiece of open design, a platform for adaptability, the iPhone of housing. I even put Aravena on the cover of the magazine I was then editing, with the cover line 'Housing for the billions'. Was I right?

Walking to Quinta Monroy, I start to get a feel for the real Iquique. Away from the high-rises on the beach, it is a rather ramshackle city. Many of the houses look cobbled together, as though an army of beachcombers and DIY hobbyists decided to settle here. It's clear from the cars parked outside them, however, that these are middle-class homes, not the poor ones that an outsider might take them for.

Quinta Monroy itself is only four blocks from the beach. That fact explains why this small plot of land is worth three times what social housing can normally afford. Here, the residents are one block from a supermarket and close to their jobs and to social networks. If they hadn't managed to settle here, the likeliest alternative would have been in Alto Hospicio, a barrio up on a dusty plateau forty-five minutes away.

As soon as I get there I recognize it, not just from the photographs but also from the mild taste of disappointment that accompanies travelling thousands of miles to see something that is simply what it is – a handful of cheap houses, not the Pyramids. The light is not as flattering as in the photographs, the views not as artfully composed, and my very presence here – a tourist at a non-attraction – somehow incongruous. This is when it pays to remind yourself that you are witnessing the manifestation of an idea, not a masterpiece.

The houses are arranged around communal courtyards. This configuration alone distinguishes Quinta Monroy from the rest of the housing in Iquique, where there is very little in the way of communal space formally inscribed into the city. Inevitably, some of these have been gated off, as is often the case when public space is next to private property in South America. The courtyards make for protected playgrounds but also car parks, and judging by the array of 4×4s lined up in them, vehicles are greater status symbols than houses in Iquique.

The extensions are of varying quality. Some owners have really gone to town, with balustraded balconies and nice windows. Other add-ons look like slum shacks wedged between concrete houses. I approach a man in mirrored

Ray-Bans and a baseball cap sucking on the last of his cigarette. He looks like he's about to tell me to get lost, but then
flicks his fag into the road and invites me to take a look
at his apartment. He's in his late forties and his name is
Marco Toledo.

The ground-floor apartment is dark, the concrete and
breezeblock walls are unpainted, but in other respects it
is well appointed. There's a large display cabinet adorned
with fresh carnations and tchotchkes. Marco's wife is sitting
at the computer, on Facebook.

A mechanic who keeps the trucks running at the local
copper mine, Marco occupied the site illegally, like the
other residents in Quinta Monroy. He built a shack and
then claimed legal ownership of the land after living there
for the required five years. He agreed to Aravena's proposal – the residents were shown various typologies and
they agreed that this was the best. The apartment was just
one six-by-six-metre room when he and his family moved
in. However, the ground-floor models were the easiest to
extend, since they didn't require building vertically, so he
quickly expanded into the void and divided up the space.
Later he added a large bedroom out back, as well as a second
bathroom. He did all the construction work himself, after
work. With four bedrooms, there's now enough space for
his wife and their six children.

It was slightly annoying, he says, having to live with his
upstairs neighbour's construction noise, but he knew what
to expect with this housing model. Everyone was in the
same boat, so he didn't mind too much. He even helped his

neighbour out. 'It's not good for people's minds to live in small spaces,' he says.

I ask him whether, after six years, he is happy there. 'No,' he says. 'Because you can change the houses but you can't change the Chileans.'

His complaint seems to be not with the houses themselves but with the locals' suitability for them. 'Chilean people are selfish,' he says, 'they don't think of the community.' For instance, each upper-storey apartment has its own private staircase into the courtyard. This is one of the key features of Elemental's design, because it avoids communal areas where no one is responsible for maintenance. But Marco points out that while there are twenty houses around this courtyard, there is not enough room for twenty cars. So he proposed removing some of the staircases and creating a deck access walkway around the upper storey. His neighbours wouldn't agree to it. To him, that was symptomatic of their attitude generally: a refusal to think communally that ranged from playing music too loud to trying to colonise bits of the courtyard with private gardens.

Marco hopes to move his family out of Quinta Monroy next year, preferably to the south of Chile where he was born. Thanks to this house, he now has some social mobility. He paid 180,000 pesos, or just $400, of his own savings for it, and now he estimates that it's worth $50,000. That seems optimistic to me, but even at half that, it's an accumulation of capital that he couldn't have dreamed of when this patch of ground was covered in rickety shacks.

I feel lucky to have found Marco. He is civic-minded and

ambitious, and an articulate guide to the pros and cons of life in Quinta Monroy. That he is moving on makes him, in a sense, the perfect example of a man who has been empowered by his home. For him, Elemental's housing solution is merely a stepping-stone. That's something that Aravena is proud of. And it's certainly a different dynamic from traditional social housing in Latin America. It is not a zone of exception like Alto Comedero, exempt from the property market. On the contrary, it uses rising property values as a tool of social mobility. Aravena has often argued that, while most social housing reduces in value, and is thus an expense, Quinta Monroy is an investment. Perhaps it is no surprise to see such a market-oriented model emerge in Chile, the country in Latin America most in tune with free-market capitalism.

Quinta Monroy has been a divisive project among Latin American architects. Despite a history of government initiatives to support self-building in Chile, Brazil and elsewhere, many feel that it places onerous demands on the residents. They feel that governments should build houses, not half-houses. Is it right that hard-working people with the scarcest of resources should have to finish building their homes themselves?

John Turner would no doubt have approved. He felt that, far from seeing it as a burden, people derived a great deal of personal satisfaction from self-building, however ramshackle the result. In *Freedom to Build* he wrote: 'When dwellers control the major decisions and are free to make their own contribution to the design, construction or management of their housing, both the process and the environment produced stimulate individual and social well-being.' Turner could be accused of romanticising the tough conditions in which the urban poor live, and he has been. Aravena, too, got complaints from some residents at Quinta Monroy who felt daunted by the task of having to do their own construction work. 'You studied this, we didn't,' some said.

What's interesting is that I rarely hear this criticism levied outside of Latin America. I've sometimes wondered whether one of the reasons why Aravena's work was so lauded in Europe and America was because of a collective sense of relief that finally someone was tackling the question of social housing again. Moreover, it seemed to fit a new zeitgeist. In Turner's day, the DIY survivalism of the *barriadas* was mostly seen as an invidious symptom of underdevelopment. In today's discourse, it fits neatly into the pervasive, internet-driven mantra of 'participation'. In the early twenty-first century, participation is the watchword of everyone from media conglomerates to local government. Whether you are adding your tuppence-worth to a newspaper comments section, customising your own product or volunteering at a local library that government cuts threaten to shut down, participation is, in theory, beginning to vie with consumption as our new state of being.

This notion of housing as a 'platform', as an 'open' system that allows poor people to help themselves, that allows for spontaneous 'customisation' – all this is part of the appeal

to Western observers. It's fashionable Silicon Valley rhetoric permeating the urbanism of Latin America. Given the
subtext of that rhetoric – which sounds social but is in fact
entrepreneurial, favouring private power over government
responsibility – I think one might retain a healthy scepti-
cism. But if one accepts the fact that the majority of housing
in the world is self-built, then surely Aravena's solution is a
valuable compromise: half a house is better than no house.
It's true that it is deeply pragmatic. Instead of challenging the politics of a subsidy that is inadequate, he accepted
it and designed a creative solution. The genius of Quinta
Monroy was the way it reframed the question: not what
kind of a bad house to build, but how much of a good one?
Its greatest value, though, lies in the way Aravena didn't
design a one-off solution but a replicable system. And
systems designed for extreme scarcity are what the urban
peripheries of the world need, not nice houses.

Having said that, Quinta Monroy has obvious drawbacks.
While it is clever housing, it is questionable urbanism.
It might work on a city block in Iquique, but extended
to the scale of the slums it would be a dispiriting monoculture. In that sense it is very different from PREVI. It
allows for growth but doesn't provide a diverse streetscape,
with a mixture of scales and housing types. Thus it suffers
from the same problem that plagued so many of the
modernist housing estates: as if the only way to produce
housing in quantity is to abandon the principles of good
city-making.

Designing for Scarcity

'I really appreciate that I was trained in an environment of scarcity,' says Aravena, sitting in his office in Santiago. 'Somehow it's a very efficient filter against what's not strictly necessary.'

It's true that the power of his model stems from its irreducible logic. But, to me, the process he went through to get it built is crucial to its message. The activist architect initiates the process that might lead to an intervention. That means hectoring the government for an opportunity to act, and, more often than not, it means engaging with the arcane world of planning legislation and financial models. And that is what Aravena did, re-engineering the loan system to make it possible for the people of Quinta Monroy to buy their houses. That is a fairly political act.

Yet, the result is pragmatic. Though a descendant of PREVI, it lacks the idealism. And while it is completely unfair to compare the humble Quinta Monroy with one of the most ambitious housing projects of the 1960s, the comparison is rather eloquent on the situation in which architects engaged in social housing now operate. That idealistic moment in Belaúnde's Peru is long gone, and pragmatism is the order of the day. If anything, Quinta Monroy is the true descendant of the Dom-ino House, the flexible housing system designed by Le Corbusier in 1914. Corbu thought he would make his fortune by selling two-storey concrete frames and letting people fill in their own walls. Although he never managed to get his business model off the ground, the Dom-ino method is not so different from the way most favela housing is built these days, making it – ironically – one of the most successful housing models ever. But in the hands of the master architect, it exemplified the tension between the pragmatic half-solution and the idealism of citizen participation.

Does Aravena see himself as an idealist or a pragmatist?

'I'm not changing the conditions, I'm accepting the conditions. So you might use words like "pragmatic,"' he says. 'But it's also arrogant to an extent, because we're so confident in what we're doing that we don't need to change the conditions and we'll still prove to everybody that things can be better. And if we succeed in that there will be no reason for not changing things right here and right now.'

From Aravena's window, on the twenty-fifth floor of the Santa María tower in the Providencia district, you can see all the way to the edge of the city and the Andes beyond. From up here it seems a city without qualities – prosperous, pleasant, not troubled by squalor nor uplifted by any urban splendour. The city's only drama is the glowing wall of mountains to the east. Notwithstanding its nearly five centuries of history, the city could be less than fifty years old. Indeed, that is not so far from the truth. Santiago's rapid growth began in the 1960s with an influx of rural migrants. And it is only twenty years since the neoliberal economic reforms introduced under Pinochet's dictatorship turned this from a capital city into a city of real capital. During the 1990s Chile had the fastest-growing economy in Latin America, and it was on that wave of free trade agreements and copper exports that many of these smart new residential towers were built. At the other end of the residential spectrum, Santiago's poorest residents have seen their fortunes improve alongside everyone else's. But it has been a rocky road, and the history of social housing in Chile is one of experiments and political gestures, among which Aravena's half-a-house model is merely another, and a less extreme one at that.

If Aravena's critics feel that asking the working class to build the other half of their own houses is draconian, they need only look back to Operation Sitio, the policy adopted by the centrist government of Eduardo Frei between 1964 and 1970 to cope with the pace of urban migration. Nicknamed Operation Chalk, the most comprehensive state housing programme in Chilean history involved literally outlining plots of land in chalk and letting people build their own houses on them – which added up to 65,000 plots in Santiago alone. So there is a history of self-building in Chile that, unlike the informal settlements that would come later, was legal and effective. However, when Salvador Allende was elected in 1970, he scrapped the self-building programme, arguing, like a good Marxist, that it was onerous to force workers to use their leisure time to house themselves. Asserting housing as a basic human right, he resumed a state-sponsored building programme. The Soviet Union even donated a prefabricated housing factory that churned out concrete panels round the clock.*

---

* The story of the Soviet I-464 system is told by Pedro Ignacio Alonso and Hugo Palmarola Sagredo in 'A Panel's Tale', in Patricio del Real

It was noble paternalism, but short-lived and ultimately hopeless. During Allende's three years in government, the number of people living in *campamentos* – informal settlements – rose from 60,000 to 800,000.*

After General Pinochet ousted Allende in 1973, he handed responsibility for housing back to the private sector and banned the land invasions, forcing the existing *campamentos* to become denser and denser. Pinochet forcibly removed tens of thousands of families from profitable parts of the city to make way for market-driven gentrification. It was the same combination of brutal authoritarianism and liberal economics deployed by dictatorships across the continent. However, in 1979 the junta introduced the housing subsidy system that is still in use today. In the 1980s developers built around one million units speculatively, in three-storey housing blocks. In that sense, the subsidy proved far more effective at reducing the housing deficit than Allende's centralised idealism. But that housing is now recognised as some of the worst in the country.

With the return of democracy to Chile in 1990, the centre-left Concertación government resumed a massive housebuilding programme and over the subsequent decade drastically reduced the housing deficit. But, as was inevitable given the focus on quantity, the buildings were of poor quality, uncomfortably small and often located one or two

and Helen Gyger (eds), *Latin American Modern Architectures: Ambiguous Territories*, Oxford: Routledge, 2013.

   * A statistic cited in Paola Jirón, 'The Evolution of Informal Settlements in Chile', in Felipe Hernández, Peter Kellett and Lea K. Allen (eds), *Rethinking the Informal City*, Berghahn, 2010.

hours from the city centre. As John Turner pointed out, raising the material quality of the home is not the same as improving the owner's quality of life, and often results in the reverse: a mortgage the family can't really afford and a much longer commute to work. Furthermore, the new occupants of these social housing blocks enjoy less sense of ownership and community spirit than they did in their informal housing, where at least there was a sense of collective achievement and solidarity. So does the idea of housing as a basic right cause more long-term problems than it solves?

Chile is an interesting context in which to ask that question, because these days it has the housing deficit more or less under control. Indeed, before the terrible earthquake of February 2010, the government had hoped to reduce the number of squatter families to zero in time for the bicentennial celebrations in September of that year. The current housing deficit stands at about 100,000, which is nothing by Latin American standards. So the focus ought now to shift to the quality of life enjoyed by people in government housing. The fact is that Chile no longer needs a housing solution as drastic as the one Aravena pioneered in Iquique. Thanks to its copper, the country has grown rich. It has the highest income per capita in Latin America, and no public debt. Within five years of Quinta Monroy being built the national housing budget has doubled – twice.

The evidence of that is written all over Aravena's subsequent housing projects.

He parks his VW Beetle outside a row of houses in Lo Espejo. They look similar to the ones in Iquique, but they are different. That's partly because the structures are made of brick rather than concrete, but mainly because the 'voids' have been filled in a consistent style. The owners of these houses didn't have to finish them off themselves – at least not the exteriors – because they were built just after that first doubling of the housing budget from $500 million to $1 billion in 2007. So, with a larger subsidy available than the design anticipated, there was enough in the kitty for the construction company to complete the facades. All the residents had to do was divide up the interiors. The great advantage of this model is its density – in this case, thirty families on one square kilometre – and that can be useful on city-centre sites where the land is expensive. But with government subsidies currently at $15,000 per home – double that available in Iquique – this model of a two-tier development (one home on top of another) with voids for expansion is rapidly becoming unnecessary. It is a design that evolved out of scarcity, not plenty.

It's the same story at Renca, built a year later in the northwest of Santiago. Here, Elemental moved a squatter community of 170 families across the road to a legally purchased site that used to be a clay pit. The beauty of this development is that it's a twenty-minute drive from the city centre, and so residents are still close to their jobs and schools. Unlike Iquique, the residents could only extend by adding another floor within the house. The principle of adaptation is the same, but it places much less of a burden on the residents, since adding an internal floor is palpably easier than completing the shell.

To me the houses look better, more inviting, but Aravena finds them less interesting. He doesn't like the fact that the owner's interventions aren't expressed in the facades — almost as if the key to the design is hidden behind a completed shell. There are outward expressions, however, beyond the ones Aravena anticipated. People have added their own balconies and porticos, with terracotta-tiled eaves and Swiss-chalet-style gables. The residents of Renca are perhaps only marginally better off than the ones in Quinta Monroy, but you can feel a shift in affluence, an aspiration to bourgeois style.

Driving on, the next development is even more successful and Aravena is yet more uncomfortable with it. Lo Barnechea is the richest district in Santiago, and when President Piñera came to open Elemental's housing here in the summer of 2010, he was astounded that government subsidies could achieve such high-quality architecture. Not only had the subsidies doubled again since Renca, but the 150 families here — who work as maids or gardeners in the neighbourhood — had more savings than Elemental's previous clients. I must say that I, too, am impressed. This doesn't look like social housing, it looks like a middle-class development. The houses are made of brick with pitched roofs and arranged around courtyards. In this instance the residents hardly had to do a thing. These are complete houses, with no voids. They were designed so that residents would have to subdivide them vertically by providing their own second- and third-storey flooring, but even that hadn't been necessary in the end. How could you wish for a better result, I wonder.

'I'm not interested in this place,' says Aravena. 'When you have that much money the quality comes out as architectural language. I'm not interested in that.'

But surely, I argue, if you are a family moving in here, you just want a completed house, not the added hassle of having to build the other half yourself, with construction work on the weekends and parents sleeping in the same room as their kids. Is it that Aravena simply doesn't find this challenging enough? That it makes him feel like any old architect?

'I prefer to go to an environment where there's not enough money, and instead of producing a tiny house you build half of a good one,' he says. 'And by doing so you're not only making a more efficient use of the scarce resources, but also creating an open system that allows for families to keep on adding in the way they want.'

It strikes me that this 'the way they want' is the crux of our debate. Do the residents here really want room to expand more than they want an easy life? These are 70-square-metre homes, whereas the standard for social housing in Chile is 40 square metres, so it's not as though they were starting off with insufficient space, as was the case in Iquique. Isn't it a precious intellectual argument to put the desire for an 'open system' above the appeals of a whole house? Is flexibility worth more than wholeness, if wholeness is provided at a sufficient scale? If the owners are given a complete house with room to expand even further, then that's an added bonus, but what I find difficult to accept in Aravena's argument is that he wants to see the residents' input reflected on the buildings' skin. He wants his half-a-house solution to take a visible form, and that seems like a contradiction from a man who claims not to be interested in architectural language.

Chile may be too rich for Aravena's housing system, but it still has its moments of crisis. The earthquake of 2010 left thousands of people homeless in the southern city of Constitución. When I visited, a group of angry citizens had blocked the road into town. They'd been living in emergency shelters for the last eight months and they were protesting against the slowness of the government response. The city itself was still pockmarked with empty lots where buildings had collapsed and the remains had been bulldozed out of sight. Elemental was hired to create a new masterplan for the city, but it was still too early to see the fruits of that project. Some time after my visit, however, Elemental built 500 houses, or, rather, half-houses. These followed the same logic as in Quinta Monroy, but they were wooden-framed and pitched-roofed, like rows of saw-toothed terraces. And they looked all the more uncanny for that, each house like a child's drawing that is only half coloured in.

The Constitución housing is a project on almost the same scale as PREVI, but it took the worst earthquake in Chile's recent history for it to be necessary. For that reason Aravena is increasingly looking to other countries, where the scarcity is greater. 'There's too much money here,' he says. And it strikes how rare it is to come across an architect who wants a smaller budget. But the fact is that he and

Iacobelli – who, incidentally, left Elemental to become vice-minister for housing – have devised a system that could revolutionise social housing in countries that need such a revolution far more than Chile does. 'All that toughness, all the rigour required in the Quinta Monroy approach, is the healthiest thing in a project. If you're trained under those conditions then wherever you go it's fine,' says Aravena. Elemental has now tested the design in Monterrey, Mexico, and is developing projects in Guatemala and Peru. These are places where Aravena can still make a difference.

3

Rio de Janeiro: The Favela Is the City

All this money for the Olympics, but to do what? To create what kind of city?

Jorge Mario Jáuregui, in conversation with the author.

In December 2010, I was sitting in a café in São Paulo watching an incredible scene unfold on the TV news. A squad from BOPE, Rio's police special forces unit, was crawling through the undergrowth with machine guns, attempting to surround a favela in Complexo do Alemão. With live rounds whizzing past him, a terrified reporter was doing his best to get as close to the action as his camera crew would let him. This, you could see him thinking, was award-winning stuff. Urban warfare, the scoop of his dreams.

The military-style siege was part of a campaign by the state of Rio to 'take back' the favelas, and rid them of the drug traffickers who treated them as their fiefdoms. BOPE action in the favelas was perfectly common, but this was a widespread and strategic programme of 'pacification' aimed at sending a very clear message that government and the rule of law were back. With the two greatest shows on Earth – the World Cup and the Olympics – coming to Rio in quick succession, it wouldn't do to have vast zones of poverty and criminality, no-go areas even for the police, on such obvious display. The city's image was at stake.

In May 2013, the German magazine *Der Spiegel* ran a feature about European migrants moving into the favelas of Rio. 'Gringos in the slums', read a shocked headline. And, indeed, it is a remarkable turn of events. Here are Italians and Portuguese fleeing recession-hit Europe for the slums of Rio – a sort of reverse colonialism with its tail between its legs. Even a decade ago, no one would have dreamt that such a thing was possible. Yet, after all, the favelas are much safer than they used to be, and they have the best views in town and the cheapest rents. What's not to like?

On one level this is a non-story. Europeans moving into a few favelas in the choicest locations is of little consequence, considering that there are around one thousand favelas in Rio. And yet it is of enormous significance to the perception of these long-vilified settlements. The prospect of gentrification reveals them to be desirable real estate at last, and thus subject to the same market forces that make Rio home to some of the highest property prices in the world. This highlights an essential paradox faced by the municipality with regards to its various slum upgrading programmes: is it possible to improve quality of life in the favelas without subjecting the residents to a process that will force them out altogether?

Rio is changing fast. In the run-up to the 2014 World Cup and the 2016 Olympics, the city faces the prospect of having to build more infrastructure in half a dozen years than it did in the previous fifty. It's not just the millions of dollars being spent on stadiums; whole neighbourhoods are being re-imagined. In Porto Maravilha, the port zone, for instance, miles and miles of new streets, pavements, tunnels and rail tracks are being laid. And the property developers are on the march. In the port, Donald Trump has a multi-billion-dollar plan for five office towers that would form the heart of a new business district. On the other side of town, the wealthy suburb of Barra da Tijuca will be transformed by the Olympic Park. Developers are lining up to build luxury condominiums, while the area's favela residents are on the verge of being relocated. Across the city, tens of thousands of slum dwellers are being evicted from their homes to make way for World Cup and Olympic projects.

Following London's example, there is much talk of an Olympic 'legacy'. Can anyone really take this notion seriously? And why is it that the one and a half million citizens of Rio who live in favelas are always treated to 'urban acupuncture', while a two-week global spectacle warrants mega-projects and massive infrastructural investment? Something is wrong here.

In June 2013, by sheer chance, I was in Rio during the largest popular protests Brazil had seen in decades. Triggered by a small hike in the bus fares, a million people took to the streets of the city. Both the pundits and the government initially struggled to pinpoint what the demonstrators were calling for – there were so many issues to choose from. Some decried political corruption, others the huge sums being spent on World Cup and Olympic stadiums at the expense of public services. It felt like half the city was at work designing placards: 'We want FIFA-standard schools and hospitals,' was a common refrain.

President Lula had raised 40 million out of poverty, swelling the ranks of the middle class, and now the middle class was demanding its rights. It was like a collective political awakening. Even here, in the home of the beautiful game, football stadiums were being denounced as frivolities. It was a watershed moment, not least for Rio, famous for its laid-back, beach-loving cariocas, because it demonstrated for the first time in a generation that the citizenry is brimming with political potency.

The *cidade maravilhosa*, the marvellous city, has another nickname. *Cidade partida*, Rio is sometimes called – the divided city.* Juxtapositions of extreme poverty and wealth are part of what make it instantly recognisable. The favela of Vidigal and the neighbouring Sheraton Hotel, the favela of Rocinha adjacent to the condominiums of São Conrado – it's the stuff of postcards. This is not the standard centre-versus-periphery dialectic; here, those living on the margins can be right in the centre. The question of how to integrate these opposing pieces is one that Rio continues to struggle with. Mayor Eduardo Paes has said that he plans to upgrade every favela in Rio by 2020. Yet his key strategy, Morar

---

* *Cidade Partida* is the title of a popular book by Brazilian journalist Zuenir Ventura.

Carioca, the most ambitious slum-upgrading programme Brazil has ever embarked upon, is in limbo.

Architecture books will assert that the one radical city in Brazil is Brasilia. A capital built from scratch according to strict modernist principles, it is the very definition of the formal city. It is also rigid, misguided and outmoded. No: Rio, the birthplace of the favela, is far more radical. The favelas may not be modernism but they are the byproduct of modernity. In their spontaneity, energy and resourcefulness, they represent an aspect of urbanity that is only now coming to be appreciated. And in its varied approaches to tackling urban poverty, Rio has been a laboratory unlike any other in Latin America. Most of those approaches have failed but, in the failures and the successes alike, there are lessons that cities across the developing world could learn. Because the challenges Rio has faced, and continues to face today, are the challenges of urbanism in the twenty-first century.

Amid the maelstrom of competing agendas – the poor demanding a right to the city, the middle classes clamouring for public services, the gentrifiers in search of a better life, the developers hunting profit, the politicians chasing votes, FIFA and the International Olympic Committee – one question needs to be kept in mind: who is the city for? Because, as we speak, Rio is engaged in a struggle for the soul of the city, and the stakes couldn't be higher.

The First Favela

'Do you know what those people up there in Canudos have done?'
Epaminondas Gonçalves murmurs, banging on the desk. 'They're
occupying land that doesn't belong to them and living promiscu-
ously, like animals."

In his novel *The War of the End of the World*, Mario Vargas
Llosa tells the story of a community of peasants in Canudos,
in the northeast of Brazil, who fall under the sway of a mys-
terious figure called the Counsellor. Led by this saint-like
character, they establish a utopian community in which all
property is communal and money is forbidden. Canudos,
revolutionary and autonomous, is considered such a threat
to the new republic of Brazil that the army is sent north to
destroy it.

It is certainly true that in 1897 thousands of people in this
commune were massacred. The irony is that the remainder
of the army that undertook this bloody campaign returned
to Rio and founded a settlement that would, in turn, prove
to be a revolutionary force in city-making. They founded
the first favela. Named after a fava bean plant that happened to grow abundantly there, this favela was located
on a hill just outside Rio, subsequently named Morro da
Providencia. *Morro* means 'hill'. As many of the original
favelas were on hillsides, it's a term that has become almost
synonymous with informal settlement, and is defined in
opposition to the *asfalto* (asphalt) of the so-called city

---

*   Mario Vargas Llosa, *The War of the End of the World*, Faber and Faber,
1985.

The Nonoalco-Tlatelolco housing estate in Mexico City, designed by Mario Pani, 1964

The Piedrabuena housing in Buenos Aires, designed by Manteola, Sánchez Gómez, Santos & Solsona and completed in 1980

Tomás García Puente

Milagro Sala at a Tupac Amaru rally in 2011

Tomás García Puente

Guardians of the pool, Alto Comedero, Jujuy

A Che-branded house in Alto Comedero, Jujuy

Row houses in Alto Comedero, Jujuy

Elemental's houses in Quinta Monroy, Iquique

The Quinta Monroy houses after the residents' expansions

Four decades of expansion and restyling at PREVI, Lima

The living room in a Knud Svenssons house, PREVI

Cristóbal Palma

Cristóbal Palma

An expanded Charles Correa house, PREVI

Locals in front of some extended James Stirling houses, PREVI

The new rail line and the demolition at Manguinhos, Rio

Affonso Reidy's Pedregulho housing in Rio, designed in 1947

The cable car in the Complexo do Alemão, Rio

proper. This dichotomy between the hill and the asphalt has come to define Rio, and it is one that the city must address at all costs.

Today, Morro da Providencia is in the heart of the city. From this promontory you can look down on Rio's Central Station on one side and Porto Maravilha on the other. It's one of the smaller favelas – about 4,000 people live here – but it's a microcosm of the challenges facing hundreds of others across the city.

The steep cobbled street that winds its way up to Providencia stops outside a brand-new and as yet unopened cable car station. Cable cars are not novelties in Rio – there's been one taking tourists up to the Pão de Açúcar for decades – but they are becoming a prominent feature of favelas. Providencia is the second to have one installed, and there is a third planned for Rocinha. It was the success of the cable car in Medellín, Colombia, that triggered this trend, but in Rio it is much more controversial.

I ask a lady leaning out of her window what she thinks of the new arrival. 'We don't need it,' she says. 'They didn't ask us if we wanted it, but since they destroyed our only plaza, let's put it to work.'

As if to prove her point, a Sunday mass is taking place outside the cable car station, with the congregation packed together in what is left of the square. You can see why locals don't exactly welcome this invasive structure. Eating up precious public space, and installed without consultation, this is not the way favela upgrading is supposed to happen.

So centrally located, Providencia is sure to be a hit with tourists, and people here suspect that that is the real market for the cable car. This favela was 'pacified' in 2010, which means that it now has its own Police Pacification Unit (UPP). And though the drug dealers are still here (their guns just aren't tucked into the tops of their jeans anymore), it is now one of the safest favelas in the city. Indeed, there is a metal trail embedded in one of the streets, marking the route that the tourists are supposed to follow as they soak up authentic favela life. There were even plans to build a hotel here, and dozens of houses at the top of the hill are marked for demolition to make way for it, but they may yet escape that fate. Following the demonstrations earlier this year, the mayor has put a hold on all evictions, fearing more popular unrest. But either way, the cable car risks turning Providencia into an open-air museum. The absurdity is epitomised by a new viewing platform, which projects out over one of the community's garbage dumps. How can the city be investing in tourist infrastructure here when it doesn't even collect the rubbish?

These are just some of the tensions that define the city's relationship with its hundreds of favelas. The intentions behind its interventions are sometimes noble and oftentimes not. The strategies can be astute or crass, their advocates committed or corrupt. If any city has taken measures, good or bad, to tackle informal settlements, it is Rio. And yet it is as though those in power haven't quite grasped the scale of what they're up against.

There are 1.4 million people living in Rio's favelas,

accounting for 22 per cent of the population within the city limits. Across Latin America, nearly a third of all city dwellers live in informal conditions. Across the world, 85 per cent of housing is built illegally. In other words, squatters and *favelados* build more square miles of city than governments, developers, architects or anyone else. Some estimate that by 2030, some two billion people, or a quarter of humanity, will be squatters. So when are we going to recognise that favelas are not an aberration, but the primary urban condition? When will we come to terms with the fact that the favelas are not a problem of urbanity, but the solution? When will we accept that the favela *is* the city?

A History of Failure

When Le Corbusier first visited Rio in 1929, he made some remarkable sketches of an alternative layout in which the city was just one continuous ribbon of a building with a highway running along the top of it. It was one of the most radical urban designs ever committed to paper. It was just an idea, of course – but there is a building in Rio that is reminiscent of it. Perched on a hillside in São Cristovão is the Pedregulho social housing block, designed by Affonso Reidy in the late 1940s. Similarly serpentine, it's a tiny section of Corbu's fantasy.

With its sensuously curved facade, Pedregulho belongs unmistakeably to the heroic tropical modernism of the 1950s for which Brazil is so often celebrated. Pedregulho was meant to project progress and modernity, but it was also warm and inviting. With its panoramic views, distinctive form raised up on pilotis both at its base *and* at its midriff, and overlooking a large swimming pool (now empty), it would be luxury housing almost anywhere else. But when I visit, my taxi driver is reluctant to let me out of the car, so concerned is he for my safety. The building is in a state of disrepair, and does, I confess, feel somewhat menacing.*

On the open-air platform, I follow the cries of 'Halleluyah!' to the door of an impromptu Evangelical church. Outside it I encounter Esteban, a muscular thirty-four-year-old who looks like a model. 'There used to be people dealing drugs in the corridor, and the police were constantly raiding us,' he says. 'But there are no problems now, even though people still think of the place that way.'

Esteban takes me into a friend's apartment where a family is cooking Sunday lunch. In the kitchen, three women are expertly negotiating the narrow space and the steaming pots. Six people, from three generations, live in this one-bedroom flat. 'We're a community in this building,' says the grandmother; 'everyone looks out for each other.' But who looks out for them, I wonder. At the entrance to the building, I passed a car with broken windows next to a heap of uncollected rubbish bags. The jungle surrounding the building is pressing forward. Pedregulho is, and feels, disconnected from the surrounding neighbourhood. Part of

---

* Incidentally, Pedregulho makes a cameo appearance in the film *Central do Brasil* (*Central Station*), where it's the home of a couple who take in street children to sell their organs.

the problem is that nobody knows whether it's the city or the state of Rio de Janeiro that owns the land. And you can see the abdication of public responsibility wherever you look. It's the perennial problem of housing estates in Latin America. But Pedregulho, with its 274 apartments, was as noble and as ambitious as social housing in Rio ever got.

The history of governmental and municipal efforts to find a solution to the favelas is a long catalogue of failures. Since for the better part of the twentieth century they were considered illegal, and thus undeserving of services such as electricity and running water, the solution was often slum clearances. These were particularly popular during the military dictatorship of the 1960s and 70s. Between 1960 and 1975, 175,000 residents were evicted from dozens of favelas in Rio, which, according to the architectural historian Roberto Segre, was 'without doubt the largest urban "cleansing" operation that has taken place in the country'.*

In the 1960s the favelas were considered breeding grounds of communist revolt. In the grip of Cold War paranoia, the US was on guard against future Cubas in the making, and sponsored mass housebuilding programmes in Brazil to help eradicate the favelas. One of these was Cidade de Deus, or City of God. It is no coincidence that it resembled the American suburban model of detached (albeit rudimentary) houses arranged in neat blocks around playing fields. From the mid 1960s to the mid 1970s, the government built 40,000 such homes, resettling nearly 30 per cent of Rio's

---

* Roberto Segre, 'Formal-Informal Connections in the Favelas of Rio de Janeiro', in Hernández et al., *Rethinking the Informal City*.

favela population far away on the outskirts. And like City
of God, many of these new settlements soon became favelas
in their own right. Part of what motivated this mass uproot-
ing was the belief that if people were made homeowners
they were less likely to become revolutionaries. However,
more punitive than progressive, it was a hopeless strategy.
Between 1970 and 1974, for instance, the number of favelas
in Rio nearly doubled from 162 to 283.

If slum clearances and mass housing strategies did little
to dent the housing deficit, it was because the government
was treating the symptoms of urban poverty rather than the
causes. And when it was finally accepted that the National
Housing Bank simply couldn't build fast enough to cope
with the scale of the rehousing, the evictions began to stop.

In the 1970s, a new ideology promoted by John Turner
and others was beginning to recognise the advantages of
self-built squatter settlements. The mass housing schemes
had been justified with the argument that people needed a
roof over their heads, whereas in fact people already *had*
roofs. Turner's support for self-building wasn't merely
pragmatic, it was ideological – he believed that those best
placed to meet the needs of the poor were the poor themselves. And that notion caught on.

With the gradual return of democracy to Brazil in the
early 1980s, government policy became one of precisely
that, helping the poor to help themselves. It began with
Operação Mutirão, a sponsored self-building scheme,
which provided materials and technical assistance but
relied on settlers to do all their own manual labour. This

was short-lived, however, proving too bureaucratic and ineffectual. So the government conceded even more paternalistic control and resorted to what are known as sites-and-services schemes, where it simply handed over designated plots of land with some basic infrastructure and let people get on with it.

The 1980s came to be known as the 'lost decade'. Rio's favelas ballooned. As ever, this was linked to an economic downturn, in this case the decline in industrial output thanks to a combination of failed policies and competition from the Far East. With rising unemployment, the favelas in the city's northern industrial heartland took on a new proportion. The number of *favelados* rose by 50 per cent, leaving a third of the population living in poverty. Government self-help schemes were simply not geared up to handling the scale of informal growth. But just when policy-makers were throwing their hands up, they were offered a lifeline in the form of a new liberal economic ideology.

From the late 1980s onwards, with the Washington Consensus spreading south through the arm-twisting of the World Bank and the International Monetary Fund, the neoliberal agenda took control. Government's job was to cut spending, privatise, and let the housing market regulate itself. In effect, Turner's argument for self-determination was turned on its head by politicians who, now relieved of housing obligations, no longer had to pick up the ruinous bill. And as the economy boomed, the effects were supposed to 'trickle down' to the poor. But after two decades of that experiment, we all know that neoliberalism only widens the gap between rich and poor, and that was certainly the case in Brazil, one of the world's most unequal countries. More recently, Lula's financial aid programme, the Bolsa Familia, went some way towards addressing that inequality; but while it boosted consumer power, it did nothing to alleviate the urban manifestation of poverty.

In Rio, nearly a century of federal, state and municipal policies have failed to eradicate the social inequality of the favelas. There are several reasons why. For one thing, those policies were rarely capable of matching the scale of the problem. And if they were, they failed because they erred too much in one direction or the other: they placed too strong an emphasis either on architecture (as with the mass housing programmes) or, conversely, on economic policies that ignored the spatial dimension altogether. In other words, they addressed either the symptoms or the causes, but never both at the same time. There is no one solution to the social divisiveness of the favelas. Rather, it needs to be approached with social measures tackling poverty and spatial interventions improving the quality of the urban fabric. Only a combined strategy, operating at the scale both of the individual favela and the entire city, can possibly succeed.

In the end, that lesson was learned. In 1994 Rio launched what was then the most ambitious and influential slum-upgrading programme in Latin America, and probably the world. It was called Favela-Bairro, a name that declared the scheme's ambition to turn slums into city neighbourhoods.

From Slums to Neighbourhoods

In the early 1970s, at the height of the dictatorship's zeal for slum clearances, one man was forging a different path. His name was Carlos Nelson Ferreira dos Santos, an architect and anthropologist. Influenced by the ideas of John Turner, Carlos Nelson fought for the favelas to be accepted as functioning pieces of the city. This was at a time when the government was trying to restrict people from working with the *favelados*, and when those who undertook community projects in the favelas (even if it was UNICEF) sparked rumours about communist groups stirring up trouble in the slums. But Carlos Nelson, who had links to the *soixante-huitards* in Europe, was one of the original activist architects.

His key intervention was in Brás de Pina, a favela of 900 families in the industrial northern zone of the city. Working for an NGO called CODESCO, the community development company, he designed a plan for improving quality of life in the favela. Simply by removing some of the houses and opening up the walkways, he improved circulation and helped create a healthier neighbourhood. But more than the insertion of space itself, it was the methodology that was radical. Carlos Nelson was one of the first architects to develop participatory design, consulting the community on its needs and working in collaboration with a team of social workers. It was a far cry from the authoritarian mass housing schemes that were busily relocating the urban poor to the city fringes. This was the first time a favela had been treated as a piece of city worthy of an architect's attention, and not as a potential tabula rasa. In short, it was the first slum-upgrading project.

It would take two more decades for that strategy to be adopted. In the 1970s and 80s, design was simply not one of the tools being used to tackle informal urbanisation. It was as if architecture had become the scapegoat for the inability to control the sprawling favelas: modernist housing blocks had failed to deliver on their promise, and so architects were out of favour.

It wasn't until the Favela-Bairro programme that design was reprised as a crucial weapon in the battle to integrate the favelas into the city. In the 1990s, there was a paradigm shift in the perception of informality. The favelas started to be treated not as outlaw territory but as useful pieces of the city. A new discourse started to emerge around informal settlements, which redefined them not as places of illegality but of resourcefulness. Rather than erasure, what they required was enhancement. And that didn't just mean introducing electricity, sanitation and other services which they had previously been denied or had to steal; it meant designing in some of the spatial qualities of urbanity.

The absence of a spatial understanding of the favelas is exemplified by the fact that heretofore they had not even been included on any official maps of Rio. They were voids. And yet in 1994 there were 661 favelas in Rio, home to more than a million people. Rather than treating those uncharted territories as blank slates, as the modernists would have done, this more sensitive approach left the street pattern and the houses intact, and instead operated within and around them. This was a new departure.

Launched under Mayor Cesar Maia, and the brainchild of architect Sérgio Magalhães, then head of the municipal housing department, Favela-Bairro would operate in nearly 150 favelas. Funded in part by the Inter-American Development Bank, it was the largest slum-upgrading programme, with the highest political profile, in Brazil. The aim was to improve all of Rio's medium-sized favelas, along with dozens of smaller ones and several of the biggest, by 2004.

Beyond the scale of its ambition, what was innovative about Favela-Bairro was the way it operated on multiple planes at the same time. Absolutely central was the notion that the informal had to be connected to the formal city, with roads, staircases and funiculars that would improve mobility in and out of the favelas. At the same time, public spaces were inserted into the crowded streetscape. Plazas and meeting platforms were used to create a sense of breathing space, but also to induce civic pride and encourage a sense of community values. In fact these were often deployed around the edges of favelas, to break up the physical and psychological barriers between poor and middle-class areas. They were bridges of sorts, connecting segregated neighbourhoods and softening the boundaries between them. Beyond that, new public spaces and community buildings were supposed to serve as demonstrative symbols of improvement – making the favelas look more like the rest of the city, thus lessening the stigma attached to them.

Of course, there is a politics to slum upgrading, with vying ideologies and strategies. And aspects of Favela-Bairro were controversial. Some critics felt that the aesthetic approach of inserting symbols of urbanity smacked of authoritarian planning and threatened to weaken the identity of the favelas. Indeed, 'urbanity' is so loaded a concept that the urbanist Saskia Sassen has since coined the term 'cityness' as a more inclusive alternative to describe urban qualities that do not conform to the Western ideal. But at the time, the architects behind the programme argued that, on the contrary, challenging the perception of the favelas, visually, was crucial to their acceptance as ordinary neighbourhoods. This was a concept that would later prove influential in other Latin American cities. But, for now, Rio was setting the agenda when it came to breaking down the barriers of a divided city.

Jorge Mario Jáuregui

'In the '60s and 70s, there was belief that the *new* would be enough to solve the problem – Brasilia, big housing projects, etc.,' says the architect Jorge Mario Jáuregui. 'There was still this idea of Le Corbusier's that architecture could prevent the revolution. Today, we no longer think that. The question is different: not how to prevent the revolution but how to put the social aims of the project at the top of the agenda.'

Jáuregui is sitting in his office in Botafogo, at a desk strewn with papers, smoking a cigarette. With his nicotine-tinted moustache, he cuts a rakish, old-school figure. On his wall is the famous map of South America upside down, drawn by the Uruguayan artist Joaquín Torres García in 1943. Torres García's vision of an artistic school of the South that would supplant the traditional bias to the North never quite came about, but there is an argument that it is now happening in architecture and urbanism.

'What is the role of the activist architect today?' he continues. 'To establish relations with people, to force doors open, to impose a dialogue, to provoke.' Jáuregui gestures out of the window. 'Just outside here is the favela of Doña Marta, but we have no contact with it. And they have no contact with people who live in the formal neighbourhood, only as cheap manual labour. The favelas are the *senzalas* of the twenty-first century, where the slaves lived on farming estates in the colonial period. This dialectic continues today: in the formal city the *senhores* live and in the informal the slaves – they exclude each other but depend on each other.'

Jáuregui is an Argentinian who fled the military dictatorship in the early 1980s. As an activist in the leftist youth movement Juventud Peronista, he fit the profile of the kind of dissident being 'disappeared' by the thousands. The day after some soldiers ransacked his house – luckily, while he was out – he escaped to Brazil, leaving his wife and infant son to join him later. Not knowing anyone in Rio, Jáuregui visited Oscar Niemeyer, who offered him a job in Algeria working on a housing project, but he didn't go because he couldn't speak French. He only expected to stay in Brazil for a couple of years, but the return of democracy to Argentina brought with it hyperinflation and so he stayed. Today, he is one of Rio's most influential architects.

He made his name in 1994 with the redesign of the pedestrian zones in and around Rua do Catete, near the beachfront district of Flamengo. This was just when the Favela-Bairro programme was beginning, and he would go on to become one of its most active proponents. He worked on the upgrading of more than twenty favelas. Often, these were small interventions to dignify the public realm or to improve mobility: turning a dirt track into a covered staircase in Salgueiro, creating a small plaza in Vidigal, building a housing scheme in Macacos, or otherwise inserting football pitches, paved streets, crèches.

The aim of the Favela-Bairro programme was not just to improve the quality of life in the favelas, it was to raise the perception of the favelas in the urban imaginary. In this respect it was far more complex and nuanced than any upgrading programmes that had come before. The challenge was to integrate them into the city without diluting their identity, and this was a delicate balancing act.

The Favela-Bairro programme achieved great things: it lifted the urban quality of the favelas, boosted civic pride, and raised the value of property (a thorny issue I shall tackle further on), with very little displacement of residents. But, with twenty years' hindsight, it was not an unqualified success. It was assumed at the time that improving the public realm would trigger a spontaneous improvement of favela housing by the residents themselves, and that did not often occur. Despite high approval ratings among residents, the process in many instances was also not as participative as it should have been, and so counts as a paternalistic achievement rather than a community one. Finally, the biggest failure of all was the naïve notion that upgrading would have any impact on the narco-traffickers who dominated the favelas. It would take two decades, and the arrival of the Police Pacification Units, for that issue to be tackled head-on.

Leaving the comfortable clutter of his office, Jáuregui and I drive to Complexo da Maré, a cluster of favelas in the north of Rio, for a meeting with a group of community leaders. As we're making our way there, the president of Brazil is across town in the favela of Rocinha. It's the final month of his presidency and he's inaugurating a new housing project, designed by Jáuregui. Why, I ask him, isn't he there shaking Lula's hand and enjoying his moment of glory? 'It's just politics,' says Jáuregui, 'and it's too hot for standing around.'

At this casual response, my respect for Jáuregui doubles. Here's a man who doesn't have time for photo opportunities with the president. But it turns out that he has other reasons for not attending. 'They changed some of my plans in a way I don't like,' he confesses later. 'There was supposed to be a plaza there, but they didn't build it. They missed the whole point of the project. I wanted to create something cultural, integrated – they only created buildings.' It's a classic tale of urbanism in Rio. Politicians and construction companies understand the value of housing, but too often not the space around it.

In Maré, Jáuregui takes his seat in a circle of NGO members and community leaders, mainly women. He starts outlining a plan to bisect the favela with tree-lined boulevards. The circle starts throwing questions at him. What about kids who skate, can they have their own route? Can we have a crèche for working mothers? Can we have a big welcome sign and a map on the main road, because nobody knows how to find us here?

These people know Jáuregui. He's been working in Maré for fifteen years, they trust him. The reason he's here is because he wants to propose regenerating Maré as part of the new Morar Carioca scheme. 'Making contact with the community is the first step to a successful project,' Jáuregui tells me. He hasn't been commissioned, he's initiated this himself, and it would be pointless to embark on a design without understanding what the community needs, and who the stakeholders are. 'You need to see the community through their eyes,' he says. This is basic participative design, and the very essence of the activist architect's method.

On the way back from Complexo da Maré, we take a detour to Manguinhos to visit one of Jáuregui's more recent projects. Manguinhos is home to 55,000 people. One of the poorest favelas in Rio, it is known locally as the 'Gaza Strip'. Jáuregui was tasked with a new master plan for the area as part of the federal Growth Acceleration Programme (PAC). An initiative of the Lula government, PAC was a massive national scheme to stimulate the economy through infrastructure projects, with a budget of 504 billion reais ($231 billion) for the period 2007–10.

The bulk of the money went not to slum upgrading but to major infrastructural projects across the country, and so the first phase of Jáuregui's intervention is fairly modest. We pass some new, boxy housing blocks that look, frankly, cheap. He is not proud of them. As in Rocinha, the contractors and the private investors value-engineered his design, simplifying the facade and reducing the size of the apartments. 'The construction companies are a mafia,' he says.

Next to the housing, however, is a large square with trees and a fountain, and facing on to the square, in a former army barracks, is Manguinhos public library. Inside we are greeted by delicious air conditioning, a bright and spacious layout and rows of bookcases – well-stocked bookcases. In the fiction section you'll find everything from Stephen King to Nabokov and Joyce. But there are also shelves of political science, photography and architecture. The art criticism section (Panofsky, Greenberg and Danto among others) would put my local library in London to shame. I'm not sure whether the teenagers using the computers are aware of the full extent of the treasures here, but they are certainly clicking away with gusto.

The library is impressive, but the much more ambitious phase of Jáuregui's plan involves reconnecting the favela with the city around it. Part of the problem with Manguinhos is that it is completely cut off from the surrounding neighbourhoods by a railway line and the six-lane

Avenida Leopoldo Bulhões, otherwise known as Death
Avenue because of the number of accidents on it. These
two transport arteries form a brutal barrier, and Jáuregui's
scheme attempts to dissolve it by reducing the size of the
road and lifting the rail lines up on legs so that the whole
area becomes permeable to pedestrians. At the same time,
under and alongside the railway will stretch a mile-long
park that he sees as Rio's version of Barcelona's Ramblas.
Jáuregui describes it as the most important urban legacy of
the Lula era. Will it work?

Manguinhos

Three years later, I return to Manguinhos to see what
became of Jáuregui's plan. The library is still in good condition, although I notice the fountain in the square has
stopped working. There's a new row of kiosks painted in
Miami pinks and blues, which are supposed to stop people
trading out of their own homes, but they're all shuttered.
The most dramatic change, however, is that the railway, as
promised, is now raised up on arched legs. There's a prom-
enade underneath it, and a modern station with a swooping
roof. If you focus on that image, it's as though the architect's renderings have sprung to life. But adjust your gaze
to what's directly in front of the station, and you'll notice
that there is no park. Instead, there is what looks like a
war zone.

Rows of houses stand in ruins. Dozens of buildings have
been demolished, ripped away from others that used to

adjoin them. Staircases and living rooms are exposed, interiors turned into jagged exteriors. Here and there, in a field of rubble, stands an isolated house. And this is the tragic part – some people are still living in this carnage. I pass a couple drinking beer outside what's left of their home, the music cranked up to full volume as if to drown out the view.

What happened here is that 172 families had to be relocated to make way for the new park. Except that the process seems to have stalled. The woman showing me around, who prefers not to be named, used to work for the PAC and was in charge of this project. She quit, she says, because she couldn't cope with what she saw happening to people's lives. I notice a banner hanging out of a nearby window. It reads: 'PAC kills'.

Walking through the first row of ruins, we enter what is still a bustling favela community. But most of the houses within the first couple of streets have numbers spray-painted on them, which means they're condemned. Some are marked because they're in the future park, others simply because they're falling down. However, all evictions have been put on hold for the time being, as the mayor is keen to avoid any more protests. He may not realise that residents are already painting their protest banners on the very day we visit. Apparently the UPP (the pacification force) now overseeing Manguinhos killed an eighteen-year-old the other day by smashing his head against a wall. People here are outraged. But, this moment of political expression aside, life here is in limbo. The sewage is overflowing in the street. Stench and rubble – these are the new norm.

My guide explains that there are a number of reasons behind what's going on here. One is that part of this community, the part that will become the park, falls under state jurisdiction, while literally the next street is the city's responsibility. And there is no coordination between the two. But the bigger problem seems to be that in such cases the demolition team has to collaborate with social workers – a sensible policy, only in this case the social workers' contract has expired and the demolition cannot continue without them.

Such are the mundane causes of the tragic scenes around us – all of this because of bureaucratic incompetence. It is a stark reminder that you can design all the masterplans you like, but if the administrative process that's supposed to deliver an urban renewal project doesn't function, then lives get ruined. In Brazil, the bureaucratic machinery needs redesigning as much as the urban fabric.

One of the houses standing alone in the rubble has a smartly tiled facade and a hanging chair out on the balcony. My guide says it's the most beautiful house in the area, and the owner was offered an unprecedented 138,000 reais ($63,000) in compensation. She's lucky, but she didn't accept it because she says she can't find anything of comparable size for that money. It's standard practice to compensate people for their construction costs but not for the value of the land, which they don't own. That's why buying another house is so difficult. If she doesn't accept the offer soon, her case will be referred to the attorney general and she'll just get the 50,000 reais that is mandatory. It's an invidious choice.

These are the daily realities of urban improvement in Rio. There are dozens or even hundreds of other sites across the city where people will be forced out against their will and insufficiently compensated.

'They're just relocating poverty,' my guide says.

An Olympic Legacy?

In 2010, Mayor Eduardo Paes announced that all of Rio's favelas would be upgraded by 2020. It was a bold statement, and one that the Brazilian architecture community met with optimism rather than disbelief. The mayor's primary tool in this sweeping transformation was an urban renewal programme called Morar Carioca – Carioca Living. With 8 billion reais of funding, it was the most ambitious slum regeneration project ever launched, dwarfing Favela-Bairro.

In the same vein as its predecessor, Morar Carioca was to continue the process of stitching the favelas into the urban fabric of Rio. However, one of the weaknesses of Favela-Bairro, in hindsight, was that it did too little to improve the quality of housing in the favelas, and this new programme was to address that shortcoming. A major national competition was launched, and forty architects were chosen to carry out projects in 100 favelas. If Favela-Bairro had shown the world how to take the first steps in integrating slums, here was a comprehensive sequel promising deeper change. It was an exciting moment.

Three years later, however, there is almost no sign of Morar Carioca. It still appears in PowerPoint presentations by the mayor's chief urban adviser, Washington Fajardo, but with precious few details. My initial suspicion was that the funding had somehow been diverted to one of the major infrastructural projects lined up for the 2016 Olympics. If that's so, I thought, then can one even begin to talk about an Olympic 'legacy'?

There are rumours, however, that the reason for Morar Carioca's stasis is political. Much of what has been achieved in Rio in recent years was down to a rare aligning of interests between Mayor Paes and state governor Sérgio Cabral, both members of the centrist PMDB party. But following the popular protests, Cabral is a lame duck, and now the PMDB risks losing the post to a rival candidate from the governing Workers' Party (PT). And with the municipal housing body, SMH, also run by a member of PT, the mayor is concerned that if Morar Carioca goes ahead, the PT will take the credit. So it is most likely on hold until after next year's election. This is the kind of political point-scoring that suffocates so much potential in Latin America.

With the city's flagship programme in mothballs, where does this leave its housing policy? The answer is, back in the bad old days. At this moment, the primary producer of housing across the country is a programme called Minha Casa Minha Vida, or My House My Life (a name that harks back to that 1960s impulse to derail the revolution with home ownership). Launched by President Lula in 2008, the programme was supposed to build a million homes across Brazil by 2012 – which it did – and another million under his successor Dilma Rousseff by 2014 – which is still some way off. The problem with Minha Casa Minha Vida is that its ambitions are quantitative, not qualitative. Lula set up the programme after the 2008 downturn in the knowledge that it would create jobs and boost the construction sector (worth 10 per cent of the economy). As an SMH official confessed recently, 'Minha Casa Minha Vida is more about generating jobs than cities.' In other words, homes are merely the byproduct.

The result of this policy is that millions of poor-quality homes are being built far out in the peripheries of Rio, São Paulo and other cities across the country. Contractors don't even need an architect on board to get funding from Caixa, the National Housing Bank – an engineer's signature will do. And you can tell. These flimsy towers and rudimentary housing blocks have no architectural aspirations at all. For the poorest, MCMV is providing worse housing than was built at City of God in the late 1960s. History is repeating itself, and the result is yet more urban sprawl.

The lessons of John Turner, PREVI and even Favela-Bairro appear not to have been learnt. The notion of conveniently located, self-built, adaptable housing has been rejected in favour of the construction industry's profits. I spoke to a veteran of Brazilian social housing strategies, Ephim Shluger, who spent thirty years working as an architect for UNICEF and the World Bank, and he painted a very clear picture. 'A poor family is sold a 45-square-metre house with no roof slab so they can't expand upwards – so where are you going to grow?' he says. 'Not only are these houses unfit for the *favelados*, but they can build themselves a 45-square-metre house for 27,000 reais, whereas the government can't do it for less than 53,000 reais – so why should they pay double?'

Shluger argues that the government is simply ignoring the fact that 50 per cent of all housing being built in Rio is informal, and that self-built, incremental dwellings are the very DNA of Brazilian cities. For him, MCMV housing programmes merely compound poverty by pushing the poor outside of the city. Worse, their unofficial purpose is to provide lines of credit to the construction companies that are so politically influential. 'The objective is not housing, it's to get the government re-elected,' he says. 'It's diabolical.'

This is a perennial problem. Mass housing has long been tarnished by corruption and electioneering. It also seems to be that when housing is built in volume, the principles of good urbanism, or what we might call 'cityness', are thrown out of the window. And when the emphasis is on sensitive urbanism, as in Favela-Bairro, the need for housing is neglected. Morar Carioca was the first scheme intended to redress that balance. One can only hope that it is put back on track soon, and given the necessary means to fulfil its promise.

Meanwhile the World Cup and the Olympics are looming, and Rio is in a state of nervous anticipation. The city is embarking on its most significant transformation in decades. The question is, who will benefit?

In Porto Maravilha, the old industrial port zone, the municipality has unleashed a whirlwind of development by selling off nearly 5 million square metres of land on the national stock market. This is an area five times the size of London's Canary Wharf, in a city with the most expensive office rents in the world. But setting aside the financial windfall, what measures is the city taking to prevent it becoming as elitist and disconnected from the surrounding context as Canary Wharf? The answer is not entirely clear. A third of the population of the port area lives in favelas. How will these people benefit?

Driving along the elevated highway above Avenida Brasil, you can peer through the broken windows of one derelict warehouse after another. All these will go, as will the elevated highway itself, which is scheduled to be dynamited any day now. Replacing the flyover, city officials are proud to announce, will be the world's most extensive Bus Rapid Transit (BRT) network, one of whose four corridors has already opened. This system of public transport with its own traffic lane was pioneered in Brazil, in Curitiba, then championed in Bogotá and exported as far afield as Cape Town. So it feels appropriate that it should find its fullest expression yet in Rio. The city is laying 152 kilometres of bus lanes, heading through the port to the poorly served northern zones, as well as west to the main Olympics site in Barra da Tijuca. Officials claim it will serve two million people a day.

It is clear that public transport is the city's key Olympic legacy. It's not just the buses – there will also be 28 kilometres of new tram lines. But, while improved mobility is paramount, some of this infrastructure is designed to benefit the same old vested interests. Extending the metro line west to Barra da Tijuca, for instance, will be useful for the two weeks of the Olympics, but thereafter it will serve a mere 200,000 people, at the cost of billions of dollars. Who benefits? Well, the construction company that manages the metro line, for one. Also cashing in will be the developers hoping to exploit Barra's new connections to the beaches of Ipanema and Copacabana. Instead of concentrating the city, the municipality is stretching it out to open up new development opportunities.

We may well ask why the Olympic Village, the Olympic Park and the Media Village are all being located in Barra in the first place. Surely, if there were any lesson to be drawn from London's Olympic legacy concept, it would be that the investment should fall in the poorest, most undeveloped part of the city. In London's case it was the East End, in Rio's it would be the industrial north zone, where Manguinhos and the complexos of Alemão and Maré are located. That hasn't happened.

Barra is an unashamedly wealthy part of town. Laid out to an auto-centric masterplan designed by Lúcio Costa in the 1960s, its highways are lined with gated communities and shopping malls. It reminds me of parts of Florida, with its well-watered lawns and its Subway restaurants. There's even a New York-New York mall, with a fake Statue of Liberty and Eiffel Tower, and a piece of ersatz Venice, a copy of the copy in Las Vegas. Down the road is the ungainly new City of Music designed by Christian de Portzamparc, the largest concert hall in Latin America.

The exception in Barra is a favela called Vila Autódromo. This community of 500 families was slated to be removed in its entirety to make way for the Olympic park and a future luxury development. The residents were to be relocated to – guess what? – a Minha Casa Minha Vida housing development. Only stiff resistance from the community and a subsequent court order in their favour prevented the evictions from going ahead. Residents even worked with urban planners on a counter-scheme to avoid their removal, and at the time of writing the mayor has been forced into finally negotiating with them, although the outcome is as yet unclear.

Are we back in the realm of evictions as a state policy? Is top-down planning that serves the interests of developers and construction companies still the order of the day? Is the opportunity of the Olympics being wasted? In June 2013, a million people took to the streets of Rio to protest against the lavish spending on World Cup stadiums and Olympic projects. Already, these are the most politically charged Olympics of recent memory. Not since the last Latin American games, in Mexico City in 1968, when the students were massacred in Tlatelolco, have they served as such a potent political platform. In a sense, the Mexico City games – and that symbolic protest in Mario Pani's modernist housing estate – coincided with the end of the architect's tenure as the visionary masterplanner bestriding the city with god-like power. Five decades later, Rio is supposed to symbolise a different kind of city and a new era, with a new breed of architect sensitively supporting the needs of disenfranchised communities. But even in the age of the activist architect, urban acupuncture and so-called participatory design, there are powerful forces in the way of an equitable city. And unless the protesters keep taking to the streets, the politicians and their friends will remain as unaccountable as ever.

What Kind of City?

The favela that I watched BOPE laying siege to on the TV news in December 2010 now goes about its business under the watchful gaze of the UPP. New police stations grace the top of each of its hills, and next to each one is a cable car station. This is the Complexo do Alemão, a cluster of fourteen favelas, and home to 80,000 people. Once one of the most dangerous neighbourhoods in the city, Alemão is now a popular tourist destination. They say more tourists ride the new cable car line over Alemão than the one up to Sugarloaf Mountain. After all, carp the cynics, what better way to take in the notorious favelas than looking down from the safety of the air?

Modelled on the Metrocable in Medellín, this new cable car system cuts an impressive silhouette against the landscape of Alemão. It is, for sure, a demonstrative symbol of investment in this long-neglected favela. And yet it is difficult to judge how effective it actually is. On the day of my visit, there seem to be very few other people using it, but it's noon, not rush hour. Running for 3.5 kilometres, the cable car covers what would take two hours to walk in a mere sixteen minutes. And yet it's only operating at a third of capacity, transporting some 10,000 people a day. In which case, was it worth $200 million? I wonder what's going to happen when the cable car in Providencia opens, offering tourists a more central and much more compact experience.

While city officials say the Alemão system is on track to reach full capacity, I've heard numerous explanations as to why it's underused. Some argue that it's only helpful to those who live near the stations, others that it can't compete with the motorcycle taxis and vans that do a brisk trade in Alemão. I can only think of one reason why cable cars are suddenly the big thing in Rio. Carving roads through the favelas means evicting and resettling thousands of residents, and politicians simply don't have the stomach for it. By contrast, cable car pylons touch the ground lightly, requiring relatively few houses to be removed, while gracing the skyline picturesquely. It's the politically sensitive, brand-conscious mode of transport. Residents of Alemão say they weren't consulted. Residents of Rocinha, who also have a cable car heading their way, are fighting it tooth and nail. So who's benefiting?

'It's good for the construction company,' says Jailson de Souza e Silva. 'If they had asked the population of Alemão whether they should spend 300 million reais on it, they would have been against it. There were much more intelligent ways of spending that money.'

Jailson is a rare figure. He comes from the Complexo da Maré, one of the largest and poorest favela complexes in the city, and yet he is a successful academic. Associate professor at the Fluminense Federal University, he belongs to the first generation of *favelados* even to attend university, let alone teach in one. For more than a decade he has been running a community organisation in Maré called the Favela Observatory, with a group of like-minded activists.

'We built a specific viewpoint combining the life experience of the peripheries and access to academic language,' says Jailson. 'We're the first to look at the favelas not as a question of need but of social experience.'

Having spoken to architects, activists and politicians, there is no one I would rather have fielding my remaining questions than Jailson. He is one of the very few who understand the full extent of the transformation Rio is experiencing and who can address its social legacy from the position of an insider.

I know that he has been a vociferous critic of so-called pacification, a policy that many consider to have been a historic success, and so I ask him to explain his reservations. 'The term itself is horrible,' he says. 'The city allowed the privatisation of security by criminal groups, and now the favelas have been turned into a combat arena in the war on drugs, so that favelas have become the territory of the enemy. The problem with "pacification" is that it instils the idea that it was the people of the favelas who made it a war zone and thus need pacifying.'

There is no doubt that the logic of military occupation creates a dangerous 'us' and 'them' mentality that goes against everything the city should be doing to combat urban segregation. There is also no doubt that the UPP forces have committed countless abuses, including that murder in Manguinhos. And yet pacification has returned a semblance of the rule of law to the favelas, and with that has come a degree of normalisation. But what comes with normalisation? In Alemão and Providencia, it was a largely unwelcome cable car. In Rocinha, Vidigal and other favelas in the Zona Sul, the beachy south zone, it has brought gentrification. Is there anything that can be done, I ask, to counter the pernicious effects of rising property values?

'If nothing is done soon, the Zona Sul will be just for the middle classes,' he says. 'It's important that the poor and the middle class live together, but the state thinks the market should rule.'

And there are powerful pressures bearing on the state. The international entities funding the regeneration programmes, including the World Bank and the Inter-American Development Bank, stipulate that title deeds should be granted to *favelados* so that they can be taxed, and so that urban economic growth can march on unabated. That hasn't yet happened, due to a combination of bureaucratic inertia and judicial reluctance. But many feel that, title deeds or not, the outcome is inevitable. 'My bet,' writes David Harvey, 'is that, if present trends continue, within fifteen years all those hillsides now occupied by favelas will be covered by high-rise condominiums with fabulous views over Rio's bay.'* Harvey's opinion is that the poor,

---

*   David Harvey, 'The Right to the City', in *Rebel Cities*, Verso, 2012.

out of need, are easily persuaded to sell their homes at too cheap a price.

Jailson's solution would be not to give the *favelados* in the Zona Sul the right of ownership, and instead to levy a social rent system. This is a standard and, in my opinion, reasonable foil to Hernando de Soto's argument that the only thing the *favelados* lack is access to the capital embedded in their homes.[*] For it is that very right, and the speculation that accompanies it, that ultimately forces the poor out of the centre of the city. 'The state has to recognise that housing should have a use value and not an exchange value,' says Jailson, sounding like a Brazilian David Harvey. 'They should offer the right of use, not of ownership. Capitalism doesn't prohibit that.'

On the question of the Olympic legacy, Jailson is as sceptical as I would have predicted. 'The Games are just a business,' he says. 'The main challenge is that they serve the city and not the other way around. During the Pan-American Games [in 2007], the city served private interests, and unless the popular demonstrations are strengthened, we'll have the same situation.'

The good news is that, unlike some people I've spoken to, Jailson seems to trust Mayor Paes's instincts. He points out, for instance, that Paes tried to spread the Olympic activities around the city rather than limiting them to Barra, where it most benefited private interests. Paes challenged Governor

---

[*] Harvey has another, succinct counter-argument: that de Soto ignores 'the fact that poverty is abundantly in evidence in societies where clear property rights are readily established'. Ibid.

Cabral on this but evidently couldn't go far enough, because he feels he owes his election to Cabral.

Jailson now claims to have the mayor's ear, and Rio's Olympic Committee is now asking him to be a consultant. In this fragile calm after the summer's political protests, politicians of every stripe are keen not to cause the next spark, and people like Jailson have suddenly become valuable allies. This alone is a turn-up for the books. It is a special moment when a *favelado* has a measure of political influence. I have no doubts as to what Jailson can do for the mayor; the question is, what can the mayor do for him? He has radical ideas, and one of them is to open a university in Complexo da Maré, hosting 1,500 students. Urban interventions are one thing, but it's hard to imagine a more powerful symbol of transformation than a university. 'We have to recognise the new centrality of the favela,' he says.

Finally, I ask him what is the most optimistic thing he can draw from the shifting landscape that is Rio in this febrile moment. He doesn't even hesitate. 'Each day people like me have more presence in the city. When I was a boy it would have been unthinkable – it was always the middle class that spoke for the poor. Now we have economic and cultural mobility. Rio today is so much better than it was twenty years ago.'

4

Caracas: The City Is Frozen Politics

En socialismo las grandes obras las haces tú.
[In socialism the greatest works are done by you.]
— Roadside graffito in Caracas

Landing in Caracas is to enter a time warp. As soon as you exit the airport you're confronted by vintage Americana: Jeep four-wheel drives from the 1990s and muscle cars straight out of a 1970s Hollywood chase scene. Only a country with the world's cheapest petrol could keep these things running. The drive into town is peppered with outmoded culture of a different kind: propaganda. Vast murals welcome you to the República Bolivariana de Venezuela, sometimes depicting Simón Bolívar himself, South America's nineteenth-century Liberator, or more often his would-be successor, Hugo Chávez. A socialist republic redistributing the profits from the world's largest oil reserves – it's an admirable arrangement.

However, Caracas itself shows no outward signs of that

redistribution. It's a segregated city with a decaying infra-structure, home to what may be the largest slum in the world, Petare, one of a network of barrios occupying the hills that circle the capital. Approaching along the airport highway, you can take in the disparity at a glance: two con-centric cities, one on the valley floor and another clinging to the valley walls and hilltops that surround it. The formal city nestling in the folds of the informal city.

With a population of 6 million, Caracas is not one of the largest cities in Latin America, but it has the highest per-centage of slum dwellers. An estimated 60 per cent of its citizens live in the barrios. Venezuela has one of the most urbanised populations on the planet (close to 90 per cent), a situation exacerbated by an economy that relies on the oil industry and government bureaucracy for employment, at the expense of agriculture and other sectors. Caracas alone has a deficit of 2 million homes, which has grown by about a million since Chávez came to power in 1998. The govern-ment needs to build 100,000 homes a year just to keep the deficit stable, and it is averaging about a quarter of that.

Caracas suffers from more than a chronic housing short-age, however. The city fabric is badly run down. Driving across town, you're likely to take one of the sunken express-ways built by Robert Moses, New York's own master builder, in the 1950s. The underpasses and overpasses that carve up the city are the legacy of Venezuela's heyday as the richest country in Latin America. In addition to being choked with traffic, they are also prone to flooding. Even the most prominent landmarks can languish in casual disrepair.

The Parque Central Complex, with its twin towers that were once the tallest skyscrapers in South America, is one of the symbols of the city. Built during the oil boom of the 1970s, one of the towers is still blackened from a fire eight years ago and is only now being refurbished.

The urban policies of the Chávez era were mostly initiated at the whim of the president himself – a statue to a revolutionary here, an expropriation of a building there. This gestural, populist politics was played out live on his own TV show, *Aló Presidente*, in one of the most seemingly transparent and theatrical political performances imaginable. Admirably, Chávez used Venezuela's petrodollars to lift millions out of poverty, but he did so mostly with handouts and material goods. Very little went into the urban fabric or civic culture. The two fastest-growing forms of housing are slums and gated communities, the latter for the 'boligarchs' growing rich under the Bolivarian revolution. With such segregation, it's no wonder crime looms so large in the popular imagination. This is a city where you'll see metal grills on a window ten storeys up a tower block – not protection against an actual threat, but the symptom of a state of mind.

Caracas's unruly image, with its tales of kidnappings and gun crime, can leave the tourist ill at ease. When I arrived in spring 2012, however, I would have made slim pickings for a mugger: I had no money. I couldn't withdraw cash from an ATM because the government has set artificial exchange rates for Venezuela's currency, the bolívar, that foreign banks simply don't recognise, while locals just use the black market. Amid all the visible decay of the city itself, this logistical snafu was even more revealing about the state of things. In my first week, I latched onto a distinctive piece of graffiti as a guide to the nature of the place. I would see it everywhere, so that it became a nagging presence in my peripheral vision. It said simply: '*caos*'.

Frozen Politics

'This is a fake revolution, corrupt as hell,' says Alfredo Brillembourg as we drive through downtown Caracas. Brillembourg, alongside his Austrian partner Hubert Klumpner, is one half of Urban-Think Tank, an architecture practice that has been operating in this city since 1998. What began as a research practice into the nature of the barrios ended up delivering by far the most significant urban legacy of the Chávez era, a cable car system connecting the slums in the south with the city centre. Besides that triumph, however, trying to make a difference in Caracas has proved frustrating, to say the least. And today I'm getting a crash course in just how easily things can go wrong.

As we cruise down Avenida Lecuna, Brillembourg keeps pointing at clunky, plum-coloured buildings. These were supposed to be community centres and offices for the government's *misiones* programme. The 'missions' are quasi-governmental organisations that deliver support to poor communities and keep the Bolivarian message strong among Chávez's grassroots support base. In 2008, U-TT was commissioned to design the scheme, part of a grand plan to rebrand Avenida Lecuna as Avenida Socialista. U-TT devised a series of densely programmed buildings, housing gyms and other facilities alongside offices connected directly to key metro stations. But when U-TT refused to join the official United Socialist Party of Venezuela, the government kicked them off the project and handed the plans over to their own contractor.

In the end most of the buildings were turned into apartment blocks, appropriated to ease the housing crisis. The community facilities were ditched and the buildings now have a cheap, shoddy feel. But Brillembourg is phlegmatic. Laughing, he calls them 'exquisite corpses' – one part U-TT and one part standard-issue contractor, the kind that siphons the cream of the budget into an offshore account. That's how things work here.

The fact that U-TT refused to join the party was partly a matter of principle, but mainly one of realpolitik. It was in their interest to remain neutral because they were working with various district mayors in the city, some of them belonging to other parties, and they wanted to protect those contracts. In a polarised city where everyone is on one side or the other, picking sides has consequences.

'It's not the architect's job to be party-aligned,' says Brillembourg. 'We want to knit the city back together, not divide it up! But we were naïve because either you're with him or against him.' The 'him' in question is of course Chávez. Such are the invisible forces that determine what does or does not happen in the city. Not for the last time, Brillembourg uses a phrase that is almost a U-TT mantra:

'Urbanism is frozen politics.' The city, in other words, is the product of countless negotiations, political allegiances and secret trade-offs. It's a rhetorical flourish of the kind that Brillembourg excels at. An energetic orator, he could almost go toe to toe with El Comandante himself when it comes to marathon lectures full of ideological zeal. But he is also a realist, and he knows when to back down. 'We threatened to sue them for taking our designs, but the contractor said, "If you sue us you'll never sleep another night in this city."'

As we're driving, Rafael, one of the U-TT team, gets a call alerting him to an impromptu gig a few blocks away. Local rapper Canserbero (Spanish for Cerberus, the guardian of Hades) is in full flow. When we get there – an abandoned lot behind a disused bullring – hundreds of people are jumping up and down, hands in the air. A sweaty, boyish figure is booming into the mic. The song, *Jeremias 17-5*, is a street-wise epic full of bitter experience, and his fans know every word of it. 'Cursed is the man who trusts another man,' they sing along. Canserbero's lyrics record lives of violence and hardship. He preaches disillusionment and defiance. In *A Day in the Barrio*, he sings: 'Power can corrupt any human / Capitalism, socialism, communism were practiced / But the result was almost the same.'

The crowd laps it up, hands bobbing. This patch of gravel, only a few blocks from the government complex of El Silencio, has erupted into a joyous critique of a city both vividly alive and unliveable. It is Caracas in microcosm: spontaneous, passionate and cynical. And it's as if the bouncing bodies sense that a city this fucked might be the place to invent the city of the future.

Revolutionary Ideals

In the U-TT office in El Rosal is a framed photograph of Cuban architects and artists shoulder to shoulder with revolutionaries in fatigues and berets. This group portrait, taken in front of the domed National Art Schools building shortly after it was completed in 1965, depicts the architectural community and the new political regime joining forces to support the noble cause of culture. Revolution and the arts, in other words, were not mutually exclusive. It's a poignant image because it represents an ideal that Urban-Think Tank has never had the good fortune to experience in Caracas.

The built legacy of the Bolivarian revolution is slim indeed. Governmental housebuilding schemes have been woefully inadequate. In spring 2012, with an election looming in November, Chávez is desperately trying to get some housing projects finished so that in his campaign he'll be able to say he completed the 40,000 units that he promised this year. When the need is particularly urgent, after flooding or landslides, he simply expropriates buildings and turns them over for makeshift housing: an office block here, a shopping mall there. Later in the year, he'll propose a $140-million mausoleum for the remains of his hero, Bolívar. But again this is political theatre, not urban strategy.

In U-TT's early years in Caracas, they did all sorts of commercial work, from private houses to a swanky office building for the Banco de Venezuela. But they were drawn to the barrios. In the 1990s this was not a fashionable preoccupation, especially for two well-heeled architecture graduates from New York's Columbia University. Brillembourg was the son of a wealthy Venezuelan family whose farms were expropriated by the Chávez government, and Klumpner a Salzburg native who had trained under the once radical Austrian architect Hans Hollein. They were perhaps unlikely candidates for the work they subsequently embarked upon but, living in Caracas, the realities of a deeply segregated city were too brazen to ignore. Using the Brillembourg family driver and gardener to gain access, they started visiting the barrio of La Vega. This initiation into the way that the majority of the city lived was a career-defining experience. '[It] compelled us to rethink how we had been trained and to what purpose,' they wrote. Tweaking the title of Venturi, Scott Brown, and Izenour's seminal text on Las Vegas, they defined a practice that they called Learning from La Vega.

In the absence of a revolutionary urban policy, U-TT has always relied on initiating its own projects. In the early days these were modest and unglamorous. In 2003, Brillembourg and Klumpner tested the idea of bringing what are known as dry toilets or compost toilets into the slums, where there are most often no sewerage systems. They designed the toilet as what they called a House Core Unit, the starting point for a self-built house. It was a pragmatic proposal but one that, implemented across the barrio, had the potential to dramatically improve the living conditions of its residents. The more idealistic position to take would have been to lobby for the installation of proper infra-structure, but, given how unlikely the chances of success, U-TT considered that almost an abnegation of responsibil-ity. 'Considering ideal conditions is a waste of time,' they wrote in their 2005 book *Informal City*; 'the point is to avoid catastrophe.'*

In 2003, U-TT launched its first properly funded research project in the barrios of Caracas, inviting international artists such as Marjetica Potrč to collaborate on projects, including that dry toilet. The results became *Informal City*, which remains one of the best, most accessible books about informality in Latin America. It set out clearly that barrios were not merely a problem awaiting a solution but extraor-dinary self-regulating systems, places with qualities. Above all, they were facts on the ground, an urban condition too pervasive to be reversed. 'The planned city can neither eliminate nor subsume the informal qualities and practices of its inhabitants,' wrote Brillembourg and Klumpner. 'The informal persists; its inherent strengths resist and deflect efforts to impose order. The totally planned city is, there-fore, a myth.'

In engaging with the informal city, U-TT developed a methodology of maximising the amount of social activ-ity that a tiny plot of land could deliver. The strategy was

---

* Alfred Brillembourg, Kristin Feireiss and Hubert Klumpner, eds, *Informal City: Caracas Case*, Prestel Publishing, 2005.

tested out on the Mama Margarita children's shelter in 2001. Working with a local church, U-TT built a home for street children on an unpromising site under a flyover in Petare. Taking over this disused space was precisely the kind of opportunism displayed by the *buhoneros*, the street vendors. Already U-TT was using the tactics of the informal city, developing a street-vendor style of architecture. By building a football pitch on the roof, the architects gained two productive storeys out of an otherwise dead space. This technique of maximising the potential uses of a space is one they were to deploy across the city – or at least they would have, if politics and the dark arts of the Venezuelan construction industry hadn't got in the way.

In the little barrio of La Cruz stands a building that U-TT calls the 'vertical gymnasium'. What is a simple modernist box from the outside becomes a riot of colour and structure when you enter. There is a sports court on the ground floor on which some grannies are practising tai chi – a sedate enough scene, if it weren't for the elaborate red structure over their heads. Suspended in mid-air is a running track circling the edge of a three-storey open space. This building is, in the best sense of the term, a piece of Latin American High Tech. Walking in off the street, the space is baroque by local standards, and generous in the extreme. As well as the running track, there are changing rooms on the second floor, gym equipment, a climbing wall, offices on the third floor and once again a football pitch on the roof. Up here, with a view over the district of Chacao, some kids are practicing with their trainer. The football pitch used to be at street level, and the local community wanted a roof over it so that the kids could play in the rain. U-TT's instinct was, why stop at a roof?

There was much hype after the gym was built in 2004 about its dramatic impact on local crime statistics. Violent crime fell by 30 per cent more or less overnight, according to U-TT. Walking around La Cruz today, it's easy to see why. This is a micro-slum on the edge of Chacao, the richest district in Caracas. Virtually incorporated into the city proper, it's the kind of barrio tourists can wander around in – there are even street signs. Ask residents of La Cruz whether the gym has lifted quality of life in the community, and they'll reply: '*¡Claro, claro!*'

There is no denying that it's a wonderful asset, but it's clear that as a one-off this kind of urban acupuncture is only gestural. It would have to be tested in bigger slums and implemented at some kind of scale. And that's precisely what U-TT set out to do. When I visited there were gyms under way in the neighbourhoods of Baruta, Los Teques, San Agustín and El Dorado. But as I write, only the one in La Cruz has been completed.

In Baruta, in the south of Caracas, the gym is still merely a metal framework. It was commissioned by Henrique Capriles, now the leader of the opposition party, when he was still mayor of Baruta in 2005. The construction should have taken six months, but for the last three years this skeleton structure has sat in limbo. Showing me around, Klumpner explains that the contractors took the advance that was meant for buying materials and instead bought dollars. With Venezuela's runaway inflation, they like to keep their money stable. Meanwhile they slow down the construction process and invent reasons to request more funds. 'The thing that guarantees that a project goes forward in other countries is the thing that guarantees it doesn't go forward here,' says Klumpner.

Like the gym in La Cruz, the one in Baruta was built on top of a football pitch, which means that while the project is stalled the local kids have lost the only amenity that was available to them. The contractor was at least fired, but the municipality won't be suing because of course the local politicians were in on the deal. It makes me angry to see the effects of such institutional corruption. On a neighbouring hill stands a half-built social housing project that is stalled for similar reasons. Meanwhile, from this hillside you can look into the plush gardens and swimming pool of the Italian Club, a famous hangout for the Caracas rich set. The vertical gym over in Los Teques also has a swimming pool – it's been nearly finished for two years now. Klumpner shrugs. 'Not finishing a project is the best business here,' he says.

23 de Enero

It was not always thus. In the 1950s, the military junta headed by Marcos Pérez Jiménez embarked on a vast programme of investment in the infrastructure of Caracas. Expanding Venezuela's oil production, the dictatorship poured money into construction projects, using American cities as his model and American expertise to make Caracas the most modern city in Latin America. Jiménez was another dictator fond of bulldozing the barrios. During the 1940s the population of Caracas had doubled, swelling the slums around the periphery. The regime's response was to forcibly decant the barrio dwellers into a social housing project on a scale that the continent had never seen. It was to be called 2 de Diciembre, the date in 1952 when Jiménez seized power. And in just three years, from 1955 to 1958, the estate was ready to house 60,000 people in one fell swoop. It was more than double the size of Pruitt-Igoe in St Louis, which had also just been completed, and which would become infamous when it was demolished twenty years later.

It is one of the ironies of Latin America that military dictators were so much more effective at building social housing than their democratically elected counterparts. Of course, operating by diktat makes it easier to divert government funds, steamroll opposition and bypass due process. But it was also a function of the historical moment: the dictatorships held sway during a period – from the 1950s in Venezuela to the early 1980s in Brazil – when mass housing schemes were still seen as the answer and had not yet been discredited. As we saw in Argentina, the dictatorships were also ruthless at using housebuilding to buy loyalty, especially among the military. Still, it is counter-intuitive that a regime as corrupt and despised as Jiménez's should have produced what remains ostensibly the most ambitious urban social legacy of any Venezuelan government. When he was finally ousted in 1957, the estate was renamed 23 de Enero – 23 January, the date of democracy's return.

The architect who designed 23 de Enero was Carlos Raúl Villanueva. A graduate of the École des Beaux-Arts in Paris and a disciple of Le Corbusier, Villanueva was Venezuela's most prominent architect. He had recently completed the campus for the Universidad Central de Venezuela, one of the most gracious modernist campuses in the world. And now, with funding from the Banco Obrero, he had the chance to build his tour de force. He conceived of 23 de Enero as thirty-eight *superbloques* supplemented by dozens of medium-sized blocks, providing over 9,000 units. These were to be scattered evenly across a terraced hillside to the west of Caracas, with acres of green space in between. The very picture of modernist utopia, this was paternalistic politics as spectacle.

However, in the confusion after the overthrow of Jiménez, and before it was even completed, 23 was squatted by an estimated 4,000 families. This rather set the tone for how the estate was occupied over the coming years. With the Banco Obrero losing out on so much rental income, 23 was never properly administered or maintained. When the *superbloques* became overcrowded, new arrivals began building their homes in the verdant spaces in between, a fact that successive governments did nothing to prevent. Gradually, Villanueva's high-rises were like modernist breakwaters in a sea of slum.

Now a World Heritage Site, 23 de Enero is merely a more extreme case of what happened to any number of blighted housing estates in Europe and America. The reasons were the same: administrative failure, a short-sighted faith in built objects over the long-term processes of management and maintenance. The architecture was hardly to blame. However, the spectacle of 23 today makes a mockery of the notion that the government could squeeze a ballooning population into industrialised 'superblocks'. It is also symptomatic of the absence of an alternative housing plan, and thus an indictment of every government ever since.

The fate of 23 is best surveyed from the top of one of the blocks. The terraced slopes in between the blocks have been invaded by a wave of tin-roofed *ranchos*. Instead of 60,000, now close to 100,000 people live here. When I visit, what strikes me is that 23 has metamorphosed into a strange new typology. Rather than the defeatist image of modernism overrun by the barrio, it's as though the informal city has become the connective tissue joining together what were once isolated tower blocks. This is a hybrid of the formal and informal cities – of the planned and rational with the spontaneous and rhizomatic. Ironically, far from slowing down the growth of the slums, 23 became the framework for a slum – the concrete skeleton that the barrio has now fleshed out.

My guide is a pony-tailed resident called Merwill, who grew up here. His building has just had new Chinese-made elevators installed, and they even play Muzak. As we ride up to the sixth floor, we're subjected to the unmistakable saxophone of that doyen of lifts everywhere, Kenny G.

We could be in a mall in Florida, except that this lift only stops every four floors, so we take it to the eighth and walk down two flights. The outside of Merwill's apartment is lined with fake bricks, like a suburban semi, and there's a bulbous 'pigeon-chest' grill over the window. Inside it's fairly large, until you realise that nine people live here. Merwill's own bedroom is tiny, with just a single bed on which he, his girlfriend and their son sleep. His parents are in another room, his sister and her daughter are in another, and his brother and his girlfriend are in another. 'This is normal for 23,' he says.

Merwill, who is thirty-one and works for Avila TV, a new 'urban' station that frequently airs programmes about life in the barrios, grew up around drugs and violence. There used to be twenty-five other kids in this block of his age, but most of them were killed. Getting into music saved him, he says. 23 is famous for its music. Several renowned salsa musicians live here. First and foremost, though, it is notorious as a stronghold of radical left-wing politics. Stigmatised by successive governments, it was the site of many a gun battle between residents and the police. But it has always been a bastion of the Bolivarian revolution. In 1992, when Chávez was planning his failed coup attempt against the government of Carlos Andrés Pérez, he set up his headquarters in 23. With the Miraflores Palace, the seat of government, just down the road, he could look down from the hillside at his intended target. Then, in 2002, when a US-backed coup ousted Chávez for a mere forty-eight hours, one of the reasons why he was so quickly restored to power was because the residents of 23 marched down to Miraflores en masse to protest.

The walls of 23 are plastered with murals honouring the various heroes and martyrs of the revolution. 'Death is a risk that every revolutionary must take,' reads one. It remains a hotbed of radical activity, with armed pro-Chávez groups such as La Piedrita and Los Tupamaros carrying out vigilante justice and the occasional politically motivated attack. 23 is also home to several of the missions through which Chávez keeps his support base pliant. They do make a difference, and according to Merwill have drastically reduced the amount of crime in 23. As he leads me out of the estate, we run into an eccentric sculptor who, spotting a foreigner, gesticulates wildly and sings the praises of the neighbourhood. 'There's absolutely no need to leave the barrio – it's the university of life,' he cries. On the way out, Merwill picks up his four-year-old son from school. Today, the boy says proudly, he learnt about Bolívar, and then starts singing a song about Che.

For U-TT, 23 is a touchstone. Emblematic of a time when Venezuela was the most modern country on the continent, it is a reminder of the days when governments could muster vast resources for social housing. But it is also symptomatic of how unsuccessful the centralised, paternalistic approach to housing was. And thus it's a place that evokes nostalgia, but with optimism. For U-TT, this new hybrid settlement, a collision of the formal and the informal, seems to hold greater potential. Now that Villanueva's rigid vision has been corrupted, it has also been humanised. 'The barrio around 23 cements it together as a real neighbourhood,' Brillembourg told me. It's a statement that rejects the idea of the city as a rational, ordered place and welcomes spontaneity as its intrinsic quality. It's a statement that accepts the essential, messy nature of Caracas.

The Activist Architect Is an Extrovert or Nothing

A motorcycle gang led by a short, tough guy called Rommel is taking Alfredo, Hubert and I up to the barrio of Cota 905. The streets are a blur as we cling to the backs of the motorbikes. One of the U-TT team and a young German film director are in tow, filming the scene for a movie about … well, I'm never quite sure what the movie's about. Ostensibly it's about informal cities, but it's also about the life and work of U-TT, but really it's about Alfredo. A film buff of sorts, Alfredo is obsessed with making a movie about the twenty-first-century city. Since U-TT took up a professorship at the prestigious ETH architecture school in Zurich, Alfredo has been pumping resources into the film project. And one of the reasons why this visit to Caracas in the spring of 2012 is so hectic is because now that they spend less time in Caracas, every spare minute is spent documenting the extremes of Alfredo's native city.

The motorcycle scene is a nice touch, somewhere between *Easy Rider* and *The Motorcycle Diaries*, but it's also the only way to get up to Cota 905, as the alleys are too narrow for cars. This is a pilgrimage of sorts. Ten years ago U-TT organised a basketball competition here, but today every one of the youths who took part is dead, the victims of crimes of one kind or another. U-TT tried to initiate a vertical gym here, but they didn't succeed. Recognising a passing sports coach, they try and revive the project. The coach is enthusiastic, but ultimately there are divided opinions in the community about how to use the proposed site. Alfredo and Hubert strike up this kind of speculative conversation whenever they can. They bring to mind the Dutch architect Aldo van Eyck, who built hundreds of playgrounds in Amsterdam after the Second World War. But van Eyck had the municipality on his side, providing sites and funds. U-TT's is an endless process of self-initiation: keeping conversations alive, winning over the community, seeking government funding. Only a small number of projects ever get off the ground, and we've seen how most of those end up mired in routine corruption.

Here in 905 is the first time I see Alfredo and Hubert in action. Spotting some kids playing basketball, quick as a flash Alfredo is shooting hoops with them, for all the world as if he were fifteen and not fifty. A group of girls singing is an opportunity for him to conduct. A passing mother is a conversation. Every moment he's engaging, taking the temperature. Hubert is doing it too, though as a European you get the sense he's had to learn how, it's not in his blood like Alfredo. The activist architect is an extrovert or he is nothing. You have to be comfortable in the community, and if the community is not instantly comfortable with you, then it takes charisma to win them over. 'The architect,' says Alfredo later, 'is a social connector. That is the main role.'

It strikes me in 905 that the residents appear to lack for nothing in material goods. They have TVs and computers. I see a woman in army fatigues checking her BlackBerry. But all of this is misleading. Because of Venezuela's hyper-inflation, there is no incentive for ordinary people to save money. It has to be used while it's still worth something, and consumer goods are where it goes. At the bottom of the hill I notice a lengthy queue for the bus that will take residents the long way round to the top of 905. That is the nature of poverty in Caracas, not a lack of goods but of infrastructure.

Back in the U-TT office, downtown, Alfredo and Hubert are having a huge row. They're shouting and waving their arms about, and then suddenly Alfredo is laughing – he's in stitches. He's been play-acting, provoking Hubert just so that they could have a fight captured in the film. 'The way we get things done is through fights,' he once told me. Alfredo's film is turning into *opera buffa*, and Hubert looks world-weary. He accuses Alfredo of being emotion-ally unstable. Alfredo, to be fair, is going through a painful divorce, and it seems likely that he's a little unhinged. 'I haven't lost myself, I've found myself!' he counters.

Hubert drives me to Baruta to see the FAVA school for autistic children, which U-TT has just completed. This is not a slum project, it's for a private client, and the highly polished building is set in manicured gardens. A terrazzo walkway spirals around the edge of the school, enclosing classrooms, playrooms and all manner of learning facilities for the children. After just five minutes with the principal, it is clear that this is a well-run institution. And then it dawns on me that the reason why Hubert brought me here was not just to see a U-TT project, but also to prove that it is possible to get projects finished in Venezuela. Listening to him talk about the angle of the spiral ramp and the colour schemes best suited to autistic children, it also becomes clear that, if Alfredo is the dynamo who gets projects off the ground, Hubert is the finisher. He is the one in the U-TT duo with the patience and the attention span to see projects through.

It would be a cliché to say that Alfredo is south and Hubert, the Austrian, is north, but inevitably there is some truth in it. Alfredo comes from the 'soap-opera culture' of Latin America, as he calls it, whereas Hubert married into it, and some of its craziness has rubbed off on him. Alfredo, though, embodies the contradictions of this continent, with its extreme wealth and poverty. One minute we're staying with his eighty-year-old mother in the Country Club neighbourhood, with servants and a stuffed lion that she shot in Africa half a century ago, and the next we're in the barrios discussing vertical gyms and dry toilets. He's bourgeois and he knows it, but he can play the man of the people when he needs to. As Néstor López, a former managing editor of Caracas's *Daily Journal* – we'll meet Néstor soon – told him: 'You're a good bourgeois. The best revolutionaries are good bourgeois. Bolívar was a good bourgeois.'

The Brillembourg family's farms were expropriated by Chávez, and yet U-TT continued to work with the government. 'Despite what they were doing to my family, I kept engaged in the political process,' says Alfredo. This bipartisan spirit has made them more effective in Venezuela than most of their counterparts, even though they have occasionally been burned by it. Venezuela is a political minefield, and they've picked up all kinds of survival tactics. 'We always avoid the inauguration ceremonies,' says Hubert, 'otherwise next time you're in a photo with the wrong people and then the new regime associates you with the opposition.'

'We understood the desperation of a city with five municipalities, five police forces and two mayors competing against each other, and we had to traverse those boundaries,' says Alfredo. 'We can be invisible. We can walk through walls, because we're not carrying an ideological flag. What killed Neruda's poetry, what killed so many Latin American writers, was when they became aligned with political ideologies.'

By its own definition, U–TT has to tread a fine line, being politically engaged while being perceived as politically neutral. It is a rather different challenge to the one faced by the last generation of socially motivated architects in the 1960s and 70s. Thinking back to two of his heroes, Alison and Peter Smithson, Alfredo claims that they were sidelined because 'they didn't engage in the politics enough'. This is simplistic, but what I understand by it is that for the Smithsons and other modernist builders of social housing, the going was good when they could count on governments seeking them out, but not when it was the other way around. Being an activist architect means engaging in the dark matter of politics to make your case when the politicians have no particular plans in mind.

By and large, the Venezuelan architecture community does not seek out these challenges, partly because of the social stigma attached to the barrios, but also because of a traditional high-culture education which taught them that architecture is the design of refined objects. Indeed, ignorance of the barrios is widespread among the residents of formal Caracas. The *Guardian*'s former Venezuela correspondent, Rory Carroll, summed up this relationship between the formal and informal cities with biting clarity. 'At dusk, when the valley was fed and had ice in its scotch, the buses took visitors back up the slopes to home and a supper of beans and rice. The hills knew the valley intimately, how it liked its towels folded, its juice squeezed, its steak seasoned. The valley knew the hills not at all.'[*]

In their attempt to know the hills, U-TT are rare but not alone. The architect Teolinda Bolívar, at the Universidad Central de Venezuela (UCV), has been studying the barrios for thirty years. A pupil of Henri Lefebvre, she even took him to the barrios when he visited Caracas in the 1970s, and was instrumental in making the barrios a topic at UCV. And, in 1999, Josefina Baldó and Federico Villanueva, also at UCV, began a research project funded by the World Bank that was supposed to lead to a $150 million slum-upgrading programme in Caracas. It was useful research, but the World Bank pulled the plug on funding the actual upgrading.

---

[*] Rory Carroll, *Comandante: Hugo Chávez's Venezuela*, Penguin, 2013.

Baldó and Villanueva, whose strategy consisted in ret-
rofitting the slums with 'good architecture', were less of
an influence on U-TT than Bolívar. Her prolonged social
engagement with the barrios was an inspiration. And
trying to see the barrio as she did, through the needs of
its residents, U-TT ended up producing the most effective
mechanism yet in the transformation of informal Caracas:
a piece of transport. Up to this point, Chávez had been the
first president to recognise the barrios as a political force –
as the population that elects the president – and he rewarded
his supporters with social programmes and handouts. But,
despite this generosity, he never really facilitated their role
as the economic backbone of the city, the labour force that
Carroll deftly described. As U-TT understood, rewarding them as productive citizens would mean making them
more mobile.

The Metrocable

The Caracas Metrocable is the most significant urban
legacy of the Chávez era. Despite all the petrodollars that
Chávez spent on his social projects, very little went into
civil infrastructure. The cable car line is a glorious exception. The first leg, running from the Parque Central metro
station up to the hills of San Agustín, connects one of the
largest barrios in south Caracas directly to downtown. As a
symbolic act alone, it joins two pieces of the city that were
socially and psychologically worlds apart.

Cable cars have become something of a familiar sight

in Latin American cities. In Caracas, Medellín and Rio, it's as though they have become the default method for negotiating the hilly barrios, *comunas* and favelas. The origins of the Caracas Metrocable lie in 2001, at a conference on human settlements at the United Nations General Assembly in New York. Brillembourg and Klumpner were in a public debate with Hernando de Soto, questioning his thesis that the slum dwellers should be given legal titles to their houses. Firstly, they argued, it would be more productive to give them cooperative titles over the land rather than private titles that would incur all kinds of taxes that the slum dwellers could ill afford to pay; secondly, what use was a legal title at all to a house at the top of a hill that was inaccessible? The real solution, they said, was infrastructure.

On the panel with them that day was the engineer Guy Battle. He agreed with Brillembourg and Klumpner's argument, and *Informal City* included a proposal developed by Battle and U-TT for a cable car system connecting Parque Central and San Agustín. At that point it was just an idea. But a few years later that idea gained traction through a series of chance encounters. Klumpner happened to know the Austrian ambassador to Caracas, who happened to know the mayor's director of planning, Mike Menéndez. Through Menéndez, word of the cable car reached the ears of the mayor, Juan Barreto, who took a shine to the idea. So, in 2006, U-TT and Menéndez organised a high-powered conference on the future of Caracas, which was when the concept was to be formally presented to the mayor. Getting his blessing should have been a formality, but of course it couldn't be that simple.

Venezuela being Venezuela, when Mayor Barreto found out that the key instigators of the cable car scheme were not functionaries in his office but two independents that might be able to claim the glory that was rightfully his, he wanted them thrown out of the conference. A number of delegates insisted that U-TT remain, including one Néstor López, of the *Daily Journal*, who, shortly after the conference, was found outside his home with both his legs broken.* Reluctantly, the mayor let them stay, on the condition that they remained silent. Luckily for U-TT, in the room were delegates from Doppelmayr, the Austrian aerial lift company that was already busy restoring Caracas's original cable car, which used to carry tourists up to the Humboldt Hotel on Avila Hill in the 1950s and 60s. Doppelmayr's representatives encouraged U-TT to lie low during the conference and rest assured that they had a partnership. Even more luckily – Venezuela being Venezuela – the project turned into a political hot potato.

It so happened that on the day of the conference Chávez was in Vienna for a meeting of OPEC and his first trade talks with Austria. There, the Austrian ambassador sold the idea of the cable car to the president (along with a shipment of Austrian-made Glock pistols for the Venezuelan police), who decided that it was too important a project to be left to the mayor. Insisting that it fall under the aegis

---

* I'm not alleging that these two events are connected, but Brillembourg tells the story as if it's no coincidence.

of the government-owned metro company, Chavez swiftly relieved the hapless Barreto of his golden egg. Finally, in 2007, the metro company hired Doppelmayr to build the cable car and U-TT to design it.

In San Agustín

Five years later, I'm flying over the barrio of San Agustín in a gondola labelled '*Libertad*'. Through the plexiglass windows the towers of Parque Central are receding, and beneath me the hillside is a carpet of corrugated rooftops. The Teleférico para Transporte Masivo Interurbano, to give it its official name, was opened in 2010. It now takes about five minutes to get from Parque Central to the top of San Agustín. Previously the only way to get there was by climbing a concrete staircase for the equivalent of thirty-nine floors – a journey that took up to forty-five minutes.

The municipality had imagined building a winding road up to San Agustín, but the community was against it, because it would have meant demolishing a third of the houses on the hillside. The cable car, by contrast, meant that very few people had to be rehoused, and is arguably a better way to negotiate such steep terrain anyway. There used to be just one bus that wound its way from here to El Silencio, to the west of the city centre, but now residents are connected to the heart of the metro system at Parque Central. And at 50 centavos the Metrocable is a quarter of the price of the bus.

There are five stations along the cable car line, dotted along the hilltops, and the journey from first to last takes less than fifteen minutes. That is a fact worth dwelling on for a moment. Two-hour commutes for the poor are part of what make Latin American cities so socially divisive. The right to the city is not just a question of housing – as it stands, most of the residents of Caracas have already met their own needs in that regard. The right to the city is also a right to mobility, a question of how long it takes to get an invalid to a hospital. For the barriers in segregated cities are not just social and psychological: they are marked as much by physical distance and journey times. But unlike housing, mobility is a responsibility that only government can assume. For this reason, some of the most effective urban policies in Latin America have been transport policies, from the BRT networks in Curitiba and Bogotá to the cable cars of Medellín. The answer to a divided city is integration, and there is no integration without transport connections.

As in Rio, Caracas's cable car has come in for criticism. U-TT's film crew isn't allowed to film in the stations, because the metro company has become touchy about the press. Some of the newspapers have been arguing that the Metrocable is underused considering how much it cost, and that it stops with the slightest gust of wind. And while it's true that it's not yet operating at full capacity, it's still moving 1,200 people per hour. The difference from the Complexo do Alemão is that there aren't more effective alternatives already in place.

All the gondolas on the line have graphic monikers by the Swiss designer Ruedi Baur: *Amor*, *Equidad*, *Humanismo*, etc. – a kind of humanitarian sloganeering. The first station to swallow the good gondola *Libertad* is Hornos de Cal. From here, one of the smaller stations, the line turns to follow the hilltops before entering the much more impressive summit station of La Ceiba. With its exposed metal structure holding up a great barrelled roof, La Ceiba is a piece of High Tech architecture transplanted to the barrio. Its technical language is appropriate to a piece of engineering infrastructure, but it also carries more than a hint of the techno-utopian futurism that Archigram turned into pop icons in the 1960s. Archigram's progeny turned High Tech into the language of airports and banking headquarters. But in Caracas it has been reinvented, in vertical gyms and Metrocable stations, as part of the language of the barrio.

That homage to the 1960s extends to U-TT's terminology. They describe the social amenities they've designed at each station as 'plug-in programmes' (think Archigram's Plug-in City, where living capsules are slotted into a kind of mainframe). This is the other aspect in which the Metrocable differs from Complexo do Alemão. Here the stations are not just isolated transport nodes protected by UPP stations, they are meant to serve as communal hubs, with a vertical gym or a library or a community centre.

As we pull into La Ceiba, it becomes clear that the community centre that was supposed to occupy the base of the station has been bricked up. Brillembourg doesn't seem too concerned that his light, open structure has been turned into a useless box, because the potential is still there. Similarly, the vertical gym nearing completion next door looks nothing like it was supposed to. The plexiglass brise-soleil have also turned into brick walls, but again Brillembourg seems thrilled to see it take shape. He's resigned to the fact that U-TT has very little control over the details. 'It's all about imperfection,' he told me later. 'We need to question the role of the architect as the producer of perfect objects.'

At La Ceiba we're met by community leader María Eugenia, who offers a very different perspective from the critics in the newspapers. She says that the cable car has sparked a growing sense of self-esteem in San Agustín. 'The kids even dress differently now,' she says. It's true that there is a tangible sense of transformation at work in the barrio. We pass a few people renovating the outside of their homes and I notice several 'For Sale' signs. According to Brillembourg, San Agustín is densifying, a natural consequence of new infrastructure. It's hard to tell, though, because there is no accurate population count. Somewhere between 45,000 and 65,000 people live on this hill. The For Sale signs suggest some upward mobility now that San Agustín is becoming more desirable, but it's hardly in the throes of gentrification.

Crime is still a major problem. The day before our visit a girl was killed at Hornos de Cal station. Things seem to have become worse in Venezuela in recent months, partly thanks to the government's flirtation with Colombian guerrillas and the promotion of armed militias to 'defend' the revolution, some of which finance themselves through drug running. According to the *El Universal* newspaper, there were 19,366 homicides in Venezuela in 2011 – that's 67 per 100,000 (compared to 8 per 100,000 in Chile and 9 per 100,000 in Peru). Many of the shoot-outs involve children of between ten and thirteen.

Today, San Agustín is echoing with salsa from some untraceable window. Within minutes we come across kids playing basketball, and, like the competitive dad, Alfredo is straight in there, bobbing and jumping. Then he's chatting to random passers-by on the street; Hubert too, less frenetically. This is their extrovert face, the activists playing men of the people, building their social capital.

We join a small group drinking Polar beers at an impromptu bar outside someone's front door. One man sitting with us left San Agustín to live in the city, but he still likes to come back and be with his friends. 'Once you adapt to a way of life it's difficult to give it up,' he says. The barrio has its comforts – it is not necessarily a place people are desperate to escape from. Similarly, you can't underestimate the attachment to houses that people have built for themselves. These houses are hard won. Indeed it's more expensive to build a house in a barrio than it is in the city centre – for a start, you have to transport the materials up the hill, and the materials themselves are more expensive because, unlike a construction company, you're not buying in bulk. What makes it worthwhile, of course, is that the land is free.

As it happens, one of the ladies in our group, Carolina Rico, had her house expropriated to make space for one of the cable car pylons. She was given a new apartment but she, too, comes back regularly to hang out, even though this is where she saw her husband shot in front of her. Six years ago some men broke into her house, made him kneel down and shot him in the head. She doesn't know why, and she describes the scene matter-of-factly. 'I'm used to seeing corpses,' she says. Everyone seems to have a story about death. As a few drops of rain become a sudden downpour, we retreat into the house to hear the owner telling how the mason who built it was killed by a group of delinquents. He got caught in the crossfire. People around us shrug their shoulders. It's most often for no good reason, they say.

Are they grateful to Chávez for the cable car? 'It's not a present,' says one man. 'We elected him to do things like the Metrocable. He should have done a hundred of them.'

The question is whether the Metrocable is merely a prelude to the formalisation of San Agustín, or the beginning of a different evolution for the settlement. U-TT feel strongly that this hillside barrio could be an experiment in an entirely different kind of city. Connecting the informal to the formal is one thing, it is undeniably progress of sorts. But if the next phase of the process is to incorporate them into the system – giving them property deeds, taxing them, plugging them into the grid and making them pay for water and electricity – then we already know where that process leads. That way lies debt, gentrification, displacement through rising land values – the standard machinery of the city as a generator of surplus capital. Incorporating them into that system would be a failure to recognise that the problem is the system itself.

This is not stale Marxist theory, however. U-TT's alternative vision for the hill is not socialism but a model developed by the Manhattan elite. They propose to divide up the hill into cooperatives, in the manner that wealthy New Yorkers build and manage their apartment blocks. In this model, the government would grant communal rather than individual leases, and residents would group together, perhaps a dozen neighbouring houses at a time, and take joint loans for the improvements they want to make. Instead of being plugged into the grid, San Agustín could be a district that operates off the grid, with solar power and a degree of autonomy. 'Why can't models developed for the elites function for the poor?' asks Brillembourg. 'Our idea was to take the worst place in the city and make it the most unique place in the city.'

This was a line of thinking that began in Petare. With Teolinda Bolívar's research to hand, they noticed that people in Caracas's biggest barrio tended to parcel land among family and friends. Often this was territorial, with tight-knit groups of Colombian or Peruvian immigrants forming clusters. It struck U-TT that if those families grouped together, they would have a much better chance of securing a loan against the value of a larger piece of land than against merely their own. Of course, in order to get this financing system off the ground, the government would need to give the squatters a legal right to the land. And that's when Brillembourg and Klumpner started to think in terms of leases, like the ones that cover most of the London property market. Instead of owning the land, they would have the right to it for a certain number of years.

The advantages of the cooperative idea over Hernando de Soto's argument for legal ownership are numerous. Firstly, it sidesteps the problem of gentrification while rewarding pioneers who raised the value of land by urbanising it. Secondly, cooperatives may well be a more effective way of getting whole hillsides upgraded in a structured fashion. 'The atomisation of communities into individual owners doesn't make sense in a large upgrading scheme – what good is one shack upgraded on a hill that doesn't have a plan?' says Brillembourg.

Although he doesn't couch it in such terms, it occurs to me that what Brillembourg is describing sounds like a kind of heterotopia, a place where alternative systems – where difference – can thrive. Perhaps linking the barrios to the formal city and its systems is not radical enough. After all, the barrios were generated by their spontaneous logic, without government assistance. Having achieved that much, surely a different organisational logic can be allowed to operate there. To achieve this, however, would require the architects to engage at the policy level. But U-TT didn't get that far. Their vision for San Agustín was to be developed as part of the all-encompassing Avenida Lecuna scheme. This was supposed to be an urban loop that brought formal spaces to the barrio and informal features – market streets in the air – to downtown. But of course U-TT was fired from that scheme.

The irony is that, having been denied in Caracas, U-TT

is now developing a scheme along very similar lines in South Africa. In Cape Town's Khayelitsha township, the architects are working on a cooperative model that revolves around rooftop solar panels. The idea is that the government provides leases of fifteen years, against which the owners can secure microcredit loans for construction, while the solar panel eventually generates income by feeding excess energy back into the grid. If it works, it would be the basis of a cooperative and sustainable model of urbanism – a heterotopia indeed.

That project is indicative of the fact that, these days, most of U-TT's experiments are abroad. Two vertical gyms in Caracas are progressing slowly, but otherwise the city appears to be in a downward spiral. Inflation has hit nearly 50 per cent, the highest in Venezuela's history, and supermarket shelves lack the most basic goods – newspapers have been reporting a chronic toilet paper shortage. Meanwhile, Chávez's successor, Nicolás Maduro, has just created a Vice Ministry of Supreme Social Happiness. It sounds like satire.

But wherever Brillembourg and Klumpner end up working, Caracas was the wellspring of all their ideas. It frames their world view. 'We're starting to see that Caracas is everywhere,' says Brillembourg. 'We found it in Bangkok, in Amman, in São Paulo, in Nagaland in northern India. And in all these places, the city is in the control of kings, businessmen, industry – the club. We need to unfreeze the city!'

5

Torre David: A Pirate Utopia

On 9 April 2012, hundreds of policemen raided Torre David in the hunt for Guillermo Cholele, an attaché to the Costa Rican embassy in Caracas. Cholele had been kidnapped and his family had received a phone call demanding a ransom, which the police apparently traced to Torre David. But Cholele was nowhere to be found. The next morning he was released, and had apparently never been in the tower. Nevertheless, the newspaper headlines had succeeded in further vilifying its residents, who live there illegally and, according to popular opinion, contribute to the blighting of central Caracas by defiling one of its most prominent landmarks.

Two weeks before the raid, I'm loitering on Avenida Urdaneta outside the solid steel gate of Torre David. With me are Urban-Think Tank and their film crew, who are hoping to resume their documentation of life in the tower. But the gate remains closed. Today, we aren't going to be allowed in. Sometimes it's like that. The residents are wary of outsiders and especially journalists. Despite living in the third tallest skyscraper in Caracas, they don't want to draw undue attention to themselves. The head of the squatter's association, known as El Niño, doesn't trust us. He's twitchy about some of the coverage the tower has been receiving in the papers, and he's worried that if Chávez loses the forthcoming election they'll all be kicked out. But his deputy, Gladys, a calm, religious woman in her mid-forties, is more accommodating. It's a lengthy round of good cop, bad cop – she says yes, he says no. Today it's no.

It's a frustrating moment. All of the tower's mysteries lie behind that steel door, all of its experiences remain latent. I have yet to climb forty-seven flights of stairs to gaze upon the city from the helipad. I have yet to watch a basketball game from the vertiginous perspective of the eighteenth floor. I have yet to step over gaps in the concrete floor plates and feel my stomach make a dash for my throat. I have yet to hear tales of gruesome falls from appalling heights. I have yet to hang out with a guy called Frankenstein.

The Pioneers

On the night of 17 September 2007, during a torrential downpour, hundreds of drenched citizens appeared at the gate of the Torre Confinanzas, a derelict skyscraper. This flash mob had been organised by a group of squatters who'd put the word out that they were going to make a move on the tower, which had stood empty for more than a decade.

They must have made a pitiful sight because – or so the creation myth of the tower has it – the security guards opened
the gates and allowed this sodden mass to seek shelter
inside. There was no turning back. These refugees from
the barrios and from other squats around the city rolled out
mats and pitched tents, staking a claim to their piece of the
ground floor. Soon their families and friends arrived to join
them. They stayed there for weeks, waiting to see if they
would be evicted, exploring the rest of the tower's forty-
five storeys. As they began to feel more secure in their new
home, they initiated a new phase of the occupation, dis-
persing into the tower itself, cleaning it up and allocating
themselves apartments. Today, 3,000 people live in what is
known as Torre David, the tallest squat in the world.

Torre David is a conspicuous presence in Caracas.
Standing in the central district of Libertador, it is a prominent feature of the city's skyline. Depending on which side
you view it from, it can appear just like the postmodern
skyscraper that it was intended to be, its silky skin of mirrored glass merely pockmarked here and there with missing
panes. But, like Jekyll and Hyde, one face contradicts the
other. The more distinctive facade has almost no glass at
all, just exposed concrete and gaping windows framed by
some very irregular brickwork and the odd laundry line.
This side is impossible to categorise: it is neither skyscraper
nor slum, but some novel hybrid. Has a city ever seen one
of these before? Not quite. Squatted residential towers are
perfectly common – São Paulo, for example, has several –
but a corporate skyscraper, a would-be financial head-

quarters in the business district? Perhaps only Caracas, with its volatile combination of economic turmoil and demagogic politics, could give birth to such a chimera.

How did it happen? Simply put, the tower is the product of the last Venezuelan boom and one man's excessive optimism. It was the brainchild of the developer David Brillembourg (a distant cousin, it should be pointed out, of Urban-Think Tank's Alfredo Brillembourg). He planned to build one of the most luxurious office complexes in South America. But the scheme was fraught with risk. Venezuela was entering a period of prolonged economic turmoil. In 1989 it had re-elected President Carlos Andrés Pérez, who instituted a series of free-market economic reforms along IMF guidelines, including selling off national companies, abandoning oil subsidies and freeing interest rates. These were to prove disastrous. Inflation and unemployment soared, and petrol prices doubled. The result was the Caracazo, a day of protests and chaos that ended with hundreds of dead. It would be more than a decade before Venezuela's economy recovered.

Yet in 1989 David Brillembourg was confident that demand for office space in the financial heart of Caracas was still rising. His Centro Financiero Confinanzas would be the pride of the city. Its five adjoining structures, of which Torre David (or Edificio A) is the tallest, would house the offices of the Banco Metropolitano de Crédito Urbano and Brillembourg's own Grupo Confinanzas, along with a luxury hotel lined in Italian marble, executive apartments with a swimming pool, a ten-storey car park, a helipad and twenty-three state-of-the-art Schindler elevators (that last item is worth remembering). Designed by the architect Enrique Gómez, the complex was to cost $82 million. It was scheduled to be completed in July 1994. But in April 1993, fifty-five-year-old Brillembourg died of natural causes. Then, the following year, Venezuela's financial sector was crippled by a wave of bank closures and Grupo Confinanzas declared bankruptcy. Torre David, named after its owner, was nearly completed when it was seized by FOGADE, the government reserve fund, along with the rest of the group's assets.

For thirteen years Torre David stood empty. FOGADE's attempts to sell it off were unsuccessful, and meanwhile bits of the facade and other useful construction materials were pilfered by occasional squatters and looters. A picture of dereliction, the tower became a memorial to the failed hopes of the boom years. Many still see it so. But on that rainy night in 2007, it began a process of existential transformation. Here is an emblem of speculative finance capitalism that has been taken over by those who were disenfranchised by the neoliberal policies of that era – the poor. Is there not a certain poetic justice in that? Could we not say that what would otherwise have been a symbol of exclusive luxury is now a symbol of the redistribution of wealth? Is this not a more equitable outcome?

The squatting of Torre David is a direct consequence of Chávez's demagogic politics. For years his rhetoric implicitly encouraged the apppropriation of 'idle' property, from farms to golf courses, and a series of decrees gave squatters and those living on illegally occupied land in the barrios more and more legal rights. Moreover, after catastrophic floods in late 2010, when thousands of *caraqueños* were left homeless, Chávez introduced an emergency law giving the government the right to seize land and property either for temporary occupation or to build housing. On one level this was a swift and populist way of compensating for a deficit of two million houses in Caracas alone. But in practice, one of the weirder consequences of that emergency law is that a shopping mall two blocks from Torre David is also being squatted, along with dozens of other buildings in Caracas. Hardly the best way to run a city. While such populism ostensibly empowers the people – at the expense of any sense of order in Caracas – it does so in the most fragile and illusory way, without legal substantiation. Worse, this tacit condition depends on the figure of the patriarch, one whose body, at the time, is riddled with cancer.

So Torre David is an accident of circumstance, the bastard child of economic collapse and a revolutionary socialist government – let's call it a rip in the economic and political fabric, one more symptom of Caracas's abnormality. But since this accident exists, what can we make of it? Urban-Think Tank has been studying the tower because they see in it a potential new model of urban living. They call it an 'urban laboratory', one that may be of crucial value to cities of the future. From São Paulo to Shanghai, the cities of the world are pincushions for speculative office towers that are surplus to requirements, empty castles in a game of fictitious capital. The Torre is an early trial in how they might be put to better use. For why should the poor be forced to live in slums on the periphery of the city, when there are empty high-rises in the centre?

Communal Ideals

Finally, a few days later, we get the call. There will be a community meeting tonight, and we are invited to attend. At ten o'clock we are ushered in through the steel door, which is manned by a security detail – not professionals, but residents who know how to handle themselves. Up some steps, you are soon in what would have been the atrium of the Torre Confinanzas, a vast circular space in raw concrete, five storeys high. It would have been crowned with a glass cupola, but it remains open to the night sky like some kind of brutalist observatory. A few small palms have been planted in holes in the concrete floor, and here and there street dogs are sleeping, the first internal sign that this place follows the logic of the barrio.

We hang around for a long time, trying to make polite conversation, feeling awkward but relieved to be inside. There is a group of residents waiting for all of the twenty-eight coordinators representing each of the inhabited floors of the tower, so they can have their weekly meeting. Finally, well after midnight, the proceedings get under way. They start with a prayer, hands in the air, and end in a chorus of amens and a round of applause that echoes around the concrete foyer. Gladys, our good cop who seems to handle the day-to-day management of the tower, launches into a few points of housekeeping. And then a young man stands up. His name is Fernando, a former resident of the tower who has been invited back to address the meeting. He is wearing a red T-shirt emblazoned with the mayor of Caracas's logo, although he declares himself an anarchist. Clearly, he has the makings of a politician. This is what he says:

Good evening, my friends. It's an honour to be here with all of you today, as always. I want you to know that when we analyse the history of the world, there has always existed that human being who sees himself as part of a collective. This was true in the feudal era, when there were communes. There was a king, and, well, if the people didn't identify with this king, they organised their own commune based on their own criteria, in their own mode of organisation. But these communes were always destroyed. Who wanted to destroy them? The king.

When we took the decision to occupy this space we found several realities. Among them was this dead giant. A giant of 192 metres, dead in the middle of our capital city, with forty-five floors uninhabited. And when we arrived at the top floor and stood on that heliport and looked around, we realised that the whole population that had come to fill this land of Caracas – those who came from Los Llanos, from Colombia, from wherever they came – we realised that these people were not here in the centre, in the healthy, flat part of the city. All of those people were sent out to the outskirts, to the hills, where there is a higher level of risk. They were told: Go occupy those zones! And because of the need for housing we have deforested and damaged many areas that today we know as our barrios.

And today the elitist class of fake materialists still judge you, saying: Those are the *tomistas* (takers), those are the *bichos* (bugs). You should realise that you have overcome this social process of being accused, of being called refugees and pigs. Now you can say with pride that you are a commune, because you have never depended on the state. Your only dependence on the state is your right to organise yourselves in this space of popular power.

Christians – which I am not – sometimes talk about the easy and the hard road. Who is going for the easy road? Those who always go to the institutions to beg for help. Not you, my friends. You always go for the hard road, the road of self-management, the road of self-construction. And the fact that I'm standing here to talk to you makes me proud, you know? Yes, I work for a state institution, one that for now allows people to organise themselves. But the state is still a thing that exists to tread on the people. We are in a process where the person generating this raising of awareness among the people, Chávez, is dying. That's a reality, it's not a lie. The day that friend dies, that day many towers, many institutions, and much of what's been achieved, will be destroyed.

But I have full confidence that the Torre Confinanzas, this organisation here, will stay solid. Because you have learned to solve many problems: problems of sewage, of deaths, of conflicts. And look how happy you are now. I applaud you. See if you are not the *caciques** of today. All of you are the *caciques* of this land. They were people who lived in the collective and lived in balance with nature. We have to vindicate this system of organisation. You gave life to

---

* The *caciques* were pre-Columbian tribal chiefs, although in Spanish the word has come to mean any powerful local political figure, and can imply the use of strong-arm tactics.

this skeleton. Let's give more life, but to the earth, where we were placed. Thank you.

The meeting bursts into applause. Of course they're applauding, even I am. Invoking this atavistic, pre-Columbian tradition bypasses the standard social perceptions that define the lives of the barrio dwellers, implying that whatever cards history and the politicians have dealt them, these squatters are the rightful inheritors of Caracas and that they are empowered to exercise their own self-determination. It's a masterful performance.

As various members of the group take the floor to raise concerns or make statements – none of them quite the orator that Fernando is – it occurs to me that the residents have turned this open-air atrium into their agora. What would have been the plush foyer of a luxury office tower, the belly of a corporate speculation, has become a stage for participatory democracy. And it must be said that there is something theatrical about this scene, the way the flood-lights pick out the audience's faces in the gloom. It's like watching a performance, collective decision-making as drama.

A Spiritual Occupation

Off the atrium is a room that serves as an extremely bare church. El Niño, the tower's head honcho, is a pastor, or claims to be (some use less charitable descriptions). Either way, the residents' faith is a factor in the running of the tower, as we just saw in that meeting. Some of the practising residents are Catholics, but most are Evangelicals of some Pentecostal denomination. Indeed, the squatter's movement in Venezuela appears to be driven by Pentecostals who may see squatting as a self-justifying, spiritual duty. Rafael Sánchez, a professor at Amsterdam University College, has argued that this movement pursues 'the most aggressively voracious logic of spatial occupation', a logic that holds: 'If we do not occupy spaces we are not blessed by the spirit.' For Sánchez, what this represents is a crisis of political representation. In other words, because the bond of trust between the population and the government is broken, these communities are appealing to a higher authority. Thus, what appears to be at least partly a political act – the occupation of unused spaces in the absence of state housing – is in fact a withdrawal from political life and its responsibilities to the rule of law.

The late Venezuelan architect Tomás Sanabria used to refer to a condition he called 'ranchosis', a term he extrapolated from the *rancho*, or slum dwelling. Ranchosis, then, is the slumification of the city by those who carry the slums in their heads, no matter where they live. It is the inhabitation of a skyscraper without the facility that makes a skyscraper possible – the elevator. Ranchosis is a condition that leads U-TT to occasionally describe Caracas as 100 per cent informal. Sánchez's research would seem to support Sanabria's critique, that informality prevails because nobody respects the civic code. If there is a higher calling, of course, then the rules are easy to disobey. But the idea that religion and the law should be in conflict is a peculiar paradox.

In any event, to what extent Torre David is a spiritual occupation, I don't know. I suspect that the need for shelter trumps devotional duty. As for the withdrawal from political life, the flags hanging here and there on the structure are a demonstrative display of the residents' support for Chávez, but such displays may be as pragmatic as they are ideological. They have to support him because they believe – and surely they are right – that if the opposition gets into power they will be evicted. And yet while they exist here only by the grace of El Comandante, the patriarch whose rhetoric encourages their occupation, they know that he is dying. And that's where a higher authority becomes useful. The more autonomous they can become, the stronger their claim to the site will be after he is gone – and no doubt faith gives them strength in their collective effort.

On the other hand, I'm somewhat disconcerted to find out that religious services are called *cultos* – cults. One day Gladys told me, 'I have cult today.' Maybe something's being lost in translation here, or maybe there is more spiritual fervour than I've given them credit for.

Urban Alpinism

During the course of the week, I spend the better part of five days in the Torre. Accompanying various members of the Urban-Think Tank team, who are making a film and a book about the tower, I am the only one not busily measuring up apartments or testing camera angles. The most useful of this crew is a streetwise young *caraqueño* called Rafael, who does all the negotiating for us and is, frankly, the only one of us that the residents take seriously. With Rafael as my interpreter, the tower's modus operandi becomes clearer by the day, and what begins as a lurid, almost illicit experience gradually becomes normality.

Let's begin with the tower's most magnificent and defining shortcoming: the missing elevators. Only the invention of the elevator made skyscrapers possible, and so a skyscraper without one is, theoretically speaking, a useless typology. Bearing in mind that the Torre Confinanzas complex was originally designed to require twenty-three elevators, the fact that there are none and that the residents live as high as the twenty-eighth floor makes their adaptability, not to say stamina, all the more impressive. It's true that residents of the barrios that cover the hills around Caracas are used to hour-long climbs up winding concrete staircases to get home. But this is a new extreme. Commuting up twenty-eight flights of stairs constitutes a kind of urban alpinism. It's not even just a question of effort – the sheer tedium of that climb, day after day, in a poorly lit stairwell, must be hard to bear.

As we go up and down the main internal staircase, it's common to pass people stopping to catch their breath. One day I met a woman on the stairs pausing amid several bags of shopping. Offering to help, I picked up two bags and asked what floor we were going to, as if I was about to press a button in an elevator. 'The twenty-first,' she said. My legs got a taste of what fitness instructors call 'the burn'. But the residents have shrewd ways to get around this deficiency, and the ten-storey car park adjoining Torre David is one of them. Using the car park ramps, they can drive goods and materials a quarter of the way up the tower, often on motorcycles. From there on, however, it's all legwork.

Once, and only once, Hubert and I set ourselves the challenge of climbing up to the helipad on the forty-seventh floor.* Emerging through an open hatch onto the rooftop, we are suddenly dazzled by the 360-degree view of Caracas. From here we can look down on the neighbouring Mercantil and BBVA towers, we can take in the landmarks of the Parque Central complex and 23 de Enero, and we can see how Caracas has burst the natural borders of this valley. But most importantly we can scan the slums covering the hills around the city. The view of that periphery must be a motivating force for the residents of this tower, because by the established logic of Caracas, that is where they should be living, on the edge. And yet they have managed to make a life for themselves, against all the odds, here in the heart of the city. In that sense they've transgressed, defying their allotted place in the urban pecking order and seizing a taste of another reality. That view is a kind of power. Urban-Think Tank likes to use the phrase 'grand horizon', referring to the collective gaze northwards by the poor of the global South and their aspirations to the lifestyles of the economic North – an imaginative leap across what

---

* The last two storeys don't really count as floors, which is why we always describe the tower as forty-five storeys high.

Teddy Cruz calls the 'political equator'. But in this case that grand horizon is more literal, and refers to a realisation of what it means to raise your living standards from the precariousness of the edge to a privileged precariousness in the centre.

Self-Organisation

In an apartment on the fourteenth floor we meet Iván Morales, one of the original 'pioneers', as they call themselves. He and his wife and two kids live in a triangular-shaped apartment in the corner of the tower. This was the very first apartment to be occupied. For the first three months, the Morales family, along with all the others, lived in tents on the ground floor while they cleared out and dusted off the upper storeys. He chose the fourteenth floor for no better reason than that someone had told him it was nice up there, but he seems to have inadvertently started proceedings at the very middle of the inhabited floors of the tower, with the others gradually filling in the fourteen storeys above and below him. The view from what is now his balcony (the window has been removed) is spectacular, but with only a cinder-brick wall holding you in, standing there makes your stomach turn. His wife is on the computer browsing the internet, and there is a flatscreen TV mounted on the wall. Earlier in the day I noticed what appeared to be a fire sale of Thai-made refrigerators outside the mall down the street, and here's one of them, still in its box. He must have carried it up fourteen storeys.

Iván works for a government watchdog, in price control. Before they moved here they lived in a barrio near 23 de Enero. The only thing that bothers him about life in the tower is the services, which are obviously far from ideal, but mostly he worries about safety. He's referring to the open facades and holes in the floor that make the building a potentially lethal game of snakes and ladders. 'But thank God this building is safer than many others,' he says, referring to the relative lack of crime.

Having said earlier that a skyscraper is defined by its need for an elevator, there are of course other features without which it cannot function. The modern tower has a sophisticated nervous system that delivers air conditioning, electricity, sprinkler systems, refuse disposal, plumbing and sewage services, all of which are required to make it habitable and all of which were absent from Torre David when the squatters arrived. The fact that 3,000 people now live here is a testament to the residents' self-organisation and resourcefulness.

Far from stealing their electricity, which is common practice in informal settlements, the residents of the tower actually paid off a debt of $10,000 that the state electricity company, Corpoelec, claimed was owed by squatters during previous invasions.* So they're hooked up to the grid legitimately, though you wouldn't know it from the wooden switchbox on the sixth floor that receives Corpoelec's cable and distributes power around the building. It may look

---

* Before this serious occupation in 2007 there had been bouts of squatting in 2003.

like a shoddy high-school physics project – only the five members of the electric team are allowed anywhere near the thing – but the power supply to the apartments is fairly reliable. The water supply, on the other hand, is rather more ad hoc. In what should have been the sixteenth-floor elevator lobby is a water pump, filling a central tank with 22,000 litres of water. This tank distributes water to public taps on each floor, from which the residents run hoses into the personal tanks in their apartments. It's a system that means the residents have to use water sparingly, and consequently they consume about a third of the Venezuelan national average.

But more intriguing than the services is the tower's property management system, which is more or less opaque depending on who you talk to. The official line is that residents do not pay rent, merely 150 bolívars ($23) a month for maintenance. Flats are allocated by the management – which calls itself the Cooperativa de Vivienda Caciques de Venezuela – based on family size, not market value. When a family moves out of the tower, they cannot sell their apartment but they can charge the next owner for the improvements they've made, at a price approved by the organisation. This is a closed economy where the apartments have no market value, but your labour – as well as your materials, perhaps even your taste – is refundable. This no doubt encourages residents to treat their apartments as investments and not just temporary accommodation. Anyone is eligible for an apartment in the tower, as long as they've got the right documents – an ID card, a document from the government declaring that they don't have a house, a recommendation, and a bank deposit for the cooperative.

However, this rent-free rental scheme appears not to be fully understood by all the residents. One woman we meet – let's call her Estela – has different ideas. She appreciates living in the tower, and frames the advantages of being in the city centre in simple terms. 'I can take a cab from here at any time,' she says. 'In a barrio I can't.' Unluckily for her, she lives in what would have been the elevator lobby, with no exterior windows. She's an illegal immigrant from Colombia who came to the tower to join her nephew. But he died shortly afterwards when he fell off the twelfth floor. She claims she bought this place for 7,000 bolívars four years ago, despite what the managers say about flats not being for sale. 'They keep that quiet,' she says. Perhaps what she means is that she bought the improvements from the previous owner? 'No, some of the apartments go for 50,000.' As ever, it's hard to know whom to believe, who is right and who is merely paranoid. Either way, she is deeply suspicious of the management. 'The chief has two SUVs and two motorbikes, and he says it was God's blessing that gave him all that!' She's not the first to imply that El Niño is more gangster than pastor. But she says she has to keep quiet or they'll kick her out.*

---

*   There are more extraordinary stories than Estela's. U-TT's Daniel Schwartz told me about a young black man from Brooklyn that he met in the tower last year. They bumped into each other in a corridor and it turned out that the man was living here with his mother. On a total whim, they'd chosen Venezuela for a holiday and then lost their luggage and passports and were

There's a huge discrepancy in the standard of the interiors in the tower. Some people have furbished their flats for the long term, despite the ambiguity of whether they'll be able to stay. Many units have been remodelled and are well appointed, stuffed with sofas, fully fitted kitchens and all mod cons. Others are divided up with bed-sheet curtains and cardboard, with newspaper lining the walls. These really are squats, either because the owners are recent arrivals or because they don't want to invest in a property they don't own. If Chávez dies, or even if he offers them a replacement home, they would lose what they'd invested. This is symptomatic of the fragility of life here. There is a lifestyle divide between those who are living in the here and now, and those who cannot allow themselves to.

One apartment stands out in my memory as a vivid snapshot of the aspirations to a middle-class existence. The interior was lined with stone-effect wallpaper, and all the doors were cut into arches. One wall was even mounted with a family of flying ducks, that most parodied of suburban ornaments. We could almost be in Surrey. But the will to decorate at all costs reached new heights here. On a side table, arranged around a porcelain unicorn, was an assortment of gilded picture frames, typical enough except that the 'photos' they contained depicted clean-cut American

---

stuck here. How they ended up in the Torre is unclear. And there are darker stories. Daniel and Alfredo filmed an interview with a woman who claimed to be the illegitimate daughter of Carmen Miranda – she was clearly *loca*. Later we heard a rumour that she was pushed off the tower, and that her body lay on the ground for days until an ambulance came to pick it up. Who knows what to believe.

families, with the frame dimensions printed over the top –
a sweetly plaintive case of the frame as content. It's another
manifestation of the grand horizon, that mental picture of
the accoutrements required to live the middle-class dream.

Perhaps the only thing the residents have sacrificed
compared to living in a barrio is that once you live in an
apartment block you can't expand your property, you can
only divide it up. For now the living quarters are spacious,
but if the residents stay long enough for new generations to
grow up and have families of their own, we could see multiple families living in the same apartment, which is what
happened in 23 de Enero.

They organise their own maintenance of the common
areas, with a big clean-up once a month that everyone is
supposed to take part in. This is a far cry from the picture
the Chilean Alejandro Aravena painted of social housing
in Latin America. His justification for designing out all the
common parts in his housing model was that they are inevitably neglected, because there's never any budget for them,
and because they fall outside of anyone's responsibility.
Here, nothing is outside of the collective responsibility, and
that is perhaps (John Turner would no doubt have argued)
because the building is not technically provided by the state –
there is no one else to blame here.

A Vertical Village

In the Torre, corridors become streets. The habitual street
life of the barrio is played out indoors. A group of boys will

kick a football around, a girl will sit outside her front door having her hair straightened, neighbours will cluster for a natter. These are typical barrio scenes, reframed by smooth concrete floors, strip lighting and views hundreds of feet below to the street proper.

The other aspect of the tower's internal street life, and more evidence of its collective self-organisation, is its convenience stores. When you live in an elevatorless sky-scraper, you can't be popping out every time you need a pint of milk. Consequently, there are *bodegas* every two floors or so. They sell mainly dry goods: tinned food, rice and pasta, sweets and drinks, toilet paper – the essentials. There's hardly any fresh fruit or vegetables, and no alcohol – although residents are certainly allowed to drink. Getting caught selling alcohol, or cigarettes to minors, may result in you being shut down for a couple of days. Of course, in a vertical economy reliant on leg-power, there is a premium the higher up you go. Up to the tenth floor, shop owners have to keep prices level with those on the street, but above the tenth they are allowed to charge one or two bolívars extra.

Spending our days in the tower, we found ourselves relying on these *bodegas* to keep our energy up. It wasn't just that the street was a long way down, but getting back in required an annoying amount of coordination. So, since we were hardly going to cook ourselves rice and beans for lunch, a Snickers bar and bottle of Fanta would have to do. Rafael had a handy phrase for these occasions that always made me feel tougher than I am. '*Otra raya más para el tigre*,' he'd say – another stripe on the tiger, or another day without lunch.

There are all sorts of other services on offer in the tower, too. There's a barbershop, a copy shop and, I was amazed to discover, an orthodontist. Later I was informed that the orthodontist's services are purely cosmetic – he just adds the tracks with no wires. Apparently braces are considered a status symbol, more teeth-jewellery than correctional apparatus.

One evening, on the sixth floor, we stumble across a scene straight out of J. G. Ballard's *High-Rise*. A man is slicing the ears off a goat's head, while his companion is hacking at the carcass on a chopping block atop an oil barrel. Only the context makes it Ballardian. These are ordinary rural pursuits that just happen to be taking place in the corridor of a skyscraper.

All of this rustic colour is set against what should have been the exclusive domain of the executive. This hits home when, on the sixth floor, I happen across a concrete hollow that would have been a swimming pool. You can just picture it as a blue-tiled oasis ringed by execs lounging in deckchairs. In contrast to that vision, around the corner is a string of laundry hanging over a pool-sized puddle, the arc of clothing reflected in the water like a still from a Tarkovsky movie. This place can throw jarring juxtapositions at you.

The Edge

By and large, this building is perfectly safe as long as you stay away from the edge. The only problem is that there is so much edge. The external staircases have no handrails, or if they do they've been jerry-rigged with bits of pipe and wire. The same goes for many of the walkways connecting the tower with the lower blocks adjoining it. In the top half of the tower, on floors where the glass facade panels have been removed, it's possible to walk right up to the brink. It's not uncommon for kids to play unattended, and naturally there have been accidents. A three-year-old girl is one of those who we've heard have fallen off the tower. The few residents we asked about it denied it, but two young boys we met confirmed the rumour, adding their own imaginative flourishes. One of them said she was found in the basement eaten by sharks, the other that she was seen to come apart on the way down. (This is how growing up in a forty-five-storey construction site stimulates the imagination.) They didn't like living here, they said, it was too dangerous.

Aside from falls, here are some of the routine hazards you can expect to encounter in the tower:

1. One day, a sheet of glass is dangling from the facade. It's swinging gently in the wind, a pendulum that could be about to become an airborne guillotine. The security team scrambles, shouting into walkie-talkies and corralling everyone back inside the building.

2. We're standing at the edge of the eighth floor at the rear of the tower, when two rubbish bags whoosh past our faces, landing with

a boom on the ground. Again, the security team jumps into action, shouting furiously up at the culprit.

3. Navigating my way around the building can be extremely disorienting (at this point I haven't yet seen any of the floorplans that U-TT later draw up). But you can always tell when you're moving from one section to another by the gaps in the concrete floor plates, which are there in case of any seismic movement. Stepping over these is always mildly stressful because I can never stop myself imagining what it would be like to step hip-deep into one. Between these and all the other cavities in the floors, it's as if Gordon Matta-Clark has had a field day.

4. On the fourteenth floor one of the glass panes has a bullet hole in it, a stray from a shoot-out on the street below. But I think we should discount a wild aim from the list of ever-present dangers.

The more conventional dangers that residents might face were they still living in the barrio would be crime-related. And there seems to be very little crime in the tower, either because of the sense of collective endeavour or perhaps because of that religious conviction we touched on earlier. It's true that there are metal grills on some of the internal windows, especially those of the *bodegas*, but I suspect this is down to cultural habit more than any bitter experience of life in the tower. In Caracas you almost have to redefine 'window' as not just a pane of glass but a pane of glass behind bars. On the whole this place appears to be well run, and is far from lawless. One woman told me blithely that living here was like living in a barrio 'but much safer'. For one thing, the residents self-police, and the house rules on misbehaviour are as simple as baseball: three strikes and you're out.

The Penthouse

Frankenstein lives on the twenty-eighth floor. He is not as ugly as his name suggests. In fact, he is an occasional model. And, yes, that is his real name – if you think it's strange, he has a cousin called John Wayne. It's not clear to me whether he's so muscular because the communal gym happens to be on his balcony, or whether the gym is on his balcony because no one fancied arguing with him about it. But that's where the benchpress is, two feet short of a twenty-eight-storey drop, with no railing. By way of a demonstration, he strides over and picks up a barbell loaded with two steel wheels that used to belong to the elevator motor (it should be pointed out here that the reason why the Torre doesn't have an elevator is not because Frankenstein wanted to pump iron). As the gym (which is really just the bench and some barbells) is so high up, only a few others use it; mainly members of the security team. But to their minds, anyone who makes it all the way up here has earned the right.

Watching Frankenstein and his family sit out on their balcony, one is easily sucked into the idea that, despite being poor, they live like millionaires. This is the penthouse suite, and they have one of the most luxurious open-air views in Caracas. And yet, when you see his infant daughter playing near that ledge, you can't imagine overcoming the constant fear that something might happen to her. This is extreme living. I can see Frankenstein bounding up twenty-eight flights of stairs; but with kids in tow, it wouldn't be a surprise if his family has simply given up on the street altogether. A sort of Swiss Family Robinson, castaways in mid-air, the children only discovering the street when they come of age.

For the time being, this is the highest occupied floor. That's because residents are only allowed to claim apartments within existing internal walls, and above this floor the tower's builders didn't get around to those. And so for now the tower is full, and new residents can only move in when there's a vacancy.

The Future

After five days in the tower, it's striking how different it feels to me. This environment was totally wild when we first arrived here. How quickly one adjusts, and the outlandish becomes the norm. And yet one has to remind oneself that this is not normal, nor is it sustainable. If the tower is to evolve from an anomaly, a tolerated aberration, into a legitimate and fully-functioning piece of the city, what would have to change? For one, the residents would need some kind of legal security. Gladys has a lawyer on the case, trying to get ownership of the building for the Caciques housing cooperative. I don't know how realistic

Looking down on Hornos de Cal Metrocable station in the barrio of San Agustín

The gondolas Inclusión and Lbertád

Urban-Think Tank's first vertical gym, in La Cruz, Caracas

'The barrio – it's the university of life',
a resident of 23 de Enero, Caracas

Torre David, Caracas

Pumping iron on the twenty-eighth floor of the Torre David

An interior that aspires
to normality

The Torre's open atrium

Antanas Mockus as 'Super Citizen'

Mimes patrolling an intersection in Bogotá

The Orquideorama, designed by Plan B and JPRCR, Medellín

The escalator in Comuna 13, Medellín

The España Library-Park, designed by Giancarlo Mazzanti, in the Santo Domingo barrio of Medellín

The US–Mexico border wall meets the sea in Tijuana

Los Laureles Canyon on the Mexcian side of the border wall and the nature reserve on the US side

this is. But she also says that she's waiting until they remove some undesirable elements (I assume she means thugs or suspected criminals). She uses the verb '*depurar*' – to purify. She doesn't want those people to own their flats. If the Caciques owned the building, I wonder whether the current communal dimension would remain or whether it would lead to privatisation and, inevitably, gentrification.

Interestingly, Gladys and the residents don't want donations for the improvements they want to make. They're not looking for funding: what they want is recognition for the hard work they've put in. Self-sufficiency is the prevailing ethos of the tower. And the more autonomous it can become, the more viable it will be as a model for the future. If a right-wing government comes into power then the residents will almost certainly be kicked out; but if the tower is a fully rehabilitated, self-sustaining and autarchic entity, the eviction will be that much more difficult to achieve.

U-TT have attempted something similar to the Torre David model in the past: the Growing House. The Growing House was a project created on the request of the Anglican Church in Caracas. The Church asked them to devise a system of emergency housing for its parish, but, lacking the necessary land, it had to be built over an existing building. U-TT's response was to build a concrete framework – in effect, a short tower sitting above the building – that would allow residents to build their own apartments within it. It was a flexible, dense solution that turned the residents into developers, designers and builders all at once. The model may be ingenious but it is certainly not new. Le Corbusier's

Dom-ino House model, designed as early as 1914, was precisely that, except that U-TT extrapolated the concept into a tower.

Torre David, then, is a readymade, the accidental culmination of a century-long modernist lineage. It takes Le Corbusier's concept to its logical conclusion, from two-storey house to forty-five-storey skyscraper. It's an idea that is full of untapped potential. But the question remains: is Torre David a viable model of housing for the cities of the future?

The future is never the tidy vision we hold in our imaginations. The future is often discovered rather than invented, and Torre David's claim to it is precisely as an authentically unpredictable, messy instance of real needs superseding planning or design. What will happen to all the speculative towers we continue to throw up if they turn out not to be servicing a need but – in China, for instance – inflating a property bubble? In Europe, with our shrinking populations, the Torre's model of adaptive reuse is perfectly viable. But the emerging economies are where most of the urban growth this century will take place, and they are the ones that need this idea the most. From Caracas to Lagos, the Growing House model could be one to implement deliberately, not after the fact. We're not talking about the squatting of failed structures here but a model developed legally, either by governments or developers. For what is revolutionary about Torre David is the way it unites the formal and the informal in one structure. It may be that the next step is to accept vertical informality as a feature of the twenty-first-century city. In this vision, citizens would complete the city, its buildings would remain works in progress, and perhaps the distinction between the informal and the formal would dissolve.

Common Ground

At the Venice Biennale of Architecture in 2012, U-TT and I presented Torre David as just such a revolutionary model. The theme of the biennale was 'Common Ground', and it seemed the perfect opportunity to present the Torre as precisely that: a corporate skyscraper turned into a kind of commons. What message did we hope to convey by exhibiting a squat in the world's most prestigious architecture exhibition? The point to make was that the real common ground of the city is not being created by architects at all. In an exhibition that tried to define a common architectural culture, that tried to unite the disparate factions behind the noble cause of architecture, our message was that the real common ground was not to be sought among other architects, but with citizens themselves.

Torre David is a social phenomenon more than an architectural one. It is a paradigm of human ingenuity, adaptability and resourcefulness – of citizens exercising their right to the city. In that sense, it may be one of the 'pirate utopias' that Hakim Bey called Temporary Autonomous Zones. 'The TAZ', wrote Bey, 'is a perfect tactic for an era in which the state is omnipresent and all-powerful and yet simultaneously riddled with cracks and vacancies.' That is a good description of Venezuela. The difference is that its residents are not being self-consciously rebellious (they did not occupy the tower as an act of dissent), they just want a place to live. And so, without wishing to romanticise the tower, we presented it as an urban laboratory, a testing ground for how cities might work differently.

As soon as word of the exhibition reached Venezuela, there was an outcry. Some of the country's most respected architects began writing complaints to the main newspaper, *El Universal*. They accused us of shaming Venezuela, of romanticism – worse, of indulging in favela chic. They accused us of being *chavistas*. It was only a month or so before the 2012 general election, and many of these architects were openly supporting the opposition candidate, Henrique Capriles. For such figures, the Torre is a travesty and nothing more: a hive of crime, so they believe, and a shameful blight on the face of their beloved city. How, they asked, could we endorse squatting as a viable form of city-making? How, as one venerable architect tellingly put it, could we betray 'our class'?

For me, the squatting issue is a red herring. Squatting is a question of legality, and as we've seen, under the Chávez government squatting was not only tolerated but encouraged. Of course, the fact that the Torre's residents had to be encouraged to resort to squatting is an indictment of Chávez's housing policy, and his failure to provide enough homes for the poor. Indeed, when news of the biennale controversy reached Chávez, he feigned surprise. In a staged TV spot, he pretended to find out about Torre David by innocently asking one of its residents where she lived, and then promptly announced that he would provide homes for all of its residents. Nothing more was heard on that topic, and now that Chávez is dead, nothing more will be.

To view the Torre in terms of squatting is to define it by conventional social norms. For the Venezuelan architects who find the tower so distasteful, focusing on squatting restricts them to seeing it as just another symptom of a dysfunctional city. It limits their ability to see its revolutionary potential. Instead of squatting being seen as a symptom of scarcity, might it not be a solution? This was precisely the shift in perspective brought about by Turner and many others towards the informal city more generally. The Venezuelan architects' attitude to the tower takes for granted that it is a temporary state of affairs. But must we only see the Torre as a temporary dynamic before the inevitable return to the status quo? Or can we accept precariousness as a fluid, mobile force in the city? This is a common enough strategy in London or New York, where artists are invited to inhabit derelict spaces in the interests of driving up their value (it would be ironic indeed if the squatters in the Torre rehabilitated the building enough to make it attractive to developers again). But instead of a cynical market ploy, this might be the opportunity to acknowledge that the kind of flexibility embodied by the tower is an essential quality of the future city.

The residents of Torre David have achieved something that is almost impossible in the modern city: they have defined the nature of their own coexistence. This is an opportunity that ordinary citizens never get. It is precluded from the outset by the terms of city life. Our lives are set within the predefined borders of our properties, the finance structures of our mortgages, and the terms of our rental or ownership contracts. The notion of a structure that we can divide as we see fit and inhabit according to principles that we define – in short, the idea that we can determine our own way of life – is positively exotic.

We must be alive to such potential, because out of extreme conditions the poor will create new paradigms. Le Corbusier may have invented the Dom-ino House one hundred years ago, but it took squatters in Venezuela, acting out of desperate self-determination, to realise its true potential. People came up with the answer, not an architect. And in doing so they helped create a more equitable city. Perhaps above all else, what is so potent about Torre David is its symbolism. The squatters' direct action has subverted the skyscraper, transforming a beacon of finance capital into one of social capital. Vertical exclusivity became horizontal redistribution. Alfredo once put it better than that. He said that if the nineteenth century gave birth to the horizontal city, and the twentieth century gave birth to the vertical city, then the twenty-first century must be for the diagonal city, one that cuts across social divisions. It's a beautiful sentiment.

6

Bogotá: The City as a School

One day, in 1993, the rector of Bogotá's Universidad Nacional, Antanas Mockus, was faced with a rowdy auditorium full of protesting students. Determined to get their attention, he walked to the front of the stage, dropped his trousers and mooned them. It was an early act of what Mockus calls, borrowing the term from Pierre Bourdieu, 'symbolic violence'. And it worked. The students were stunned into silence. But the act was caught on video and later aired on the news. In the media outcry, Mockus was forced to resign. It might have been the end of his career, but it was just the beginning. The rector with the unorthodox methods became notorious, and in his disgrace he achieved the status of a public figure. The following year, he was elected mayor of Bogotá.

Mockus's first term as mayor would kick-start a remarkable period of urban renaissance. The former philosophy professor was merely the first in a sequence of extraordinary mayors who would revive not just the capital but also

Colombia's second city, Medellín. In a country that was mired in wars against the drug cartels and paramilitary guerrillas, and plagued by rampant violence, poverty and a corrupt political class, three politically independent mayors were able to offer hope of a new reality.

The first, Mockus, was mayor of Bogotá twice, in 1995–97 and 2000–03, taking an unruly city and using his unique pedagogical style to instil a sense of civic culture. The second was Enrique Peñalosa, who, between Mockus's two terms, drastically improved Bogotá's transport infrastructure, building the TransMilenio bus service, hundreds of miles of bicycle lanes, public spaces, libraries and schools. Together, Mockus and Peñalosa made Bogotá a byword for urban transformation. The third was a former mathematics professor called Sergio Fajardo. As mayor of Medellín from 2004–07, he took what was then the murder capital of the world and used new public spaces and transport links to the barrios to return it to sanity.

The politics that gave rise to these works are especially compelling. In contrast to the self-initiating role that architects have adopted elsewhere on the continent, in Colombia it was the politicians who were central to this metamorphosis. Instead of activist architects, here it was activist politicians, taking a stand against the prevailing politics.

A truly radical politics can only be set in motion by an outsider. As a Lithuanian Jew by extraction, Antanas Mockus Šivickas was perhaps already that. But as an academic he specialised in teaching methods that his colleagues considered beyond the pale. As head of the Universidad Nacional, he was derided as 'the clown rector'. As a politician he was 'the clown mayor'. This is the man who dressed up as a caped crusader called Supercitizen. He was a Dostoyevskian character, the holy fool, who made a point of always telling the truth and who dared to believe in his fellow citizens' potential for good. By the end of his two terms the homicide rate fell by 70 per cent, traffic fatalities dropped by 50 per cent, water usage was down 40 per cent, tax revenues had tripled and the city's finances were coming back into the black. A much-loved figure with approval ratings in his first term of sometimes 80 per cent, his greatest single achievement was to make Bogotá feel like a city with a future.

Philosophy Is an Intruder

'There are days when I think all this will disappear without leaving a trace,' says Mockus. 'And on some days, on the contrary, I think that there are several good seeds inside it.' He is sitting on the sofa, his hands folded in his lap, in his house in Quinta Paredes, right next to the university. In a grey suit, with his trademark beard-sans-moustache, Mockus looks like an Amish businessman. He speaks slowly, at times painfully so, one of the side effects of the medication he's taking for Parkinson's disease. His work, his legacy, these are what he fears might disappear without a trace. There are signs that Bogotá is returning to its old ways. As we speak, the previous mayor, Samuel Moreno, is on trial for corruption; new public transport services are under severe strain; the traffic is appalling. People are again talking about a city in crisis.

But the thing about Mockus is that his policies rarely left a trace, not a visible one anyway. Mayors normally measure their legacy in infrastructure and other tangible works. They like to cut ribbons. But Mockus's legacy was inscribed in the minds of Bogotá's citizens. It was internalised. His was an intervention in the moral DNA of the city.

In many respects Mockus had a conformist academic career. A mathematician who moved into philosophy, he spent ten years writing his master's thesis on Heidegger's reading of Descartes, prompting jokes from other professors that it wasn't meant to be a posthumous work.

As a professor, he was influenced by a series of intellectual mavericks. One was the philosopher Richard Rorty, who rejected the tradition of empiricism and argued that knowledge is created by people interacting with the world, not just perceiving it. A fellow philosophical pragmatist, Mockus would take very seriously Rorty's idea that you can't fully understand the meaning of what you say or do until you know all the practical consequences that result from it (like when you drop your trousers in public, for instance). Another was Paul Feyerabend, who advocated an anarchist theory of knowledge. Yet another was Stanley Milgram, who conducted a controversial experiment in the 1960s that involved making participants give people electric shocks, to prove that humans are essentially obedient.

This blend of pragmatism, anarchist method and obedience theory would influence how he approached the problems of the city.

But first these ideas were put into practice at the university. Perhaps as a result of having struggled to write his thesis, Mockus developed an alternative language to the written word, a language of actions. He became adept at subverting social norms, and made a point of disrupting habitual thinking. By the time he was made rector of the university, he finally had the authority – or the social recognition, he would say – to give vent to his non-conformist self. A reformist dean, he allowed students to pay what they felt they could afford, and found that many were willing to pay more for their education. But he had a problem with decorum. He would ride into faculty meetings on a bicycle. He would get an auditorium full of students to tie their shoelaces together. He liked to combine reflection and recreation, philosophy and humour. 'Philosophy is an intruder, a sort of saboteur, which enters the conversation and prevents exaggerated normalisation,' says Mockus.

Ultimately, Mockus's talent for 'dislocation', as he describes it, would be his undoing as rector, but the making of him as mayor. Following the mooning incident and his unexpected rise as a public figure, Mockus launched his political career. Running as an independent in the 1994 mayoral elections, Mockus campaigned on the platform of 'No P' – no publicity, no politics, no party and no *plata* (money). His entire campaign cost just $8,000.* With no

---

* I've also come across $12,000, but either way it's peanuts.

advertising budget, instead he handed out *pirinolas*, a Colombian game like a spinning top. Depending on which side it lands, the *pirinola* instructs the player to add to or take from the pot. But with the next spin all the players might have to put money in (*todos ponen*) or take money out (*todos toman*). His point was that only if everyone puts something into the city can everyone get something out of it. It was playful but also an early indication of the kind of civic responsibility he hoped to inculcate. Aside from such tactics, Mockus – the professor, the eccentric, the honest man – appealed to a populace frustrated with corrupt and ineffectual politicians. They gave him a chance. In fact, they gave him 64 per cent of the vote, a landslide victory.

One of the advantages of having run as an independent and avoiding the practice of buying votes with favours was that Mockus could build his own administration. Surrounding himself with young anthropologists and sociologists, he established a kind of think tank within City Hall, the Observatorio de Cultura Urbana (Urban Culture Observatory). From this suitably academic context, he presided over what he called 'a classroom of 6.5 million people'.

The chief responsibility of the think tank was 'Cultura Ciudadana', the Culture of Citizenship programme. Its manifesto was so radical that it reads like a philosophical tract. It listed four objectives: (1) increase the obedience to coexistence norms; (2) increase the proportion of people peacefully getting other people to obey coexistence norms; (3) solve more conflicts through alternative peaceful methods; (4) improve expression and interaction between citizens through culture, art, sport and recreation.

Now, one could be forgiven for wondering what, exactly, 'coexistence norms' are. This is simply sociological jargon for the everyday rules and behaviour that comprise responsible citizenship, such as orderly queuing, stopping at a red light or not throwing litter. These sound like rather quaint concerns for a city that was ankle-deep in blood – in 1993, at the height of the war on the drug cartels, there were 4,352 homicides, or 81 per 100,000 citizens. On the other hand, it is probably no coincidence that one of the world's most violent cities produced one of the most innovative urban administrations.

Mockus was only too aware of what happens at the day-to-day level when civic norms are ignored. Bogotá in the 1990s was a tapestry of dysfunction, illustrated by the routine bribery of traffic police and the degradation of public space. Streets and even parks were being fenced off and guarded by sentry boxes, and the wealthy were retreating into gated communities. Without a sense of collective ownership, everything that should be public is inevitably annexed by private, commercial or authoritarian interests. The municipality was short of funds for maintenance, but then no city budget can compensate for the effects of a lack of civic responsibility. This, in short, is what the Cultura Ciudadana programme set out to address. The starting point was what Mockus calls 'a shared vision of the city'. Plagued by modesty (or at least a fear of its opposite), he says he struggled with the pomposity of that word 'vision'. Yet visionary he was.

Mockus's most famous intervention, and the most medi-agenic, was to replace Bogotá's traffic police with mime artists. 'I asked the secretary of transport to tell me the single rule that would alleviate traffic jams the most,' he recalls. 'And she said, if we could teach people to stop at intersections, that would be the best thing.' The Observatory spent months on this, and finally came up with the novel idea of the mime artists. There were already a few mimes working as street artists at traffic lights, but now they would be put at the service of the capital. Twenty of them were deployed in one neighbourhood on a trial basis, and Mockus announced the measure in a press conference at City Hall (far removed from the mimes, because he knew that the media would make him join in and play the clown). 'Can they impose fines?' asked a journalist. 'No,' replied Mockus. 'Then it won't work.'

But it did work. With full face paint and comical posturing, the mimes policed the junctions, stopping traffic, ushering pedestrians across and mimicking the jaywalkers. It was functional street theatre and the TV cameras loved it. It was, after all, both aesthetic and controversial. 'A critical discourse surrounded it,' says Mockus. 'People were saying it was funny, or made sense, or was a waste of money.' And within a few weeks he decided that the scheme was so successful that it would be rolled out across ninety neighbourhoods, deploying 400 mimes. It was only temporary but highly effective. Point one on the manifesto: 'Increase obedience to coexistence norms'. Tick. And with what visual humour that dry phrase comes to life. For a delicious moment, comedy was being used to enforce the law. Several months later, fed up with their corruption and sense of impunity, Mockus disbanded the traffic police altogether and replaced them with national police.

Though playful, the mimes were still representatives of authority – you might say they were enforcers by stealth. But what really interested Mockus was the second point on the manifesto: how you get citizens to influence each *other's* behaviour, without recourse to the law or the threat of punishment. And here, addressing the same traffic problem, he came up with another novel solution. He printed 350,000 red cards, like the ones football referees use. On the red side was a thumbs-down icon, and on the reverse, white side was a thumbs-up icon. The idea was that drivers could chide one another for being selfish or breaking the law, or applaud one another for their patience or generosity. His instinct was that being shamed by a fellow citizen was a greater disincentive than being punished by a corrupt traffic cop. Self-regulation by citizens was a new kind of authority, at least for Bogotá. As Mockus once pointed out, regulating behaviour is innate in humans, just as a baby regulates the behaviour of a parent by crying. Stanley Milgram's experiments with electric shocks, which Mockus had studied, may have proved that human beings are essentially obedient – but that finding can lead in starkly divergent directions. It can explain the horrors of the Holocaust or, in Bogotá's case, the roots of a civic culture.

In one of the many talks by Mockus that are online, a member of the audience likens his methods to those of an advertising agency or, more critically, the brainwashing of a dictator. Mockus replied: 'I have read *1984*. But as mayor you don't regulate people's behaviour, you build conditions for people to regulate each other's behaviour.' Fascist governments have successfully done the same. The difference, obviously, is that rather than using regulatory behaviour to bolster his own power, Mockus was using it to create a civic culture. He was restoring a sense of pride and collective ownership in Bogotá.

Mockus made physical interventions, too, such as having yellow stars painted wherever there had been a fatal traffic accident. At the time, traffic accidents were the second most common cause of death after homicides, and the stars were a kind of visual shock therapy. But by and large his policies were educational. The fact that fatalities fell from 1,300 a year to just 600 was due to a gradual rewiring of the collective brain. As he once told a roomful of Harvard leadership students: 'Bogotá was ugly but we all know very successful people who are ugly. If you can't change your hardware, you can change your software.'

Of all his achievements, the one of which Mockus is most proud is the reduction of the homicide rate. In his first term it fell from seventy-two to forty-seven murders per 100,000 citizens, and in his second from thirty-five to twenty-three. Not all of these deaths were linked to the narcotics trade, there was also a culture of casual violence. Mockus remembers as a boy reading in the newspaper about a man shot dead for making a joke about a passing stranger wearing sunglasses at night ('What's the matter, you don't like the stars?'). He took a multi-pronged approach to violence. One Christmas he held an armistice, trading toys for guns. His administration collected 2,538 firearms, which were melted down and recast as spoons engraved with *Arma fui* ('I was a gun'). Indeed he developed such a zeal for destroying weapons that a general wrote to him, reminding him that in law the military alone can destroy guns. 'It is only a small part of their profession, but the most beautiful one,' says Mockus. On a different occasion he exploited a law banning guns from public spectacles to temporarily declare all of Bogotá a public spectacle.

Another line of attack was by moderating alcohol consumption. It turned out, in the case of both homicides and traffic accidents, that most deaths occurred in the festive month of December, and throughout the year on Friday and Saturday nights. Here he parted with his ordinarily liberal, self-regulating style and adopted a rare authoritarian measure. It was, he says, one of his 'moments of certainty'. As a trial, one December he restricted the licensing hours for bars to 1 a.m. He called it the Carrot Law – a 'carrot' (*zanahoria*) is slang for a boring health freak. The slogan was, 'A carrot in December, safe in January.' It had a striking effect on murder statistics, and Mockus would resort to it more than once.

Mockus also tackled a worryingly high incidence of domestic violence. He tells me a story about visiting a hospital and encountering the children of a man who had come home drunk and set the house on fire. Thir faces were badly burned. Mockus breaks down as he recalls this. In fact he wells up several times during my visit, and it's hard to tell if it's pure emotion or exacerbated by the medication. 'And the same day I had a visit from a girl who had asked to meet me as a present for her third birthday. As she was leaving, her mother said, "I forgot to tell you, every time I go to beat her she picks up the phone and pretends to call you."' It was the casualness with which she referred to the beatings that troubled him. His solution to this scourge of family life was predictably improbable: a vaccine against violence.

It was estimated that perhaps 600,000 children in Bogotá were subject to domestic violence. 'But the number of psychiatrists was in the hundreds, and the time required to alleviate that situation … Clearly we had to invent something different.' Mockus proposed to distribute a 'symbolic violence kit' that consisted of a stuffed figure and a balloon on which the child could draw the face of his or her aggressor and then confront, either verbally or physically. This was tested on 45,000 participants under the supervision of psychiatrists who also administered drops, like a vaccine. It was a classic Mockus strategy, part catharsis and part carnival. He is quick to point out that it was not scientific, and yet it was also an introduction to real therapy if required, and 10 percent of participants were referred for further help.

The symbolic act came to be one of the defining features of Mockus's style of politics. Once, in a political debate, Mockus threw a glass of water in the face of presidential candidate Horacio Serpa, and then invited Serpa to reciprocate. Only in Mockus's hands could a seemingly aggressive act be a tool of conflict resolution, proof that antagonism need not result in violence. Symbolic acts simply became Mockus's preferred choice of communicating. For instance, in his ongoing war against the illegal fireworks industry, which maims hundreds of children every year, he got the supermarkets to sell a symbolic firework kit made up of condoms that you could inflate and burst. This was doubly effective, because it got condoms into the hands of those who normally couldn't afford them and were anyway forbidden from using them by the Catholic Church.

Politics as Performance

Mockus's method often took on a performative aspect. This was the case when he dressed up as a superhero in a red cape and yellow leotard and went about cleaning graffiti. *Superciudadano*, as his character was called, was the embodiment of everything he wanted the *bogotanos* to be, but it was also self-parody. Mockus learned to use the mass media and could get away with things that would ordinarily turn politicians into a laughing stock. To help reduce water consumption, he appeared in TV adverts showering himself and turning off the water as he soaped. It was effective: water consumption fell by 14 per cent within two months. But such antics went beyond Mockus manipulating the power of television. The will to make statements through performance seemed to be innate. Soon after being elected, he married his second wife, Adriana, in a tiger cage and the two of them rode off on elephants (a wink to the media circus that he was now entering). At times he used performances to market his policies. For instance, in his campaign against violence he staged a spectacle at a cemetery that had been emptied and was about to be demolished. He hired actors to emerge from the crypts one at a time, making tangible an invisible number of dead in the crypts beneath. The slogan was 'Let's keep them empty.'

The Colombian curator José Roca has argued that as a politician Mockus was using the methods of the performance artist. Although Mockus never claimed to be an artist exactly, art was certainly a common reference point for him. Knowingly or not, he appropriated Joseph Beuys's notion that everyone is an artist. During his presidential campaign in 2006, one of his campaign texts included the lines: 'because culture can be transformed creatively; because art liberates the individual … because each citizen can be an artist; because to exercise politics should be aesthetic.' The way Mockus practiced politics was certainly aesthetic, and not just in the sense of being media-friendly. It often manifested itself in small but loaded gestures. Once, his security team forced him to wear a bulletproof vest. In protest, Mockus took some scissors and cut a heart-shaped hole in it right over his heart. With that act, he transformed a piece of armour into a symbol of compassion. Such alchemy takes talent. It may derive from his mother, Nijole, a celebrated sculptor, whom he idolises. In fact, she lives next door. Showing me around his mother's studio, he says, 'One day my mother said to me, "You're like Dali, you can make art from anything, but you need cameras!"'

If artists in the 1970s were taking art out of the gallery and into the landscape, then perhaps Mockus can be seen as an extension of that exodus, making art a tool of public policy. Either way, his actions have influenced artists who have returned them to the context of the gallery. The Mexican artist Pedro Reyes, for instance, has incorporated the vaccine against violence into his *Sanatorium* project, a roving utopian clinic. If not exactly art, Mockus saw his acts as an alternative form of communication. What appeals to him is the idea of communicating on a non-rational level, as art does. His work as a master's student of philosophy and then as a professor had been preoccupied with the limits of rationality. A critic of Cartesian thought, he was constantly testing the limits of reason as well as those of language as a form of communication. When he dropped his trousers and bent over in front of an auditorium full of students, he was demonstrating the limits of language. But this was more than just subverting norms or communicating through actions – it was a way of taking responsibility.

Mockus's method was rooted in philosophical pragmatism. Pragmatism has come up many times in this book as a form of realpolitik, but philosophical pragmatism is not the same thing. Mockus explains it thus: 'With any theory or statement, the meaning is all the practical consequences of it that you can conceive. So if you cannot show that a new theory has different practical consequences, the two theories are the same theory with different wordings. So it strongly connects meaning with action.' In other words, thought is not just for representing the world, it's for shaping it. Mockus's anarchic method proceeded through actions, and he was constantly seeking out meaning in their consequences, just as a scientist parses the results of his experiments.

We've seen how effective these methods were. Dramatic falls in homicide rates, traffic congestion, traffic accidents and water usage, and a burgeoning civic pride. However, his impact on Bogotá, though powerful, was an intangible one. That is not quite true – in one sense it was highly material. Mockus restored the city's finances. He inherited a city with a deficit and left it with a healthy budget for urban renewal projects. He did this partly by raising taxes. Much as he had done at the university, he persuaded 55,000 of Bogotá's wealthiest residents to pay an extra 10 per cent in tax. He also sold off part of the municipal telecommunications company (and when he was accused of neoliberalism for selling off a public asset, he was able to counter that not many neoliberals are in favour of raising taxes). The other way he balanced the books, of course, was by spending very little money. In a sense, the scarcity of municipal resources forced him to innovate, but he was also looking for different outcomes than other mayors. Less interested in infrastructure and a visible legacy (and with little money for either) he focused on changing people's behaviour. And the fact that his pedagogical methods were also highly cost-effective led directly to a dramatic physical transformation of Bogotá under the next mayor.

A Man of Action

When Enrique Peñalosa was elected in 1998, he not only had a vision of what Bogotá should be, he had the money in the coffers to make it a reality. And he wasted no time. If Mockus was the professor, Peñalosa was the man of action. He was a builder, a ribbon-cutting mayor in the finest tradition, but his instincts were deeply egalitarian. For Peñalosa, Bogotá's endless traffic jams and poor public transport were symptoms of inequality. His position was that the city had given in to the car, and those wealthy enough to own one, and left pedestrians and the bus-taking poor with nothing. Even where there were pavements (by no means all of the city) they were often used for parking, allowing private vehicles to eat up precious public space. His greatest achievement as mayor was a minor revolution in transport.

In his mission to grant pedestrians 'mobility rights', Peñalosa built hundreds of kilometres of pavements. He built 270 kilometres of cycle lanes, creating the most extensive bicycle network in the developing world. He introduced restrictions to car use during peak hours, based on license plate numbers. Most famously, though, he built the TransMilenio bus service, a public transport network to replace the private buses that had had a virtual monopoly on public transport in the capital. Modelled on the Bus Rapid Transit system developed in Curitiba two decades earlier, the TransMilenio had dedicated lanes in which buses could leave the traffic eating its proverbial dust. Together with the cycle lanes, they meant that it was now the poor who moved fastest in Bogotá. As Peñalosa was fond of saying, 'An advanced city is not a place where the poor move about in cars, rather it's where even the rich use public transportation.'

Despite their egalitarian motives, Peñalosa's policies often faced fierce opposition. When he began having bollards installed on pavements so that cars could no longer park on them, he became so unpopular that the opposition party sought to have him impeached. Luckily, Peñalosa was a conviction politician, willing to court unpopularity for what he believed in. He was also a top-down kind of mayor, and, as unfashionable as that may be in an era that idealises participative governance, there are times when mayors have to play the strongman to overcome majorities that do not have the city's best interests at heart. Indeed, Peñalosa would cut an extraordinary figure had he not had the misfortune of governing in between two terms of the outlandish Antanas Mockus. His achievements, not to mention the speed with which he produced them, were highly impressive. He made Bogotá an example to the rest of Latin America, and Rio has now picked up the BRT gauntlet. And yet, while they had a transformative effect on Bogotá, bus lanes, cycle lanes and pavements were not radical in themselves – nothing that was not standard in most cities in the developed world. Compared to Mockus's pedagogical theatre, Peñalosa was doomed to look somewhat ordinary.

Nevertheless, when Mockus was re-elected in 2000, he committed himself to fulfilling Peñalosa's legacy. He extended TransMilenio and the cycle lanes and built new public spaces. While he reinstated the Observatorio de Cultura Urbana and resumed the Cultura Ciudadana programme, he also found himself completing some of his predecessor's more insensitive urban interventions. One of Peñalosa's most drastic measures was the demolition of the El Cartucho neighbourhood, a drug-ridden slum right in the centre of the city. Twelve thousand people had to be rehoused and on its site, as if to hygienically cleanse any memory of it, was to be a park. Mockus duly built it. 'I wanted continuity,' he says, 'even to finish things that I would not have done. And ... I think this park is terribly original.' When I visited the Tercer Milenio Park, admittedly in the middle of a weekday, I found it nearly deserted. With its over-prescribed pathways, over-partitioned patches of grass and seriously over-designed lamps, it wasn't a park I would spend much time in either. If Mockus describes it as original, it is because he located the medical examiner's office, where autopsies are carried out, right in the middle of it. Original, true, but perhaps wilfully so. Even though it was not his own measure, the park is one of Mockus's few disappointments.

It was not the only one. By his own admission, Mockus's policies were not particularly geared to tackling poverty or inequality. Indeed, his critics argue that even his seemingly biggest success, the drop in the homicide rate, owed more to national initiatives to combat the illegal drug trade and the paramilitary groups than to Bogotá's localised Cultura Ciudadana. That is as maybe, but it would be hard to argue, given the sum total of his achievements, that the results of the Cultura Ciudadana programme were not real. Nor could you argue that the methods were not radical. Compare mimes directing traffic and guns melted into spoons with the 'zero tolerance' policies of Mayor Rudy Giuliani, which held New York in their grip at that time, and you can see the difference between an imaginative administration and a simply authoritarian one.

What was unique about Mockus was that he redefined the role of a public administration, so that it moved beyond matters of law or the urban fabric and charged itself with resetting the belief systems of the citizenry. Mockus understood intuitively that the common good is achieved not through fear of authority but through a sense of ownership, and that a sense of belonging to a city emerges through sharing the same rules and developing the same good habits.

No doubt many other politicians understand that, but Mockus had a talent for teaching that he was able to apply at the urban scale. Which raises the question, how replicable are his strategies? Do they rely on the unique charisma of an individual? The same question might be raised of several of the activist architects in this book – how much are they necessarily exceptions? In Mockus's case, it is tempting to focus on the individual for the same reason that the media lapped him up, because he was a colourful character. But fixating on Mockus the eccentric, Mockus the maverick, risks turning him unhelpfully into a one-off. It's true that a man who entered politics by dint of baring his arse to a full auditorium will be difficult for your average face-saving politician to emulate. Mockus's panache is inimitable because it is by definition unpredictable. His core concerns, however, are eminently replicable. Any politician will tell you that, whatever the question, the answer is education. And yet that answer always implies awaiting a future generation for some improvement. The trick that Mockus pulled off was not to build a city of schools but a school that was a city.

An Intangible Legacy

Since the mayorship of Bogotá is the second most powerful political post in Colombia, it is more often than not a platform for presidential ambitions. And Mockus was no exception. He resigned before the end of his first term as mayor to run unsuccessfully for the presidency in 1998. He felt so bad about abandoning his mayoral responsibilities early that when he was re-elected in 2000 he atoned with a public whipping in a Bogotá fountain. But he ran for president again in 2006, again unsuccessfully (one of his campaign texts read: 'The campaign as art, the party as art, government as art, Colombia as art.'). Then, in 2010, as head of the new Colombian Green Party, he gave the favourite, Juan Manuel Santos, a run for his money – but finally lost. By then his Parkinson's was a matter of public record, and he is now gradually becoming less of a public figure. These days he runs a think tank and consultancy called Corpovisionarios, advising other cities on how to tackle intractable urban problems.

As the scheduled time for our meeting draws to an end, I keep making polite attempts to bring the interview to a close, but Mockus seems reluctant. He is suddenly animated, as if the medication that subdued him for the first hour or so is wearing off. His sentences gather speed and anecdotes start flooding back to him.

'Yesterday I was in a meeting of Transparency International, and I asked, "What's more serious, to steal from the government or to steal from your neighbour?" And many times I've asked people, "What's worse, to steal the communion host that is blessed by the priest, or the regular one?" And people say "It's the same, both are very serious." In Colombia we are supposed to be very religious, but looking at the answer to that question, we are not. The importance of collective actions and collective good is undermined by that sort of indifference to status. Charles Sanders Peirce and William James strongly disagreed about transubstantiation. For Peirce, a natural scientist, it was the same host before the benediction and after. For James, a psychologist and the son of a preacher, it was absolutely obvious that the host changes because it changes people's behaviour. People kneel in a different manner. Well, getting back to the question ...'

But by this time the question has escaped me.

What is more valuable, a tangible or an intangible legacy? Peñalosa built libraries, he built transport infrastructure, he expanded the public realm. In short, he left a mark. I've attributed some of that success to Mockus by virtue of him making it financially possible, but we can't overstate how important he was in opening people's minds to the idea of change in the first place. I would argue that the potential of his ideas has yet to be fully digested. It's true that his methods catered to a particular place and time, but the problems of an eroded civic culture and a dilapidated public realm are hardly specific to Bogotá in the 1990s. There are countless cities in the world in similar situations as we speak. And if Mockus deserves a chapter to himself in a book about radical approaches to city-making, it is because he was able to effect change from within citizens themselves. Without even resorting to spatial solutions, he was able to intervene in the city at the psychological level. A culture of good citizenship is not just a means to an end, it is the end. And the idea of urban change through behavioural change is far from fully explored.

Mockus knows that much of what he achieved has been undone by his successors, if not proactively then simply through apathy. The traffic is appalling, the aggressive driving is back, and street thefts and muggings are on the rise again. Even the much vaunted TransMilenio that he helped consolidate has become painfully overcrowded, arguably a victim of its own success. But aside from such tangible evidence, the sense of belief in Bogotá that he inspired has dwindled. As one prominent Bogotá architect told me, 'Eight years ago one believed in this city, now it's in crisis.' Was the Mockus effect really so evanescent?

He leaves me with a final anecdote: 'One day I saw a car break down in the middle of the street, and quickly three or four people from other cars helped to push it out of the way. Afterwards, the driver said, "Something remains." At first I didn't understand what he meant ...' Again, here, Mockus is briefly overcome with emotion. What the driver meant, he realised, was that the collective effort of citizens helping one another would leave a trace, an ineffable residue of good citizenship. Mockus's legacy, it occurs to me, is something like this. His impact was not cosmetic, you couldn't take photographs of it. But as long as *bogotanos* remember what their city was like, even fleetingly, then something remains.

7

Medellín: Social Urbanism

In 1990, the journalist and social scientist Alonso Salazar published an inside account of a war that was tearing Colombia's second city apart. *No Nacimos Pa' Semilla*, later translated into English as *Born to Die in Medellín*, was a book of interviews with teenage contract killers, gang members and vigilantes. It is a sort of portrait of hell. Dominated by the drug cartels, the city's poor neighbourhoods were in the grip of ruthless violence and fear. At the time, Medellín was the murder capital of the world. In the period between 1990 and 1993, more than 6,000 people were being killed each year. However, fifteen years later, when Salazar was elected mayor of Medellín, the homicide rate had fallen by 90 per cent. And behind that statistic lies a rather remarkable tale.

The road into town from the airport winds its way over a mountain until the city appears, cradled in a river valley cut through green hills. This is 'the city of eternal spring', famous for its lush setting and its cool, temperate climate. The road, one can't help but notice, is peppered with billboards advertising home-grown fashion labels, in particular denim brands. The centre of Colombia's textile industry, Levi's has been making its jeans here since the 1990s. But then Toyota and Mitsubishi have factories here too, and so does the tobacco giant Philip Morris. Once known as 'the Manchester of Colombia', it is the capital of the industrial heartland. Its citizens – known as *paisas* – have a long reputation for entrepreneurialism and industriousness.

What began with a gold rush was consolidated in the early twentieth century by the coffee and cotton industries, and then cigarettes, chocolate, mining – each industry run by a family monopoly – and more recently flowers. The city was and is prosperous, and even today Colombia's biggest banks are headquartered here. However, it was ironically when Medellín's industrial might began to decline that the city started to grow in earnest. With the drop in the coffee price and the rise of cheap labour in Asia in the 1960s and 70s, rural workers began to migrate to the city. From 1952 to 1977 the population grew from less than 300,000 to 1.3 million. This was later exacerbated by the war between the government and the FARC guerrillas, which has led to millions of people in the countryside moving to cities – Colombia has the second-highest internally displaced population after Sudan. Both waves of migrants swelled the ranks of Medellín's slums, or *comunas*. Of the city's 2.7 million inhabitants, about half live in these informal settlements in the hills that encircle the city.

Meanwhile, the decline of the traditional industries in the 1970s ushered in a new one, the cocaine business, which a few Medellín entrepreneurs controlled with all the acumen for which they are renowned. The legend among them was Pablo Escobar, who ran the Medellín cartel through the 1980s and early 90s. Organised crime became a haven for the unemployed, and through his semi-militarised gangs Escobar ruled the *comunas*. The off-the-scale violence statistics cited earlier were a consequence of the various fronts opened in the complex war against Escobar. On the one hand there was the government, goaded into a war on drugs by the US, but also popular militias with left-wing sympathies (and often ties to FARC) who tried to expel Escobar's gangs from their neighbourhoods. At the height of the attempts to extradite Escobar to the US in the early 1990s, he was waging a campaign of terror against the state in Medellín, killing hundreds of policemen and setting off car bombs every week. In 1993, the year Escobar was killed, the homicide rate was an unprecedented 311 per 100,000 citizens.

What was extraordinary about Medellín was that throughout this period the city was still booming – this was not the violence of economic and urban decay. On the contrary, narco-profits were filtering into the economy through money laundering and property speculation. But one of the inevitable effects of the violence was a deeply segregated city. It affected everyone, but for those in the central and southern districts the northern *comunas* were literally a no-go zone. And it was this invisible north-south border that a group of politicians and civic leaders sought to address when, finally, the citizens of Medellín had had enough of bloodshed.

On a sunny spring day, I'm sitting in the Botanical Gardens under a vast wooden canopy that shelters an orchid nursery. The Orquideorama's octagonal roof, designed by local architects Plan B and Camilo Restrepo, has become one of Medellín's most famous landmarks. As couples stroll hand in hand and kids run around bewitched by the dappled light breaching the canopy, I'm watching a photographer friend of mine shoot a cover story for an airline magazine. Earlier, we visited a spectacularly landscaped swimming pool complex designed by young Medellín natives Paisajes Emergentes, and next to it the mountain-shaped Coliseo sports complex designed by the prominent Colombian architect Giancarlo Mazzanti for the 2010 South American Games. Other stops on my friend's itinerary included a series of new parks and public squares: Parque Explora, Parque de los Deseos (The Park of Wishes) and Parque de los Pies Descalzos (Barefoot Park). Finally, the *coup de théâtre* would be the Parque Biblioteca España (Spain Library Park), a rocky promontory of a building grand-standing over the city from high up in what used to be a notorious slum.

Taxiing from set piece to set piece, it would be easy for a photographer to create an illusion of Medellín as some ideal city. Indeed, I find myself speculating what metaphor the in-flight magazine will use to denote the transition from murder capital to tourist hotspot – will it be the phoenix or the born-again Christian? In recent years the international media has been awash with stories about Medellín's dramatic transformation – 'the city that rehabilitated itself with iconic architecture and public spaces'. It is, after all, a photogenic story. Medellín has even won a slew of awards, including the Curry Stone Design Prize and, most recently, Harvard's Green Prize in Urban Design. To round it all off, in 2014 the city plays host to the World Urban Forum, where experts from around the world will gather to hear the gospel.

As with every story, there is the long and the short version. The short version plays well because it has a hero and a happy ending. In 2004 a charismatic professor of mathematics called Sergio Fajardo won the mayoral election and implemented an ambitious programme of urban design that rebuilt civic pride and brought spiralling crime rates under control. It's a story that flatters architects in particular, renewing faith in their salutary effect on the city and their social purpose. It's true that architects and urban planners feature prominently, but if anything the story is more about politics, and the power that a community possesses to effect radical change when it engages in the political process.

In the mid 1990s, long before Fajardo appeared on the scene, there was a keen sense among Medellín's citizenry that an intensive programme of reforms had to be put in place. 'The whole of society was talking about this, and we built a social project together,' says Jorge Pérez, who was head of urban planning for the metropolitan area under Mayor Fajardo. Pérez is at pains to make clear that, while architecture was the most visible tool in this process, what really mattered was the commitment of a network of politicians and entrepreneurs to building – and paying for – a new future for Medellín. This process, as much as the result, has come to be known as 'social urbanism'.

At that time there were already state initiatives being implemented that would help set the agenda over the coming decade. In 1995–96, supported by the UN, the Strategic Plan started to bring basic services to the hillside *comunas*. Then, in 1998, the Plan de Ordenamiento Territorial (the urban land use plan) set out many of the issues that would later be addressed. At the same time, Medellín's two architecture schools were being treated as laboratories, testing urban solutions to Medellín's social problems. Pérez, who was then dean of the architecture school at the Pontifical Bolivarian University, points out that it was those very students who, a few years later, would start transforming the city.

The catalytic project was Parque de los Pies Descalzos. Designed by Felipe Uribe and completed in 2000, it is a richly varied landscape of fountains, waterfalls and sand- boxes – it only takes a minute there to recognise it as an absolute fantasy zone for children. Barefoot Park helped people understand the power of public space. If it could lift the experience of the city centre, then surely it would have an even greater impact in disadvantaged neighbourhoods. And that would be Fajardo's strategy. But for Pérez, it was the consequence of a long process, of which Fajardo merely presided over the most productive period. 'He didn't invent anything,' says Pérez. 'There's a false propaganda around Fajardo that minimises the importance of the social process that happened here.'

The City in Our Skin

In the regional government headquarters on Avenida Carabobo, Sergio Fajardo invites me to have a seat. The ex-mayor is now the governor of the surrounding region of Antioquia, and, dressed in jeans and an open-neck shirt, he occupies his capacious office like a man with no interest in the trappings of power. 'Let me explain,' he says. 'Why did we get into politics? How did we create an independent civic movement [Compromiso Ciudadano]; how did we manage to make me mayor of Medellín, a city with a very well oiled electoral machine run by the traditional political parties; how did a tiny group of people get into power without having any previous experience in administration whatsoever? That's not an accident. If you don't understand that, I claim that you don't understand what happened here.'

Fajardo has the persuasive patter and commanding manner of a natural leader, but he is not a career politician. Like Antanas Mockus, he was a professor, teaching mathematics at the Universidad de Los Andes when he decided to go into politics. Unlike Mockus, though, who somehow made academia seem like the ideal training ground for politics, Fajardo makes much of his inexperience. 'Here's a guy who's a mathematician and has never held any public position whatsoever. And we get into power in Medellín – of all the cities in the world, Medellín!' he says. 'That has a very deep meaning.' Fajardo was not quite the outsider that Mockus was.* He was of the establishment, from a distinguished family – his father, significantly, was an architect and former head of planning for the city – but he was not a politician. And since the political class was not to be trusted, not being a politician would ultimately be an advantage. At the beginning, however, Fajardo and his fellow idealists who joined in the Compromiso Ciudadano movement seemed like a bunch of no-hopers. 'If you had bet with anyone here in this town in January 2000, nobody would have bet that we would eventually win the election. Nobody.'

If Fajardo labours this point somewhat, it is because he traces everything he achieved in Medellín back to the process of running for election. He, and the fifty or so concerned citizens who made up the civic movement, established a set of inviolate principles that determined everything they would do. 'We want to get into power – why? What are the problems we are going to solve?' Like an architect, as he speaks he starts to sketch a diagram. 'What we want to attack is inequality, violence and corruption,' he says, giving each vice its own box. Throughout our conversation he keeps coming back to that diagram. When he mentions building schools and libraries, he points his pen at

---

* Incidentally, Mockus chose Fajardo as his running mate in the 2010 presidential election, which they lost.

the inequality box. When he refers to new public spaces, it lingers over the violence box. It was this disciplined focus on social goals that he feels gave the urban renewal projects of Medellín their political power. But in order to implement this vision, he had to overcome target number three: corruption.

In a video conversation with the San Diego-based architect Teddy Cruz (whom we shall meet later), Fajardo described the process of running for election as 'getting the city in our skin'. What he meant by this was that he and the other members of Compromiso Ciudadano familiarised themselves with the real conditions of the city by walking from neighbourhood to neighbourhood. 'I don't know how many times I went around Medellín – on foot,' he says. 'There were parts of the city that I didn't know, or hadn't been to for years. This was a divided city, where hardly anybody on this side would dare go to the northern side of the city.' The traditional way politicians bridge such gaps in Colombia is by paying local community leaders to drum up support for them so that they can just show up in their armoured car for a quick photo opportunity. But critical to the success of the movement was that it bought no allegiances. Fajardo was not totally unknown in Medellín – he had been writing an influential newspaper column – but he claims he owed his growing profile to old-fashioned doorstepping.

It was a slow process. He didn't win the 2000 election. He lost to Luis Pérez, who initiated some key projects, including Medellín's cable car link to the hillside *comuna* of Santo Domingo, but who ultimately proved to be corrupt.

So Fajardo continued walking – 'getting in touch with communities that I had never seen before, sitting down and listening very carefully. And watching and smelling, getting the city in our skin physically.' Alonso Salazar, incidentally, was instrumental here, showing Fajardo the other side of Medellín, the real city. Come the election of 2004, he won a landslide victory. And precisely because he had bought no allies, owed no one anything, he could choose his own administration and exercise a mandate to implement his own programme. Already, that was a unique situation for Medellín.

What was remarkable about Fajardo's administration – and inevitably contributes to him having become the poster boy for the new Medellín – was the sheer quantity of projects completed in the four years from 2004 to 2007. They include: the Parque Explora, a park with a free science museum in it; the Botanical Gardens, site of the octagonal Orquideorama; ten new school buildings; five ambitious library-parks in the *comunas* of Santo Domingo, La Quintana, La Ladera, San Javier and Belén; a cultural centre in the run-down district of Moravia; and the completion and extension of the Metrocable.

It was an extraordinary burst of productivity. Public buildings and public spaces began to bloom all over the city. And while they kept the global design press drip-fed with a steady stream of captivating images, their social purpose was not always at the forefront of the media coverage. For Fajardo, however, public space was not an end in itself. Returning to his diagram, it was a tool for tackling inequality. The umbrella theme for his administration was '*Medellín, la más educada*' – Medellín, the most educated. Building schools and libraries was his way of tackling inequality, while building new parks and plazas provided a support system that addressed violence by offering citizens the chance to reconnect.

'Where there is fear, you get a fragmented society,' he says. 'The fear and violence destroy any kind of citizenship, any working together. There are no citizens living there, only individuals surviving – "save yourself". So everyone is resigned to living in their place, and public space is basically destroyed as a site of reunion for communities.'

What was most significant about Fajardo's programme was the decision to concentrate the municipal budget in the poorest districts of the city. This was an act of political will, but also an essential urban design strategy. As we've seen in Rio and Caracas, the solution to urban and social disintegration is its opposite, integration. The only way to make a city whole again is by reconnecting its segregated pieces. And this much Fajardo understood perfectly.

'We said, we are going to build the most beautiful schools in the humblest places,' he continues. 'Because building beautiful schools here means we are fighting inequality. Secondly, we are going to wash the blood of violence from our public space and we are going to come up with new public spaces that represent what we mean, which is opportunities based on education, science, technology, innovation, entrepreneurship and culture.' That list of topics comes out so fast that he essentially runs them together as one long word. This is a well-practiced spiel, but it is no less effective for that. If I take anything away from having Fajardo recount his achievements personally, it is a sense of his clarity of vision and determination.

As Jorge Pérez points out, there were public-space projects built before this administration, but Fajardo argues that they did not have the same political potency. It was the fact that his interventions were specifically aimed at equality and education, he insists, that made them transformative. 'All governments would hire good architects to design beautiful buildings,' he says. 'But if it doesn't represent a way of moving forward in society, you can do as many as you want!'

Social Urbanism

Over lunch in the well-heeled neighbourhood of El Poblado, Alejandro Echeverri fills me in on some of the detail missing from Fajardo's rousing rhetoric. As head of the Urban Development Corporation (EDU) under Fajardo, Echeverri was the mayor's chief adviser on the urban renewal process. Softly spoken and methodical, he begins by sketching out the climate in which Fajardo was able to achieve what he did. In 1991 Colombia rewrote the Constitution, giving cities more autonomy over their own affairs. It was a wise move for a country whose population is 75 per cent urbanised and spread across ten or so cities. At the same time, it opened a path for independent politicians, like Mockus and Peñalosa in Bogotá, or Fajardo in Medellín, to overcome the traditional political parties – something that would have been unthinkable before then. During the Mockus and Peñalosa terms in the late 1990s, Medellín was still struggling with a corrupt political elite complicit in one way or another with the activities of the cartels. But the events in Bogotá were a strong influence on those watching in the north.

'Bogotá was important because the leaders opened a space,' says Echeverri. 'From the technical point of view, three processes were important: the Bogotá process, the Rio de Janeiro process – especially the Favela-Bairro programme – and the reality here in Medellín.'

When Fajardo was elected, he made Echeverri head of the EDU and heaped special powers on him to make the EDU independent of the city's urban planning department, which was both inefficient and corrupt. In effect, the mayor treated the EDU as strategically as Mockus did his Urban Observatory – it was the crucible of his most significant policies. 'When he won the election we decided we had to move very fast,' says Echeverri, 'and to do that we had to have some autonomy, because if we went into the old planning structure it was very difficult to change things.'

What Echeverri is uniquely placed to shed light on is what has come to be Medellín's calling card: 'social urbanism'. What is it, exactly? The term itself is not new. It was coined by Karl Brunner (1887–1960), an Austrian urban planner working in Bogotá in the 1930s. Brunner rejected the Beaux-Arts and later modernist utopian impulse of designing cities from scratch, and called instead for a practice that recognised what was already there. In that sense, he was a good seven decades ahead of the now orthodox attitude to the informal city.

That aspect of social urbanism is certainly present and correct in Medellín in the early 2000s. But the term as it is now used has new connotations. So is it the phenomenon of architecture and public space being used towards social goals, or is it a type of urban intervention defined by a social process? Thinking back to Fajardo's emphasis on *how* his administration did things, my instinct is that it must be both – that the goals cannot be distinguished from the method. And Echeverri is quick to confirm that view. For him, social urbanism is partly about a participative way of working and partly about the message your interventions send. The building blocks of social urbanism are what Echeverri called 'integral urban projects' (PUIs). These are not buildings, but projects that incorporate multiple programmes simultaneously, from transport to landscaping, from street lighting to a cultural centre. 'So the definition of an integral urban project is one where many things are happening at the same time,' says Echeverri.

The quintessential example is Medellín's library-parks. The most famous of these is the Parque Biblioteca España, with its three monolithic towers projecting over the city from its eyrie up in Santo Domingo. But it would be wrong to think of it as just a building. It was the destination of Medellín's first cable car line, and the locus around which the renewal of the Santo Domingo *comuna* started to take shape, including a new school, new streets and new public spaces. Above all, perhaps, it was a participative process.

'We had a specific team that combined architects, urbanists, social workers, communications people, lawyers and a leader who was the "social manager" for that area of Santo Domingo. And that guy worked with the community keeping the project on the agenda,' says Echeverri. 'We also had imagination workshops every month, with children trying to think about how to make a park.' This kind of collective aspiration-raising is one of the most sensitive aspects of 'participative design', because it creates an expectation among the community. What happens when you tap people for their ideas and then you have to deliver on them?

'From the beginning the biggest problem is when someone doesn't believe you,' he says. 'That's the attitude the community often has towards politicians, they don't believe you. So you have to build confidence, and the way to build confidence is to make very small agreements with them. If you tell them they'll have a library-park, they won't believe you. But if you tell them we are going to define the design together of a small square or a small park, and in three months we'll come with the mayor and present it to you, and in six months we'll lay the first brick ...'

Central to that process of winning the community's trust was the personal presence of Fajardo. 'It was highly unusual that the mayor and all his secretaries would go to the community to discuss the proposals,' says Echeverri. 'But we also built a special network of managers of the PUIs, who had the power to make agreements and had a direct relationship with Fajardo. And the relationship of this structure with the community was one of the main things, building spaces of mediation and communication. The attitude is important.'

This is not to say that it was an effortless process. Building the library-park meant rehousing 150 people to make way for it. And so for a good six months the community was against the project. But the majority of those displaced were rehoused within Santo Domingo, and offered a subsidy to build themselves an extra storey. It was a pragmatic quid pro quo, and it smoothed the process along. 'The target is not the building,' says Echeverri, 'the target is the process during and after it.'

Make the Informal Visible

As it does in Caracas, Medellín's Metrocable starts near the city centre and cuts swift diagonal lines to the poorest parts of the city. This is Línea K, which carries you east up a hillside to Santo Domingo in three stops. The view of corrugated roofs beneath the gondola is almost indistinguishable from Caracas, but the city itself looks very different from up here, with its linear arrangement along the river valley.

Alighting at the Santo Domingo stop, I feel slightly self-conscious. I'm just another gringo tourist, parachuting in to see the famous building in the middle of the slum. But that in itself is something of an achievement. Only a few years ago, even most citizens of Medellín would not have dared set foot up here. It reminds me of something Fajardo said to me: 'Everyone who comes to Medellín wants to go to places that had never been visited by anyone before.' It was said jokingly, but he was not joking. What he meant was that he reconnected this city.

In fact, his predecessor, Mayor Luis Pérez, initiated the Metrocable project. A former chess champion and maverick populist, Pérez was looking to win votes from the poor, but it was a huge political gamble because no insurance company was willing to underwrite a cable car to a slum. With support from Medellín's metro company, and a budget of $32 million, he went ahead, and the cable car opened in 2004. It was an immediate success. Joining the main metro line, the cable car cut the commute (previously on foot) to the top of the hill from one and a half hours to seven minutes. Fajardo later extended the Metrocable, adding Linea J to access Comuna 13, the poorest neighbourhood in the city. These two single lines are less ambitious than the cable car system in Caracas, which is a genuine circuit, but they were a life-changing link from the *comunas* to the city centre. Surveyed recently, commuters from Santo Domingo said they would rather give up their mobile phones than the cable car.[*]

Heading down a set of steps towards the library, I'm about to cross a plaza where some kids are playing football. It's not what I would call a park. But then the very concept

---

[*] This survey was carried out by Professor Julio Davila at The Bartlett, who, with his students, has been investigating how the cable car has improved quality of life in the *comunas*.

of a library-park seems to be unique to Medellín. I wonder whether this hybrid typology was a tactic that made building a library in a slum seem less patronising, less overtly didactic. But as Echeverri explains the concept, it was a result of trying to do justice to the complexity of the socio-urban problem at hand, and inspired in part by the success of Peñalosa's libraries in Bogotá. In this case, Fajardo's fixation on education was combined with the idea of public space as a key tool in the reconciliation of a segregated society. It was neither one thing nor the other, but both. 'The idea of complexity was important,' says Echeverri. 'For us the main thing is to do a holistic intervention, not only public space or housing or culture but adding *more* information and complexity.'

The architecture of the library itself is at pains to suggest that it has been here all along. Like a piece of the mountainside, a rocky outcrop suitable for habitation, it is not a jarringly modern presence amid the humble self-built houses of Santo Domingo. I remember its architect, Giancarlo Mazzanti, telling me in Bogotá, 'It's not a problem to make public buildings in the barrio, but to make *good* public buildings.' Is this a good public building? In many ways it is. It is no easy act to pull off, designing something this boldly contemporary and this imposing, that nevertheless has a sense of belonging, an ease, in the middle of a *comuna*. It's clear, though, that the whole budget went on making the building a striking image. The interior is somewhat dowdier, noticeably cheaper, the windows already showing signs of deterioration.

One can nitpick with the quality of the architecture, but there is not a shadow of doubt about the message this library sends to the community: that it is valued, that it has opportunities, that it has a future. From the gaps between its three towers, visitors have a dramatic view of the city laid out before them. But it is the opposite view, from the valley below, that is most significant. The importance of the Biblioteca España is as a beacon, signalling to the city as a whole. There has been much derision of iconic architecture in recent years, but this building needed to be iconic. Its very purpose was to draw the gaze of prospering *paisas* to the hills that they had blinkered from view as if they didn't exist. The library has a <u>symbolic purpose, which is to make the informal city</u> visible.

This is a radical departure from the attitude to the slums that prevailed over the prior half-century across Latin America. For most of their existence, slums were stigmatised with illegality. Until the early 2000s, government policies discouraged consolidating slums with staircases and transport infrastructure, because they were not supposed to be there. The mid-twentieth-century view that the slums were the 'cancer' to be cut out of the city resonated into the contemporary era, not least because they were an impediment to respectable development. Now, they are awarded some of the city's choicest buildings. Suddenly, the mutually exclusive agendas of social urbanism and urbanism of the spectacle can overlap, with a common goal. As Echeverri puts it, it was crucial to make the real scale of the city 'transparent'. 'In a segregated city, where half of the city doesn't exist, it is necessary to connect not only in a physical way but in a mental way,' he says. Making Santo Domingo one of the most prominent neighbourhoods in Medellín is the definition of social urbanism.

The Public and the Private

If you drive through the centre of town on the Regional highway, you'll pass a hulking edifice doing a bad impression of the Lloyd's of London building. It's an uncanny sight, that High Tech polished-steel fire escape transplanted across the Atlantic, but it befits a building called the Edificio Inteligente. This is the headquarters of Empresas Públicas de Medellín (EPM), the public utilities company. I mention it not because of its derivative HQ but because it was central to everything that Medellín has achieved over the last decade.

The extraordinary thing about EPM is that it is owned by the municipality. The fact that it is neither private nor national but owned by a city makes it a highly unusual institution, perhaps even unique. It says rather a lot about Medellín as an entrepreneurial but also introverted and self-sufficient regional capital. Built on the local abundance of hydroelectric power, EPM is so powerful that it exports energy not just to the rest of Colombia but internationally, to Puerto Rico and the Dominican Republic. In the late 1990s the city decided that, instead of reinvesting all its profits back in the company, 30 per cent would be made available for municipal use. That means that

EPM contributes about $450 million a year to Medellín's coffers.

Having that source of income was, and remains, crucial to the city's urban renewal process. It was not always used in the most equitable way – in the early years it funded the building of highways that at least half of the populace would never use – but under Pérez it was used to fund the Metrocable and of course it made possible Fajardo's combined programme of education and reconciliation through public space. The shift with Pérez and Fajardo, then, was that EPM's profits started to be deployed in the poorest communities, namely, the *comunas* of the northeast and northwest and the relatively central but haggard Moravia.

If neoliberalism insists that utility companies are only fit to be sold off to the private sector, then many a municipal government, not to mention national ones, might look to Medellín and reconsider. The role that EPM played in the rehabilitation of Medellín is symptomatic of a political culture that has not yet bought into the Washington Consensus wholesale. This is ironic, because one of the critiques levelled at Medellín is that it embraced neoliberal development driven by profits from the narco-traffickers. Much has been made of the fact that cartel money was laundered through construction projects, that cartel gangs were involved in the 'pacification' of districts that were ripe for development and that, all in all, Medellín's establishment was in bed with the mob.* All of which was true.

---

* Forrest Hylton makes this case very convincingly in 'Medellín's Makeover', in issue 44 of the *New Left Review*, 2007, and again in the book

(American tourists are still to be seen wandering around Medellín making loud comments about how this or that building was probably paid for by drug money.) But there is no distinction in that argument between private property speculation (condominiums) and the public projects initiated by Pérez, Fajardo and subsequently Salazar. More disappointingly, there is no mention of the role played by a *public* company in funding those projects – surely that is the antithesis of neoliberalism.

In fact, Medellín has pioneered a form of public-private partnership in which the private sector's motives were, for once, not profit. If you talk to anyone involved in the urban renewal process from the early 2000s onwards, they will highlight the role of the business community in supporting the civic movement that aimed to claw back some sanity in Medellín. Beyond the millions supplied by EPM, much smaller businesses were making contributions to enhance the public nature of new facilities. Here are just a few examples: a consortium of entrepreneurs called Fundación Amor por Medellín bought a private school and donated it to the city so that Fajardo could turn it into a public one, the Instituto Tecnológico Metropolitano; nine companies subsidised the museum at the Parque Explora so that entry could be free; the creation of the Jardín Botánico relied in

---

Evil Paradises, (eds) Mike Davis et al., The New Press, 2007. In the latter, he writes that 'the democracy that Medellín's neoliberal plastic surgery allows is a "weak" or "thin" citizenship based largely on North Atlantic models of consumerism and electoral politics'. Can Hylton point to a model *not* based on consumerism and democracy that is currently flourishing anywhere in the world? Is he saying that Medellín sold out because it is not Cuba?

part on funding from a group of banks and private cultural organisations; and engineering firms helped design public buildings pro bono. What occurred in Medellín was a groundswell of civic-minded philanthropy of the likes that we have yet to see in European countries that are currently suffering through austerity policies.

For Jorge Pérez, Medellín's transformation was achieved by an extraordinary collective effort. He sees Fajardo's leadership as a consequence, rather than a cause, of that effort – so that to elevate him as the hero is to diminish the city's achievements. 'It would be better for the world,' he says, 'if Fajardo demonstrated that it was the social power of the city and the political process, not just him.'

Repaying a Social Debt

How does one measure the effects of the urban renewal process under mayors Pérez, Fajardo and Salazar? There is of course the anecdotal evidence of people who live in Medellín, who recall the bad old days with a shiver. More persuasive for the statistically minded will be the homicide rate, which in 2008 was 90 per cent lower than it was at the height of Escobar's terror campaign against the government. That sounds conclusive, but it has led to some rather simplistic analysis. 'People say architecture has reduced crime, but that's not true,' says Jorge Pérez.

The reduction of violence owed much to the government signing a treaty with the paramilitary groups and to the balance of power among the cartels themselves. After

Escobar's death, there were less killings but the city remained extremely violent. It was not significantly calmer until a new drug lord, known as Don Berna, consolidated his control over the cartels in 2003. Publicly pursued by the government but tacitly tolerated by Medellín's establishment, Don Berna kept things on an even keel, as evidenced by a worrying spike in violence in 2009–10 after he was extradited to the US – at which point, cynics were already questioning whether Medellín had in fact been transformed at all.

However, it is not merely the politics of the drug wars that Pérez is referring to. His point, much like Fajardo's, is that the power of architecture and public space to restore dignity was heavily supported by a political agenda. Fajardo in particular pumped money into education initiatives, including fellowships and the creation of innovation and entrepreneurship centres. He described it as 'repaying a social debt'. I asked the ex-mayor how he measured the effectiveness of that programme. 'I'll give you one very simple and powerful indicator that no scientist looks at,' he says. 'High-school dropouts. When we got into power in 2004, they were at roughly speaking 50 per cent. That means before the last two years of school 50 per cent of kids would drop out. That means that physically they would be sitting in the corner of one of these neighbourhoods in Medellín – lost.'

At the end of his successor Salazar's term, which continued some of Fajardo's policies, the dropout rate was down to 20 per cent. And the reason for that? 'We built hope,' says Fajardo. 'If you looked in 2004 at what kids wanted to study, they wanted to be policemen or in the army or study-ing criminology. Today they want to be medical doctors, economists, engineers and so on. So we showed people there could be alternatives. We still have a long way to go in Medellín, but that's a very powerful message for young people in this town.'

However one measures its transformation, you cannot go to Medellín today and mistake it for the city described in Salazar's book. On my last day there, I visited an outdoor escalator that was recently built on the hillside leading up to Comuna 13, in the western outskirts. As an indication of what this place used to be like, in 2002 Mayor Pérez sent in the army to try and seize it back from the paramilitary groups whose stronghold it was. The army was repelled, and it took several more assaults to gain control of the neighbourhood the following year. Thankfully, Comuna 13 is no longer a war zone. This fancy new escalator, com-plete with decorative canopy, wouldn't be out of place in a shopping mall. Medellín – and Latin America as a whole – has an uncanny ability to dislocate typologies. First cable cars are transplanted from ski resorts to tropical slums, and now the escalator is plucked from its rightful place in air-ports and department stores to the urban mountainside.

All of which is not to say that Comuna 13 is now Beverly Hills – security guards on most of the escalator landings suggest that it is still distinctly edgy – but I would not have contemplated coming here on my own before. A piece of infrastructure like this completely changes the feeling of a place. The escalator is not just a mode of transport for residents who for too long had to climb to their homes up winding concrete steps, it is a visible investment in the neighbourhood – one of the first municipal interventions that was not military. In fact, I wonder whether the guards are here to protect the community's new pride and joy as much as anyone riding it.

After Fajardo, subsequent mayors kept the city evolving. Salazar, in particular, continued the education theme by establishing a string of kindergartens. But the emphasis has shifted away from social urbanism. Under the current mayor, Aníbal Gaviria, the municipality is trying to densify the city centre, which is a necessary move because Medellín's growth is limited by the mountainous walls of the river valley. But other plans, such as building a monorail around the periphery, make less sense. Adding transport infrastructure will only encourage more people to settle on the periphery, and although the plan is to create a green belt around the city, there is nothing to suggest it would be respected. Unlike many Colombian cities, Medellín is still a place of opportunity and it will continue to attract rural migrants.

In fact, one thing that Fajardo did almost nothing to address was the question of social housing. One of the possible effects of that omission down the line may be that residents of the newly connected and embellished *comunas* will start to be displaced. Between 40 and 60 per cent of those in the *comunas* are tenants, which means that landlords can evict them as the inevitable gentrification takes hold. Building social housing around the new amenities would have been one way to keep the added value in the public sector, rather than allowing private owners to capitalise on rising prices.

However, in the real world, what was achieved under the Fajardo administration – and the speed with which it was achieved – owed much to the focus of his vision on education and public space. It is difficult to think of a programme of public buildings and spaces in recent times with the transformative effect of Medellín's. While this has made the city a touchstone for the power of architecture, we mustn't allow ourselves to be misled. The lesson of Medellín lies not in the power of libraries and plazas but in the network of political, civic and entrepreneurial agents that gave rise to them. The architecture was merely the expression of that network, and that was the source of its social capital. That, coupled with a strategy of connecting marginalised *comunas* to the city centre, is a recipe that politicians and urbanists from around the world now come to Medellín to learn.

I ask Fajardo whether he sees Medellín as symptomatic of a newfound Latin American ingenuity for solving intractable urban problems. At first, with the politician's instinct for highlighting his own achievements, he defends the 'singularity' of Medellín – a city with 'unique problems'. But soon he warms to my theme. 'These are problems of Latin America,' he says. 'In the United States, they are talking about inequality – we have thought about this all our lives. But I have a feeling that we in Latin America are coming up with different ways of looking at the world. We are coming up with our own solutions – we are a *reference* for solutions now. So I think we are an expression of a new Latin America.'

8

Tijuana: On the Political Equator

'*Estoy al límite*,' reads the graffiti in two-foot-high letters on the steel fence – I'm at the limit. This rusty wall is the edge of Mexico, and the end of Latin America. Driving along it, on a dirt road, the border is something of an anti-climax. Forget the fact that it looks like you could plough through this particular section with the right 4x4, the landscape around it is patchily inhabited and has all the hallmarks of a non-place. And yet this is the most significant line in the sand in the western hemisphere. On the other side, in the United States, is another universe.

'Isn't it amazing?' says Teddy Cruz. Five minutes ago he picked me up in a taxi at Tijuana airport, and now we're driving along the wall towards the Pacific Ocean. Down the road, we cross the suburb of Colonia Aeropuerto, nestled in a valley. Here, among the self-built houses of a shanty town, is a five-storey statue of a nude woman with a window between her breasts. La Mona is the home of local artist Armando Muñoz García, and it is the first of several surreal moments this landscape will throw at me.

Minutes later, we stop at the shore, but the wall keeps on going. Now just a tight row of steel poles, it marches on into the sea until it disappears under the waves. This place used to be called Friendship Park. Inaugurated by President Nixon's wife Pat in the 1970s, Homeland Security has put the wall right through it, making it rather less friendly. There are still a few picnic tables, though. Playing on the absurdity of this juxtaposition, some Mexican artists have had a field day here. One of them has taken the US highway sign warning of Mexican families crossing (like deer, only human) and given them balloons to carry them over the fence. Another has painted the words '*¿Estás de mi lado?*' on the wall – Are you on my side?

Cruz points to the building next to us, a bullring. 'It's great,' he says, 'the very last building in Latin America before you get to the US is a bullring.' Even though he has been studying this border zone for more than a decade, he seems to have lost none of his enthusiasm for it. Originally from Guatemala, Cruz is an architect and professor of public culture and urbanism at the University of California, San Diego. He is also the foremost theorist of the Tijuana-San Diego border in terms of what happens when the urban culture of the developing world collides with that of the developed world. Both analyst and provocateur, for him this frontier zone is fizzing with potential, and he is using it to try to redefine the architect's role in making cities.

The border between Tijuana and San Diego is the busiest land crossing in the world. There are an estimated 300,000 crossings a day – that's more than 100 million a year. In the US, the border is a volatile political topic, with both Republicans and Democrats wanting to be seen to be tough on immigration. Since 9/11 vast sums have been spent on hardening this membrane, making it less porous. And yet it is predicted that after 2050 non-Hispanic whites will become a minority group in the US. As Mike Davis wrote over a decade ago, 'These are millennial transformations with truly millennial implications for US politics and culture.'*

If this is sensitive stuff on the US side, it is the stuff of dreams on the Mexican side. Tijuana is one of the fastest-growing cities in Mexico. With a population of nearly 2 million, coupled with San Diego it forms a transnational metropolitan region of more than 5 million. As the economies of these two cities are so closely linked, it would seem to make sense not to harden the divide but to embrace their symbiotic relationship. And that's how it looks from San Diego City Hall, which recently opened a branch in Tijuana. The mayor's office even prepared a bid for the 2024 Olympics to be hosted jointly by the two cities – an idea that the International Olympic Committee is not quite ready for.

In one of those speculative reports full of foreboding about our urban future, UN-Habitat has predicted that this century metropolises will start joining up like blobs

---

* Mike Davis, *Magical Urbanism: Latinos Reinvent the US City*, Verso, 2000.

of mercury, crossing international borders to form urban mega-regions. And while this would be mostly true in the developing world, for instance in the cities of West Africa, Tijuana-San Diego is an intriguing prospect because the border is not just national but forms part of an imaginary line dividing the global South and North, the developing and developed worlds. This is what Cruz calls 'the political equator'. The question is how the two worlds on either side of it can influence each other. Can ideas as well as just labour cross that border? Can the US, which has exported a pernicious neoliberal culture to the continent below it, gain something less destructive in return? Can Southern California learn from Latin America?

Los Laureles Canyon

'This tells the whole story,' Cruz says, pointing to a slum that stretches along the Los Laureles Canyon. 'This is the last informal settlement before the end of the continent.' We're standing on a hill looking down into the canyon, where clusters of houses and parked cars line the dry riverbed and the valley walls. At one end of the canyon the houses come to a sudden stop, where the six-lane Benito Juárez highway cuts right across it. Running alongside the highway is the border fence and then, on the other side, a wildlife reserve. Shanty town on one side, national park on the other.

It's an incredible panorama. A territory bisected by a wall, like an endless blade slicing all the way to the horizon.

This landscape is partly natural and partly shaped by Homeland Security. The highway is raised up on an earth berm, which the traffic engineers do to make the border more of a topographical barrier. But it has consequences. The road has now effectively plugged the canyon, which is part of the watershed system of the Tijuana River estuary. It looks arid now, but in heavy rains the water courses along the canyon, where these houses are, and can only escape through a drain in the berm wall. As people build on these hillsides they erode the topsoil, and the rain washes the sand and rubbish from the settlements into the nature reserve on the other side of the border. 'I have pictures of what gets washed up on the other side, all the trash, tyres, dead dogs and everything,' says Cruz.

Seventy-five per cent of the Tijuana River watershed is in Mexico and the other 25 per cent is in the US. That wasn't taken into account when the border, an arbitrary line, was cut across this ancient geological system. And the water politics along this stretch of the border are complex. There is already a water shortage in the region, and it's being exacerbated by the *maquiladoras*, or assembly plants, driving Tijuana's thriving manufacturing economy. Moreover, there's a history of Tijuana's sewage ending up north of the border, and that's why, as part of the bilateral partnership between the two cities, just down the road from here (you can smell it) is the International Wastewater Treatment Plant. The first of its kind, it treats Mexican sewage in the US. This is the kind of trans-border cooperation the region needs.

The urbanist Kevin Lynch long ago drew attention to the fact that San Diego and Tijuana shared the same natural resources and must ultimately depend on each other for their survival. In a 1974 report entitled *Temporary Paradise?*, he observed that the border had turned both cities into the end-of-the-line towns of their respective nations, instead of the sister cities that they were.* But where Lynch saw Tijuana as part of San Diego's natural hinterland, Cruz is more inclined to see it from the other side of the fence.

'Eighty-five thousand people live in this settlement,' says Cruz, as we head down into the Los Laureles Canyon. Right here at the border is where this *colonia* is most established. This is where the houses are most densely agglomerated, whereas if you walk along the canyon away from the border the houses begin to thin out. The paradox of that fact is that the closer these settlers are to escaping this place, the more of a place it is. The estuary just across the highway is a stopping-off point for birds migrating north, but this particular migration ends abruptly here.

Cruz has done pioneering work in Los Laureles. He was the first to point out that the waste from San Diego's construction industry was being recycled into new homes here. Further along the valley, where the settlement is more precarious, the evidence is everywhere. 'You see those yellow walls?' says Cruz, pointing to the side of a house. 'Those are garage doors from San Diego.' Garage doors are a popular

---

* Donald Appleyard and Kevin Lynch, *Temporary Paradise?: A Look at the Special Landscape of the San Diego Region*, San Diego City Planning Department, 1974.

material in this canyon. The houses are works of assemblage, like habitable collages. Many of those on the hillside have been levelled using foundations of stacked car tyres, also imported from across the border. Elsewhere, there are whole post-war prefab houses, simply transplanted from the San Diego suburbs by truck. In crowded areas these are sometimes raised up on metal stilts, right on top of another house – a phenomenon Cruz calls 'club sandwich urbanisation'. He was so captivated by this practice that at one point he collaborated with a *maquiladora* to cheaply manufacture space frames specifically for raising up old bungalows. It was a kit of parts for building club sandwiches.

The use of readymades like this has led Cruz to describe such neighbourhoods in Tijuana as purely productive, as opposed to the consumption-based model across the border. Here, San Diego's waste is recycled to build new communities. Revealing this symbiotic relationship was one way of ascribing value to a type of settlement that is under-respected. 'This level of activity needs to be amplified if we're going to understand the sustainable city,' he says. But while Cruz celebrates such creativity, he is careful not to imply that such communities don't still need help.

Most of Los Laureles is informal, technically an illegal squatter settlement, but many of the residents have begun the process of acquiring land titles. It is a slow process through which residents incrementally buy legal status and in exchange get the utility services and the political representation that come with it. 'The land title agencies negotiate people's land titles so that squatters begin to make monthly payments, and then their papers begin to be processed so they can eventually own the land, and in the meantime the government injects very minimal infrastructure,' Cruz explains.

This is the kind of administrative process that Cruz has been at pains to engage with. For him, architectural design is far less important than the bureaucratic systems that determine whether communities are empowered or disempowered. And this is precisely one of those cases, where informal communities have the resourcefulness to build homes out of garage doors but not the bureaucratic tools – a legal address, for instance – to find employment outside of the informal sector.

In Mexico, unlike in many other Latin American countries, squatters still have rights to the land. The agrarian reforms of the Mexican Revolution created communal parcels of land called *ejidos*, on which people could squat. But during the neoliberalisation of the 1990s, the government gave people permission to sell the land, and you got developers buying it up for peanuts when it was worth millions. 'I remember a tragic article in a Mexican newspaper about how people were selling the land for enough money to buy a truck and throw a big party, and then later found themselves ending up as the cheap labour in resorts built on land they used to own,' says Cruz. 'The point is, we've gone from hyper-collectivity to hyper-privatisation, and nothing in between.'

One of the challenges of a place like Los Laureles is that shift from a public to a private ownership of the land. And this is where the canyon starts to be a source of innovation. In recent years, Cruz has been working with the environmental activist Oscar Romo, who successfully managed to create a 'watershed council' for Los Laureles, a political body solely addressing the needs of the canyon. That notion alone, of a hydrological system being given the kind of political representation of a municipal district, was groundbreaking. Crucially, it gave the community, now defined by a watershed micro-basin, a voice in how infrastructure would be brought in. But Romo and Cruz are going further. They're trying to mould local legislation so that instead of merely creating thousands of private lots, the canyon will allow clusters of families to collaborate and develop together in everyone's best interests. 'This would be a very complex system by which, with funding from this new council, maybe four families could be co-developers of their new units, and then they form a little social contract between them,' says Cruz.

So as well as bringing in much-needed infrastructure and political representation, which it is already doing, the council would also be a vehicle for a hybrid form of development, in between the collective and the private. Neither top-down entrepreneurial development nor illegal bottom-up development, this would be a third way. What is so significant about Los Laureles is that, far from being just another Tijuana slum, this marginal community is being used to explore the fertile intersection of a watershed system, a new development model and a national border – a collision of the ecological, the social and the political.

'This is *the* laboratory for me in the next five years,' says Cruz. 'The first thing Oscar and I want to do is to build a community centre slash scientific field station to work on the pollution and water issues.' The big question is whether he can get San Diego's administration to invest in a place like Los Laureles, whose trash washes across the border into the estuary, as a way of protecting its own ecological interests. 'Instead of spending millions on the wall, they could invest in this community so that the poor shanty town becomes the protector of the rich estuary.'

What's interesting is that, in developing the Los Laureles project, Cruz has been heavily influenced by what happened in Medellín. He has been studying the networks created between politicians, entrepreneurs and local communities, and the participative systems of community engagement that proved so successful there. I hadn't realised that negotiating the watersheds was also a key issue in the development of library-parks such as the Parque España, but apparently the topography and hydrology were all part of how the municipality negotiated with the community.

'This is my Medellín,' says Cruz. In fact, he even brought the former mayor, Sergio Fajardo, to the canyon to take part in an event drawing attention to the pivotal role of this community. Part tour and part art happening, he led Fajardo and the mayors of Tijuana and San Diego, along with a group of activists and researchers, through the drainage culvert under the highway at the end of the canyon. Getting the mayors to cross into Mexico through a drain was a provocative gesture (not least because it's the most unglamorous way a mayor could do it), and there was no shortage of irony, since underground tunnels are the preferred route for much of the smuggling across the border. But they were also crossing Cruz's political equator, the economic fault line that he sees as dividing the global North from the global South. Here, where the floodwater and the trash flow, Cruz made his point about the importance of Los Laureles in understanding the complexity of co-existence across this border.

As the last informal settlement in Latin America, with its nose pressed against the window of the North, Los Laureles is already symbolic. But it is also significant as the nexus of three crucial issues. Firstly, it reveals the material flows across this border: San Diego's waste flows south to be recycled into a barrio, while the barrio's waste is washed north less productively. Secondly, by disrupting the watershed, the border is undermining the stability of an ecological system. And Cruz's idea is that Los Laureles should be a micro case study in transnational collaboration, so that the barrio is seen not as a slum but effectively as the guardian of the local environment. Finally, the canyon is another potential testing ground for developing land cooperatively, much as Urban-Think Tank had imagined doing in San Agustín, so that the communal agenda is not lost in the formalisation process.

For Cruz, the collision of complex issues embodied by this easily overlooked community is of global significance. 'Any discussion about the future of urbanisation will have to begin by understanding the coalition of geopolitical borders, marginal communities and natural resources,' he says. 'That's why this canyon is fundamental.'

As we get back in the taxi, our driver (who, incidentally, used to be a *coyote* smuggling people across the border) tells us that the queue at the San Ysidro crossing is over two hours long. '¡*Dios mío!*' says Cruz. He's going to be late for a meeting at his daughter's school back in San Diego. 'My wife's going to kill me.'

When we get to the San Ysidro gateway, people are standing in line for what looks like a mile. Beads of sweat start to pop out on Cruz's forehead. But in a flash he does something he's never tried before. Instead of joining the end of the queue, he ushers me to the front where there's a separate exit for people with frequent transit visas. Neither of us have these, of course, but somehow the policeman on duty neglects to check. We pass through security, stony-faced, as if everything is in order, but as soon as we set foot on US tarmac Cruz's face cracks into a huge grin and we have to stop ourselves from bear-hugging.

'A unique monster'

The next day I leave behind the golf-course gothic of San Diego's La Jolla, home of the highest house prices in the US, and head back to the San Ysidro crossing. As a pedestrian, one experiences the border as a great knot of infrastructure, where the San Diego Freeway meets the various immigration centres, bus stations and shopping malls processing the herds of human traffic. None of which is on a pedestrian scale. Following the signs, I cross over the gridlocked freeway, through some turnstyles and on and on, expecting to meet a passport control booth, only to eventually realise that I was already in Mexico. People queue up for hours to enter the US, but apparently you don't even have to show your passport to go south of the border.

On my crossing, I recall that UN-Habitat report from a few years ago, which predicted that metropolises will soon blend together to create 'mega-regions'. One such region is in West Africa, where the cities of Lagos, Ibadan, Lomé and Accra are threatening to merge – an amalgamation that would spill across the national borders of Nigeria, Benin, Togo and Ghana. Are there strategies for transnational cities? I wonder how Tijuana and San Diego, which sit across the busiest and most socially polarized border in the world, would operate in such circumstances. Lynch's plan proposed that they share an airport and an 'Inter-American' university. It was a tactic later used by Rio's slum-upgrading programme, where shared resources were used to bridge (sometimes invisible) borders. But this is a rhetorical train of thought, not the reason I came back here. If Los Laureles was Tijuana at its most marginal, I'm curious to see what lessons the real city has to offer.

Outside a McDonald's, I wait for Raúl Cárdenas. We agreed to meet here because the golden arches are an easy landmark for a Tijuana novice like myself. And sure enough, moments later he pulls up in his silver Jetta, sporting a moustache and heavy-duty spectacles. 'Hello, my friend!'

Cárdenas is the founder of Torolab, an artist collective engaged in various community projects in and around Tijuana. An architect by training, like Cruz his work focuses on the border region but it addresses a different set of questions, to do with surveillance, literacy and nutrition. Torolab's biggest project to date is located in Camino Verde, one of the most violent neighbourhoods in Tijuana, where it has opened a food laboratory creating products that fight malnutrition and generate income for the community.

Driving along one of the main strips, Tijuana has the look and feel of an American city, only somehow less shiny. Among the KFCs and Domino's Pizzas, it has its own brand of what Robert Venturi calls 'duck' architecture – including a restaurant shaped like a sombrero – and even centres around its own version of the Gateway Arch in St Louis. Cárdenas points out a grand place called Caesar's, supposedly the real birthplace (before it was moved to Caesar's Palace in Las Vegas) of the eponymous salad.

Tijuana became a destination as a drinking and gambling city during Prohibition, until Las Vegas took its crown in the late 1930s. In 1950 its population was still only 65,000, but as Southern California started importing workers in the 1960s, Tijuana became a mecca for US-bound migrants from across the country. The population started doubling every decade. Today, even though passage across the border has become much tougher, it is still growing fast, but thanks to its own economy. This is no longer just a border town next to one of the richest cities in the richest state in the richest country in the world. Tijuana's manufacturing sector is booming, with the *maquiladoras* employing more than half of the population. This is the world capital of television assembly, and Samsung and Sony both have huge factories here.

Now that illegal border crossings are a fraction of what they were a decade ago, San Diego sees Tijuana as less of a threat, and is shedding its traditional edge-of-the-world mentality and beginning to recognise its neighbour as a place of opportunity. 'We are an economic force now in a way that we were not a decade or two ago,' said Carlos Bustamante, Tijuana's San Diego-educated mayor, recently. 'It is in everyone's interest to take advantage of that.'*

All of which is not to say that Tijuana is not still plagued by major social problems. And crime is still one of them. The steady stream of US college kids coming to party has slowed in recent years following newspaper reports, like the one in 2009, of decapitated corpses being left at the bullring. Even though things are improving, the dangerous reputation lingers.†

'Five or six years ago this place was a complete mess, like in the movies,' says Cárdenas. He was kidnapped himself, and lost a number of close friends to the violence. 'We all have stories,' he says. 'Once, my studio got completely destroyed by machine guns, just because it happened to be

---

* 'San Diego mayor building economic bridges to Tijuana', *New York Times*, 12 May 2013.

† One is reminded of Roberto Bolaño's brutal depiction of Ciudad Juárez, further along the border, in *2666* – an endless stream of unsolved murders. Tijuana's *maquiladora* hinterland, with its dusty informal communities, also fits Bolaño's description.

in the way of a gunfight. But this doesn't happen anymore. We're reconstructing the identity of this place.'

As we drive to Camino Verde, he explains that the neighbourhood has one of the highest rates of incarceration for violent crime in the city. At the same time, it has one of the highest rates of malnutrition and diabetes. That overlap inspired Torolab to initiate a food-based project that could tackle the nutritional deficit and the employment deficit at the same time. The Transborder FarmLab, as the name suggests, is part farm and part laboratory. Torolab invites scientists and top chefs to develop vitamin-rich, diabetic-safe salsas and jams that the community can sell to generate income.

'If 70 per cent of the housing in Tijuana is self-built, it's really hard to do macro-planning,' says Cárdenas, putting the project in context. 'So we try to start change at the molecular level, in people's bodies, moving to the body of the city – from nano to micro to personal to communal.'

This notion of beginning urban change at the molecular level, through the citizens' digestive tracts, is – crazy though it may sound – extremely compelling, not to say logical. The subject of people's health is almost never dealt with by architects, or at least not since modernism's obsession with hygiene. And yet it makes total sense that a community cannot be expected to look after its own interests – economically, socially or urbanistically – if it is dogged by illness and malnourishment. But the FarmLab is not just about food, it's about education and social empowerment. As part of the community participation programme that

Torolab developed, it brought in creative writing professors to help residents express who they were and where they wanted to be in their lives.

'It's a multi-dimensional approach to poverty,' says Cardenas. 'It's not just farming and food, it's about ideas and people's capacities. We're building a project about economic vocation. We're partnering with companies that will give them real jobs – that's how to feed these neighbourhoods.'

Camino Verde looks like a more established version of Los Laureles. The houses are more densely packed, but they line the floor and walls of a dry riverbed. The Transborder FarmLab stands out as the most solid building in the neighbourhood, a veritable concrete bunker. It's not much to look at, but it may gradually transform the reputation of a neighbourhood known mostly for methamphetamine labs and crime.

With solar panels on the roof, the FarmLab generates more electricity than it consumes. It's also the first place in Tijuana with real recycling ('If you divide the trash in Tijuana, you know, it goes to the same place.'). Cardenas calls it an 'urban observatory', and I'm reminded of Antanas Mockus's think tank. It's a place of research, but also a learning centre for the community where Torolab partners with Ensenada's Centre for Scientific Research to bring computer literacy to the community. 'How do you deal with the digital divide in a place with no access to technology, in a place that doesn't read and where books are three times more expensive than in the US?'

Cárdenas talks rapidly, like he's wired on caffeine, or

just can't contain his excitement. He's addicted to the taste of potential change. Having weathered the tough times, he can see imminent transformation everywhere.

'Tijuana is a unique monster,' he says. 'It's unique not just because of the border or the language or the economy, but because of the resilience. This isn't Mexico City, where you have hundreds of years of history, like the Plaza de Las Tres Culturas in Tlatelolco. Here it's closer to science fiction, to cyberpunk. If something new is going to happen, this is the place for it to happen, because we're not restricted by any wonderful history.'

I sense that Teddy Cruz sees Tijuana the same way, as a laboratory where subtle, invisible interventions – a piece of legislation, a watershed council, or, in Torolab's case, an injection of vitamins and opportunities – can have potentially radical effects. It could be that Tijuana, stationed on this global socio-political divide, is a natural crucible of new ideas, just as the fault lines between tectonic plates on the ocean floor are breeding-grounds of new life.

For lunch, Cárdenas takes me to a bright-orange street stand that does the best tacos in town. Chomping down on a taco with roasted pepper, shrimps and pineapple salsa, I notice the display the owners have laid out on the pavement – a couple of horned skulls, marigolds and candles. I forgot that today is the Day of the Dead. I was looking forward to this, because it seemed an outrageous piece of luck to be in Mexico on its most famous holiday. But I expected to see revellers in skeleton costumes. There's nothing like that, it's just an ordinary day.

'Hey, at least you had a *Día de Muertos* taco, my friend!'

Learning from Tijuana

If the US–Mexico border marks the collision of the global North and South – of the formal and the predominantly informal – then that line is less clear at Tijuana than it used to be. With the city's growing wealth, you now see expensive mansion houses a stone's throw from *colonias* like Los Laureles. At the same time, rich San Diego – which Teddy Cruz likes to call, because of the border fence, the largest gated community in the world – has its poor neighbourhoods. And San Ysidro is one.

My only experience of it thus far has been the shopping malls and factory outlet stores that line the way to the border crossing. But Cruz takes me to a community where he has been working for more than a decade. The streetscape here is noticeably more depressed, and the average household income is only $20,000 a year, which is poverty by Californian standards. Yet San Ysidro has utopian origins. It was founded by the Little Landers, the cooperative agriculture movement of the early twentieth century that believed in the modest aspiration of 'a little land and a living'. This neighbourhood is now home to a Latino community. As Los Laureles is the last *colonia* in Mexico, this is the first neighbourhood across the border. And if Cruz has his way here, it will be a testing ground for an urban strategy that is a radical departure from anything now possible in the US.

'This place is completely off the radar for the municipality, because the whole emphasis has been on the checkpoint,' says Cruz. 'So I said, let's set the agenda ourselves.'

What Cruz has been instigating in San Ysidro is a new model of participative micro-development. He has been working with a local NGO called Casa Familiar, which does everything from providing social services to creating community art projects. With Casa Familiar as the backbone of the project, Cruz set about trying to turn two under-used plots of land into a dense programme of affordable housing and social amenities.

The idea is that the plots are carved up into thin slivers, each one with distinct zoning that would allow it to accommodate a different housing typology. One of the plots, which Cruz calls Living Rooms at the Border, would become a row of small apartments, a row of larger family houses, a row of live-work units for artists, and a row of flexible units providing temporary accommodation for guests or relatives. Squeezing so many different typologies onto one land parcel is part of what's innovative about this scheme. But even more interesting is the set of social relations between them. The development would begin with a row of open structures housing collective kitchens, informal markets and community workshops. This would be the public dimension at the base of the apartment building. At the heart of the plot, meanwhile, is a 1920s stucco church that is now Casa Familiar's cultural centre, and which would be co-programmed by the artists in the live-work units. So one parcel of land is providing everything from a diverse range of housing to social amenities and a cultural programme. All of which is connected by a dense system of relations between the neighbours within the plot and the community outside it.

The other plot provides housing for the elderly combined with day care facilities for children. Here again, instead of building an old people's home, Cruz has designed a set of unique row houses providing thirteen granny flats with a childcare centre incorporated, which would be partially run by the seniors themselves. The sloping roofs of the houses alternate to create a weave-style pattern, a highly contemporary idiom that would be (given the pastiche colonial style that seems to really float people's boats here) the most original domestic architecture in San Diego.

However, the architecture is not really the topic of discussion in this case. If any architect has managed to pursue a meaningful and influential career without needing to resort to architecture, it's Cruz. What is potentially seminal about this project is the diverse set of land uses. 'We need a new concept of density,' he says. 'Density is still measured as a number of *things* – units – per acre. Why not measure it as a number of social and economic exchanges per acre?'

Cruz was inspired to think this way by studying the land uses in San Ysidro, which are often multiple and overlapping – a Buddhist temple functioning as an unofficial City Hall, a house front operating as a *taquería*. In the informal economy, as can be witnessed across Latin America, people will find a way to put even the most unpromising or unlikely places to social and economic use. By contrast, the strict regulations governing any American city strive to segregate the domestic from the economic, and categorise the city into zones suitable for property speculation rather than rich social interaction. Can San Diego learn from the likes of Tijuana?

Effectively, what Cruz is doing here is enabling a non-profit NGO, Casa Familiar, to act as a small-scale developer in the interests of the community. By transferring government funding to individuals, through micro-credit, the NGO becomes a conduit between top-down processes and bottom-up impulses. 'The community becomes co-owner or co-manager of resources,' says Cruz. 'Because the paradigm of the top down is that it just produces units for customers to occupy, but there is no social infrastructural dimension where communities then begin to shape programming, production, food.'

Cruz's plans for San Ysidro are quite well known by now, and have even been exhibited in New York's MoMA (in a display that Casa Familiar later brought to the stucco church, temporarily dubbed MoMitA). I can't help but wonder why the buildings themselves haven't yet materialised. 'Yeah, a lot of people say, "Well, when are you going to build your fucking projects?"' he says, sounding only slightly exasperated. 'Well, guess what, it's taking time to change the political structure here.'

This, really, is the crux of Cruz's project. It is also the reason why I believe he is one of the most astute architects working today. He recognises that social change and the creation of a more equitable city are not a question of good buildings. They are a question of civic imagination. And that is something that has been sorely eroded by the neo-liberal economic policies of recent decades. Cruz is a stern critic of America's steady withdrawal from any notion of public responsibility. He talks of 'the three slaps in the face of the American public' after the 2008 crash, namely: the Wall Street bailouts, the millions of foreclosures and the public spending cuts. 'It wasn't just an economic crisis but a cultural crisis, a failure of institutions,' he says. 'A society that is anti-government, anti-taxes and anti-immigration only hurts the city.'

So what is to be done? For Cruz, the only way forward is not to play by the existing rules, but to start redesigning those institutions. In San Ysidro, he has been seeking to change the zoning laws to allow a richer and more empowering community life. And changing legislation means engaging with what has been called the 'dark matter'* – not just the physical fabric of the city, but its regulations.

This is the very definition of the activist architect, one who creates the conditions in which it is possible to make a meaningful difference. Cruz himself, who has a tendency to slip into academic jargon, calls it 'expanded modes of practice'. But he backs it up with a good analogy. In his report on the Iraq War, General Petraeus said the contemporary soldier had to become an anthropologist and a social worker, and speak many languages. 'If a soldier needs to transform, then why can't architects?' says Cruz.

---

* A term coined by the architect Wouter Vanstiphout, later used in the title of Dan Hill's 2012 book, *Dark Matter and Trojan Horses: A Strategic Design Vocabulary*.

While architects have been focusing on spectacular buildings they could export to China and Dubai, the real gains were to be made on a different plane entirely, at the level of infrastructure, networks and politics. Designing a good building becomes a rather academic exercise when the entire system that allows that building to materialise is geared towards increasing social inequality. New social and political frameworks also need designing.

This is what Cruz has been doing in San Ysidro. It's not just a case of changing zoning laws (although that's difficult enough on its own). 'Designing the protocols or the interfaces between communities and spaces, this is what's missing,' he says. That means how collective kitchens, informal markets and apartments can all co-exist in the same building. It means giving people the tools they need to be economically productive, and giving them a voice in shaping how the community operates. It means levelling the playing field for what Cruz calls 'creative acts of citizenship'.

In one sense, this could be misinterpreted as just yet more deregulation. After all, extreme localism like this is more often than not associated with a right-wing agenda of devolving power (witness the Tory government's Localism Bill in the UK, which was part of the push to cut government spending). But this is not a form of deregulation that enables more privatisation. On the contrary, it would allow more collective productivity and a more social neighbourhood. Here, the architect and the NGO become developers not with a view to profit, but to improve the prospects of the community. 'We need to hijack the knowledge embedded in a developer's spreadsheet,' says Cruz.

It may seem strange to end a book about Latin American cities in a tiny community in California. But in San Ysidro lies the seed of an idea, which is that the lessons of Latin America are gradually penetrating the border wall. What Cruz is trying to do is challenge the American conception of the city as a rigidly zoned thing servicing big business on the one hand and some quaint idea of the American dream on the other. After all, the sub-prime mortgage fiasco was the product of America's fixation with private property, and the logic, as Cruz once put it, 'of democracy being based on the almighty right to be left alone behind a picket fence'. Instead, the city could be more communal, more productive. And he's drawing on the much more complex dynamics of informal economies, where no space goes to waste, where every inch belongs to a dense network of social and economic exchanges. That's the model he's using to try to transform policy in San Diego. The regulations need to be more flexible, more ambiguous, more easily adapted to people's needs. This is not a Turneresque laissez-faire attitude, but an attempt to get the top-down to facilitate the bottom-up.

And while much of that may sound somewhat utopian, the San Ysidro project has had a stroke of luck that may soon make it a reality. Cruz is now the urban policy advisor to the mayor. As the director of the self-styled Civic Innovation Lab, he heads a think tank operating out of the fourth floor of City Hall, which means that San Diego now has a department modelled on the policy units that were so transformative in Bogotá and Medellín. Indeed, in one of Cruz's first acts in the role, he is bringing Antanas Mockus's NGO, Corpovisionarios, to conduct a 'citizenship culture survey' in San Diego–Tijuana to help understand the cities' social norms and shared interests. The survey is intended as the first step towards a cross-border vision for the region that will seek to overcome a culture of polarisation and promote one of inclusion and cooperation.

What we have here is a Latin American architect, steeped in the lessons of Curitiba, Medellín and Tijuana, embedded within the administration of a major US city. And it's clear that Cruz is establishing a bridgehead for the lessons of Latin America to find new relevance across what was once an unbridgable divide. It's early days, but the implications may well be radical.

Acknowledgements

First of all I must thank the Graham Foundation for Advanced Studies in the Fine Arts for kindly supporting the research for this book. I am indebted to Deyan Sudjic, Ricky Burdett, Eyal Weizman and Peter Carl for saying the generous things about me that persuaded the Foundation to back the book with two grants. I'm particularly grateful to Peter for showing such an interest and for reading a draft, and also to Jorge Fiori for some enlightening conversations about his native Brazil. I must also thank the photographers that I worked with at different stages of this book. It's always a pleasure to collaborate with such talented people as Cristóbal Palma, Iwan Baan, Thelma Vilas Boas and Tomás García Puente. Thanks also goes to Tuca Vieira, Michael Hudler and Armando Salas for the images they let me use. My editor at Verso, Leo Hollis, had all the right instincts about how to shape this book, and I'm most appreciative. I also have to mention my friend Alfredo Brillembourg, who is not only in the book but was a sounding board and all-round enthusiast from early on. Finally, there are those who were instrumental in just making things happen in cities where I was a stranger. There are too many to mention but I am much obliged to Roberto Somlo, Jonathan Colin, Fernando Arias, José Roca, José Castillo, Adam Kaasa, Alejandro Echeverri, Manuel de Rivero, Florencia Rodríguez, Ana Rascovsky, Pancho Liernur, Julia Michaels and Ephim Shluger.

Index

Africa. *See* South Africa; West Africa

Alemão. *See* Complexo do Alemão (favelas)

Alexander, Christopher, 10, 71, 74, 75, 76

Allende, Salvador, 91, 92

Alto Comedero, Argentina, 61–6, 86

Alto Hospicio, Chile, 83

Anglican Church, 201

Aravena, Alejandro, 17, 31, 80–98 passim, 194

Archigram, 167

'Architecture Without Architects' (1964 exhibition), 12

Argentina, 8, 25, 37–66, 117–18; dictatorships, 13, 31, 151. *See also* Buenos Aires; Jujuy, Argentina

Artigas, João Vilanova, 30

Atelier 5 (architects), 73

Austria, 164

Avenida Lecuna, Caracas, 142–3, 172

Baldó, Josefina, 161–2

Banco Obrero, Venezuela, 152

Barbican, 41

Barcelona, 122

Barefoot Park, Medellín. *See* Parque de los Pies Descalzos, Medellín

Barra da Tijuca, Rio de Janeiro, 101, 129–31

Barreto, Juan, 163–4, 165

Barrio de la Cota 905. *See* Cota 905, Caracas

Baruta, Caracas, 149–50

Battle, Guy, 163

Baur, Ruedi, 167

Belaúnde, Fernando, 71, 72, 89

Beuys, Joseph, 220

Bey, Hakim, 203

Biblioteca España, Medellín. *See* Parque Biblioteca España, Medellín

Bilbao, Spain, 15

Bogotá, 19, 24, 129, 166, 207–30, 248, 283

Bolaño, Roberto, 273n

Bolívar, Simón, 139, 145, 155, 159

Bolívar, Teolinda, 161, 162, 171

Born to Die in Medellín (Salazar), 231

Botanical Gardens, Medellín, 234, 240, 253

Bourdieu, Pierre, 207

Brás de Pina (favela), 113

Brasilia, 103, 116

Brazil, 7, 12, 13, 19, 23–31 passim, 57, 99–137 passim. *See also* Curitiba, Brazil; Olympic Games, Brazil, 2016; Rio de Janeiro

Brillembourg, Alfredo, 18, 142–7 passim, 155–63 passim, 168–73 passim, 178

Brillembourg, David, 178–9

Britain. *See* United Kingdom

Brunner, Karl, 243–4

Buenos Aires, 12, 37–49 passim

Buñuel, Luis: *Los Olvidados*, 3

Bustamente, Carlos, 273

Cabral, Sérgio, 126, 137

Camino Verde, Tijuana, 272–5 passim

Canary Wharf, London, 129

Candilis Josic Woods, 8, 71, 78

Canserbero, 144

Canudos, Brazil, 104

Cape Town, South Africa, 129, 173

Capriles, Henrique, 149, 204

Caracas, 8–9, 12, 18, 22–5 passim, 31, 139–206, 241; cable car system, 162–70 passim, 247. *See also* Torre David, Caracas

Cárdenas, Raúl, 271–6

Carioca Living. *See* Morar Carioca

Carroll, Rory, 161, 162

Casa Familiar, 278, 280

Centro Financiero Confinanzas. *See* Torre David, Caracas

Chacao, Caracas, 148, 149

Chávez, Hugo, 18, 28, 59, 139–46 passim, 154–5, 162–5 passim, 176–80 passim; expropriation of farms, 159; public opinion, 170, 183, 186; Torre David and, 193, 204–5

Chile, 13, 17–18, 25, 30–1, 79–98, 169

China, 79, 80, 281

Cholele, Guillermo, 175

Cidade de Deus (City of God) (housing project), 109–10, 127

Ciudad Juárez. *See* Juárez
Civic Innovation Lab, 282
Colombia, 19, 24–5, 168–9, 171.
    See also Bogotá; Medellín,
    Colombia
Colonia Aeropuerto, 259–60
Complexo da Maré (favelas),
    119–20, 130, 133–4, 137
Complexo do Alemão (favelas),
    99, 130–5 passim, 167
Compromiso Ciudadano,
    Medellín, 237, 238, 239
Comuna 13, Medellín, 247,
    255–6
Conjunto Piedrabuena (housing
    project), 41–9 passim, 65–6
Constitución, Chile, 97
Le Corbusier, 2, 3, 8, 11–12, 75;
    counterrevolutionary idea
    of, 116; Dom-ino House,
    89–90, 201–2, 206; influence
    on Villanueva, 152; in Rio de
    Janeiro, 107
Corpovisionarios, 227, 284
Correa, Charles, 10, 71, 75
Cota 905, Caracas, 156–8
Cruz, Teddy, 20–1, 239, 259–70
    passim, 276–84 passim
Cuba, 109, 145
Curitiba, Brazil, 24, 26, 129, 166,
    223, 284

Davis, Mike, 252n, 261
Díaz Ordaz, Gustavo, 4–5
Doña Marta (favela), 117

'Don Berna', 254
Doppelmayr, 164, 165

Echeverri, Alejandro, 242–6,
    248, 250
École des Beaux-Arts, Paris, 2,
    152, 243–4
Edificio Inteligente, Medellín,
    250
Elemental, 17–18, 80, 81, 90, 94,
    97, 98
Empresas Públicas de Medellín
    (EPM), 250–1, 252
Escobar, Pablo, 233, 253, 254
Evil Paradises (Davis, et al.),
    252n

Fajardo, Sergio, 20, 235–48
    passim, 252–8 passim
Fajardo, Washington, 126
Farm Lab. *See* Transborder
    Farm Lab
Favela-Bairro, 112–19 passim,
    125, 127, 128, 243
Favela Observatory, 134
Ferreira dos Santos, Carlos
    Nelson. *See* Santos, Carlos
    Nelson Ferreira dos
Feyerabend, Paul, 210
Fiori, Jorge, 33
Florida, 130
France, 8, 75. *See also* École des
    Beaux-Arts, Paris
Freedom to Build (Turner), 86–7
Frei, Eduardo, 91

'Fryscraper', 42
Fuerte Apache (housing
    project), 39–40, 41
Fundación Amor por Medellín,
    252

Gaviria, Aníbal, 256
Giuliani, Rudy, 226
Gómez, Enrique, 179
Great Britain. *See* United
    Kingdom
Growing House, 201
Guatemala, 98
Guevara, Che, 21, 50–3 passim,
    61, 62, 65, 155
Guggenheim Museum Bilbao,
    15

Harvey, David, 135–6
Hollein, Hans, 146
Hornos de Cal Station, Caracas,
    167, 168
Hylton, Forrest, 252n

Iacobelli, Andrés, 18, 81, 97–8
Iglesia de Santiago Tlatelolco.
    See Santiago Tlatelolco
    Temple
IMF. *See* International Monetary
    Fund (IMF)
Indoamericano Park, Buenos
    Aires, 39
Informal City: Caracas Case
    (Brillembourg, Feiress, and
    Klumpner), 147, 163

Ingels, Bjarke, 14
Inter-American Development
    Bank, 115, 135
International Monetary Fund
    (IMF), 11, 57, 111, 178
International Wastewater
    Treatment Plant, 263
Iquique, Chile, 79–88 passim,
    93–6 passim

Jacobs, Jane, 11
Jailson de Souza e Silva. *See*
    Silva, Jailson de Souza e
January 23 (housing project).
    See 23 de Enero (housing
    project)
Jardín Botánico, Medellín. *See*
    Botanical Gardens, Medellín
Jáuregui, Jorge Mario, 19, 99,
    116–22
Jencks, Charles, 9, 70
Jiménez, Marcos Pérez, 150–1
Juárez, 273n
Jujuy, Argentina, 21, 51–66
Juventud Peronista. *See* Peronist
    Youth Movement

Kikutake, Kiyonori, 77
Kirchner, Néstor, 38, 57, 59
Klumpner, Hubert, 18, 142,
    146–50 passim, 156–63
    passim, 171–3 passim, 188
Koolhaas, Rem, 14
Krier, Leon, 74
Kurokawa, Kisho, 77

La Ceiba Station, Caracas, 167–8

La Cruz, Caracas, 148–51 passim

La Jolla, San Diego, 270

Land, Peter, 71, 78

'Latin American Architecture Since 1945' (1955 exhibition), 23

La Vega, Caracas, 146

Lefebvre, Henri, 3, 27, 28, 30, 161

Le Mirail, France, 8

Lerner, Jaime, 24, 26

Library Park of Spain. *See* Parque Biblioteca España, Medellín

Liernur, Pancho, 50, 51, 63

Lima, 12, 67–79 passim

Little Landers, 277

Lo Barnechea, Chile, 95–6

Lo Espejo, Chile, 93–4

London, England, 7, 41, 42, 129, 172, 205; Olympic 'legacy', 101, 130

López, Néstor, 159, 164

Los Laureles Canyon, 262–71 passim, 275, 277

Los Teques, Caracas, 149, 150

Lugano (housing project). *See* Villa Lugano (housing project)

Lula da Silva, Luiz Inácio, 27, 59, 102, 112, 119, 122, 126

Lynch, Kevin, 264

Maduro, Nicolás, 173

Magalhães, Sérgio, 115

Maia, Cesar, 115

Maki, Fumihiko, 77

Manguinhos (favela), 120–5, 130, 135

Manteola, Sánchez Gómez, Santos & Solsona, 42

Maré. *See* Complexo da Maré (favelas)

Marull, Pereyra & Ruiz, 41

Mazoni, Juana, 75–6

Mazzanti, Giancarlo, 234, 248

Medellín, Colombia, 20, 24, 208, 231–58, 268, 283, 284; cable car system, 24–5, 105, 132, 163, 166, 240, 246–7, 251

Menem, Carlos, 57

Menéndez, Mike, 163

Metabolists, 10, 71, 73, 77–8

Metrocable de Caracas, 162–70 passim, 247

Metrocable de Medellín, 24–5, 105, 132, 163, 166, 240, 246–7, 251

Mexico, 98, 266, 273n. *See also* Mexico City; Tijuana

Mexico City, 1–8 passim, 16, 131, 276

Milgram, Stanley, 210, 215

Minha Casa Minha Vida (My House My Life), 126–8, 131

Miraflores Palace, Caracas, 154–5

Mockus, Antanas, 19–20, 24, 207–30 passim, 243, 275, 284

'La Mona' (Muñoz), 260

Monterrey, Mexico, 98

Morales, Evo, 53, 59

Morales, Iván, 189

Morar Carioca, 103, 120, 125–6, 128

Moravia, Medellín, 240, 251

Morro da Providencia (favela), 104–6, 133, 135

Moses, Robert, 140

Muñoz García, Armando, 260

Murillo Bejarano, Diego. *See* 'Don Berna'

Museum of Modern Art, 12, 23, 280

Mutirão. *See* Operaçao Mutirão

My House My Life. *See* Minha Casa Minha Vida (My House My Life)

The Mystery of Capital (de Soto), 70

New York City, 171, 205, 226. *See also* Museum of Modern Art

Niemeyer, Oscar, 30, 117

Nixon, Pat, 260

Nonoalco-Tlatelolco (housing project). *See* Unidad Habitacional Nonoalco-Tlatelolco

Noro, Raúl, 53, 54, 60, 64

Observatorio de Cultura Urbana, 212, 225, 243

Ohl, Herbert, 73

Los Olvidados (Buñuel), 3

Olympic Games, Brazil, 2016, 99–103 passim, 126–31 passim, 136–7

Olympic Games, London, 2012, 101, 130

Olympic Games, Mexico City, 1968, 4, 131

Olympic Games, Tijuana–San Diego, 2024 (proposed), 261

Operaçao Mutirão, 110–11

Operation Sitio, 91

Ordos 100, 79

Ortiz de Zevallos, Luis, 72

Paes, Eduardo, 102–3, 125, 126, 136–7

Paisajes Emergentes, 234

Pan-American Games, Rio de Janeiro, 2007, 136

Pani, Mario, 2–5 passim, 12, 131

Parque Biblioteca España, Medellín, 234, 240, 244–9 passim

Parque Central, Caracas, 141, 162–5 passim, 188

Parque de los Pies Descalzos, Medellín, 234, 236

Parque Explora, Medellín, 234, 240, 252–3

Parroquia La Vega, Caracas. *See* La Vega, Caracas

Partido dos Trabalhadores. *See* Workers' Party, Brazil (PT)
Pedregulho (housing project), 16, 107–9
Peñalosa, Enrique, 24, 223–5, 243, 248
Pérez, Carlos Andrés, 154, 178
Pérez, Jorge, 235–7 passim, 242, 253, 254
Pérez, Luis, 239–40, 247, 251–5 passim
Perón, Eva, 53, 62
Peronist Youth Movement, 38, 56, 57, 117
Peru, 9, 31, 89, 98, 169, 171. *See also* Lima
Pessac, France, 75
Petare, Venezuela, 28, 140, 148, 171
Piedrabuena (housing project). *See* Conjunto Piedrabuena (housing project)
Pinochet, Augusto, 92
Plan B, 234
Plaza de las Tres Culturas, Mexico City, 4–6 passim, 276
Porto Alegre, Brazil, 24
Porto Maravilha, Rio de Janeiro, 101, 105, 128–9
Portzamparc, Christian de, 130
Potrč, Marjetica, 147
Presidente Miguel Alemán (housing project), 2
PREVI (Proyecto Experimental de Vivienda), 9–10, 16, 18, 71–9, 82, 89, 97, 127
The Production of Space (Lefebvre), 30
Providencia (favela). *See* Morro da Providencia (favela)
Pruitt-Igoe (housing project), 8, 9, 16, 45, 151

Quinta Monroy (housing project), 80–9 passim, 93–8 passim

Reidy, Affonso, 16, 107
Renca, Chile, 94–6
Restrepo, Camilo, 234
Retiro (housing project), 39
Reyes, Pedro, 221
de Rivero, Manuel, 67
Rico, Carolina, 169–70
'The Right to the City' (Lefebvre), 27
Rio de Janeiro, 12, 16, 19, 99–137, 241, 243; bus rapid transit, 129, 224; cable car system, 25, 105–6, 132–5 passim, 163, 166
Roca, José, 220
Rocinha (favela), 102, 105, 119, 121, 133, 135
Romo, Oscar, 267
Rorty, Richard, 210
Roussef, Dilma, 126
Rudofsky, Bernard, 12
Runcorn, England, 74

Sala, Milagro, 21, 51–65 passim
Salazar, Alonso, 240, 252–6 passim; *Born to Die in Medellín*, 231, 255
Sanabria, Tomás, 185
San Agustín, Caracas, 149, 162–72 passim, 269
Sánchez, Rafael, 185
San Diego, California, 20–1, 260–73 passim, 277–84 passim
San Salvador, Jujuy, Argentina, 51–66
Santiago, Chile, 89–96 passim
Santiago Tlatelolco Temple, 4, 6
Santo Domingo, Medellín, 240, 244–50 passim
Santos, Carlos Nelson Ferreira dos, 113
Santos, Juan Manuel, 227
San Ysidro, California, 21, 270, 277–83 passim
São Cristovão, Rio de Janeiro, 107–9
São Paulo, 12, 127
Sassen, Saskia, 116
Segre, Roberto, 109
Serpa, Horacio, 218
Shluger, Ephim, 127–8
El Silencio, Caracas, 144
Silva, Jailson de Souza e, 133–5, 136
Smith, Neil, 25
Smithson, Alison, 14–15, 40, 160
Smithson, Peter, 14–15, 40, 160

Soldati (housing project). *See* Villa Soldati (housing project)
de Soto, Hernando, 70, 136, 163, 172
South Africa, 129, 173
de Souza e Silva, Jailson. *See* Silva, Jailson de Souza e
Soviet Union, 91–2
Spain, 4, 15, 50, 122
Stirling, James, 10, 71, 74, 75, 78
St Louis, Missouri. *See* Pruitt-Igoe (housing project)
Svenssons, Knud, 75, 76

Tafuri, Manfredo, 14, 15
Teleférico para Transporte Masivo Interrubano, Caracas. *See* Metrocable de Caracas
Temporary Paradise? A Look at the Special Landscape of the San Diego Region (Appleyard and Lynch), 264
Tercer Milenio Park, Bogotá, 225
Tijuana, 20, 259–84
Tlatelolco, Mexico City, 6–7, 276. *See also* Unidad Habitacional Nonoalco-Tlatelolco
Toledo, Marco, 84–6
Torolab, 272, 274–5
Torre David, Caracas, 22, 175–206
Torres García, Joaquín, 117
Transborder Farm Lab, 274–5

Transmilenio, 24, 208, 223, 224,
229
Trece, Medellín. *See* Comuna 13,
Medellín
Treinta y uno (*villa miseria*). *See*
Villa 31
Trump, Donald, 101
Túpac Amaru II, 50, 52, 62
Túpac Amaru movement, 21, 30,
49–66 passim
Turner, John, 9–11 passim, 30,
68–70, 92–3, 110, 111, 127,
194; *Freedom to Build*, 86–7

UN-Habitat, 261, 271
UNICEF, 113, 127
Unidad Habitacional Nonoalco-
Tlatelolco, 1–8 passim, 16
Unidad Independencia (housing
project), 1–2
Unité d'Habitation, Marseilles,
8
United Kingdom, 11, 74, 282.
See also London, England
United Nations, 9, 113, 127, 163,
236, 261
United States, 20–1, 109, 257,
263, 281. *See also* New
York City; Pruitt-Igoe
(housing project); San Diego,
California
Urban Development
Corporation (EDU),
Medellín, 242, 243
Urban Observatory. *See*

Observatorio de Cultura
Urbana
Urban-Think Tank (U-TT),
18, 142–50 passim, 155–75
passim, 180, 185–8 passim,
198, 201–3 passim; as model
in Tijuana, 269; on myth of
planned city, 26; on urbanism,
31
Uribe, Felipe, 236
USSR. *See* Soviet Union

van Eyck, Aldo, 10, 71–9 passim
Vanstiphout, Wouter, 281n
Vargas Llosa, Mario, 104
Venezuela, 7, 11, 13, 18, 28,
31, 150–2 passim. *See also*
Caracas
Venice Biennale of Architecture,
203
Ventura, Robert, 272
Vidigal (favela), 102, 118, 135
23 de Enero (housing project),
8–9, 16, 150–6, 188, 194
Vila Autódromo (favela), 131
Villa El Salvador, Peru, 73
Villa Lugano (housing project),
40, 41
Villanueva, Carlos Raúl, 8, 12,
152, 155
Villanueva, Federico, 161–2
Villa Soldati (housing project),
37–41 passim
Villa 31 (*villa miseria*), 39
Ville Radieuse, 2

Viñoly, Rafael, 42, 46–49 passim, 66

The War of the End of the World (Vargas Llosa), 104
West Africa, 262, 271
Workers' Party, Brazil (PT), 27, 126
World Bank, 70, 111, 127, 135, 161

World Cup, Brazil, 2014, 100–3 passim, 128, 131
World Urban Forum, 235

Yamasaki, Minoru: Pruitt-Igoe (housing project). *See* Pruitt-Igoe (housing project)

Zona Sul, Rio de Janeiro, 135, 136